FOUR FLATENS

Four men. Four generations. A family history.

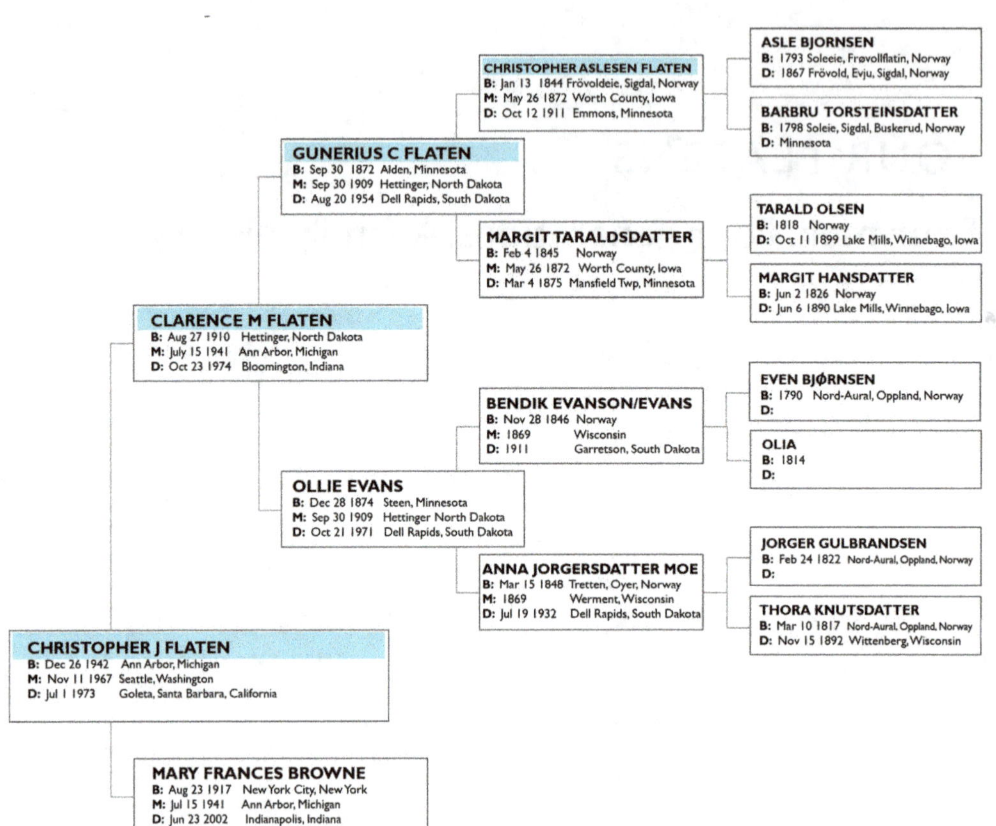

CHRISTOPHER J FLATEN
B: Dec 26 1942 Ann Arbor, Michigan
M: Nov 11 1967 Seattle, Washington
D: Jul 1 1973 Goleta, Santa Barbara, California
CLARENCE M FLATEN
B: Aug 27 1910 Hettinger, North Dakota
M: July 15 1941 Ann Arbor, Michigan
D: Oct 23 1974 Bloomington, Indiana
MARY FRANCES BROWNE
B: Aug 23 1917 New York City, New York
M: Jul 15 1941 Ann Arbor, Michigan
D: Jun 23 2002 Indianapolis, Indiana
GUNERIUS C FLATEN
B: Sep 30 1872 Alden, Minnesota
M: Sep 30 1909 Hettinger, North Dakota
D: Aug 20 1954 Dell Rapids, South Dakota
OLLIE EVANS
B: Dec 28 1874 Steen, Minnesota
M: Sep 30 1909 Hettinger North Dakota
D: Oct 21 1971 Dell Rapids, South Dakota
CHRISTOPHER ASLESEN FLATEN
B: Jan 13 1844 Frövoldeie, Sigdal, Norway
M: May 26 1872 Worth County, Iowa
D: Oct 12 1911 Emmons, Minnesota
MARGIT TARALDSDATTER
B: Feb 4 1845 Norway
M: May 26 1872 Worth County, Iowa
D: Mar 4 1875 Mansfield Twp, Minnesota
BENDIK EVANSON/EVANS
B: Nov 28 1846 Norway
M: 1869 Wisconsin
D: 1911 Garretson, South Dakota
ANNA JORGERSDATTER MOE
B: Mar 15 1848 Tretten, Oyer, Norway
M: 1869 Werment, Wisconsin
D: Jul 19 1932 Dell Rapids, South Dakota
ASLE BJORNSEN
B: 1793 Soleeie, Frøvollflatin, Norway
D: 1867 Frövold, Evju, Sigdal, Norway
BARBRU TORSTEINSDATTER
B: 1798 Soleie, Sigdal, Buskerud, Norway
D: Minnesota
TARALD OLSEN
B: 1818 Norway
D: Oct 11 1899 Lake Mills, Winnebago, Iowa
MARGIT HANSDATTER
B: Jun 2 1826 Norway
D: Jun 6 1890 Lake Mills, Winnebago, Iowa
EVEN BJØRNSEN
B: 1790 Nord-Aural, Oppland, Norway
D:
OLIA
B: 1814
D:
JORGER GULBRANDSEN
B: Feb 24 1822 Nord-Aural, Oppland, Norway
D:
THORA KNUTSDATTER
B: Mar 10 1817 Nord-Aural, Oppland, Norway
D: Nov 15 1892 Wittenberg, Wisconsin

Georgia Flaten Shaw

FOUR FLATENS

Four men. Four generations. A family history.

Shaw Studio Press | Bethesda MD

GRAPHIC DESIGN: SHAW STUDIO

Body copy: Adobe Caslon Pro | Heads: Gil Sans MT

COVER ART: Father and sons sculpture by Gustav Vigeland in Frogner Park, Oslo Norway. Photo by the author.

FOUR FLATENS

This is a work of fact and fiction. All incidents, dialogue, and characters are products of the author's research, combined with her imagination. Where real-life historical figures appear, the situations, incidents, and dialogue concerning those persons are transcribed, quoted, loosely reconstructed or partly fictional, but in each case are intended to depict actual events.

SECOND EDITION

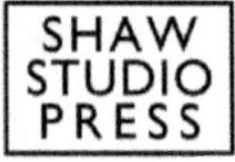

Published by Shaw Studio Press / Listed online and at www.BlueHorizonBooks.com

Shaw, Georgia

Four Flatens

ISBN: 979-8-9864075-1-7

DEDICATION

To my daughter Brigid, my siblings Kit, Larry, Peg, Brian, Liz, Marianne and Tom, their children, and our parents and grandparents.

Thanks to my husband Pat who encouraged me to write, edited my prose, and joined me in the hunt for family history. Acknowledgment and thanks to Margaret Daisley, Editor, Blue Horizon Books; to historians Sigrid Kvisle, Director, Sigdal-Eggedal Museum, Norway; Loren Luckow, Historian, Dakota Buttes Museum, North Dakota; Linda Evenson, Librarian, Freeborn County Historical Museum, Minnesota; and Bradley Cook, Photograph Curator, Indiana University Archives, Indiana, for their friendship and professional advice.

CONTENTS

PREFACE

This is the story of four Flaten men: Christopher Aslesen Flaten, Gunerius Flaten, Clarence Flaten, and Christopher Flaten. They were, respectively, my great-grandfather, my grandfather, my father and my brother. This history begins with some basic background of family lineage, but quickly proceeds to the action: that of Christopher Aslesen's immigration from Norway, his arrival and survival, and continues through the four generations with their relocation, advancement and endurance, sometimes in the face of great adversity.

Christopher Aslesen, son of a Norwegian cotter, immigrated to the U.S. to homestead in Minnesota. His son Gunerius was a photographer in North Dakota and a Depression-era farmer in South Dakota. Gunerius's son Clarence was soldier in WWII who laid down arms to build a new life in academia at Indiana University. Clarence's son Christopher was a physicist with an academic career in California.

Born in different eras, each began life with the challenge of little wealth, although each man built modestly upon that of the last generation. They were all strongly propelled by individual aspirations once they came of age. Each left his boyhood home to seek promising opportunities and adventure. All were shaped by the large events of their own times, including wars and the aftermath, climate catastrophes, and economic downturns, all of which they met with mettle.

This work began, like so many other personal histories do, after I discovered an old birth certificate in a box of family papers. After gathering many additional facts of birth, childhood, marriage, children, work, education, and military service and careers, and putting them into sequence, a long narration and an extremely satisfying order to their stories lay before me. In the process, to my surprise, I discovered facts that had never been known in my family, tales of tragedy that had become vague, and marriages and children that had been forgotten. The whole process of reconstructing their times and environment meant that these eras became exciting and alive as I pictured my forefathers making their way.

I could see the impact of world events on their opportunities and decisions, the shattering effect of unlucky obstacles on their individual hopes and dreams. I also now see that the decisions and crossroads in their individual lives are common to all men and women. While the Flatens' particular ups and downs and their time periods are what make this book an interesting tale, I hope that you, too, will be inspired by their determination to succeed in spite of the odds. In the end, we are all only partially in control of our own fate. The ability to rise up requires more than luck. It takes guts, courage, and bravery, but also music, humor, and much support from family and community.

All photographs, unless noted otherwise, were taken by my grandfather and father, who were professional photographers. Most are now the property of Indiana University Photographic Archives. I have researched the histories of towns, cities, and locations in the relevant eras in order to convey an accurate setting. I have located property plats and deeds, certificates of birth, marriage, and death, as well as original letters, obituaries, newspaper notices, and family lore to verify facts. From this, I constructed the narrative. However, when supporting documents were unable to be discovered, I tell their story as I understand it most likely happened.

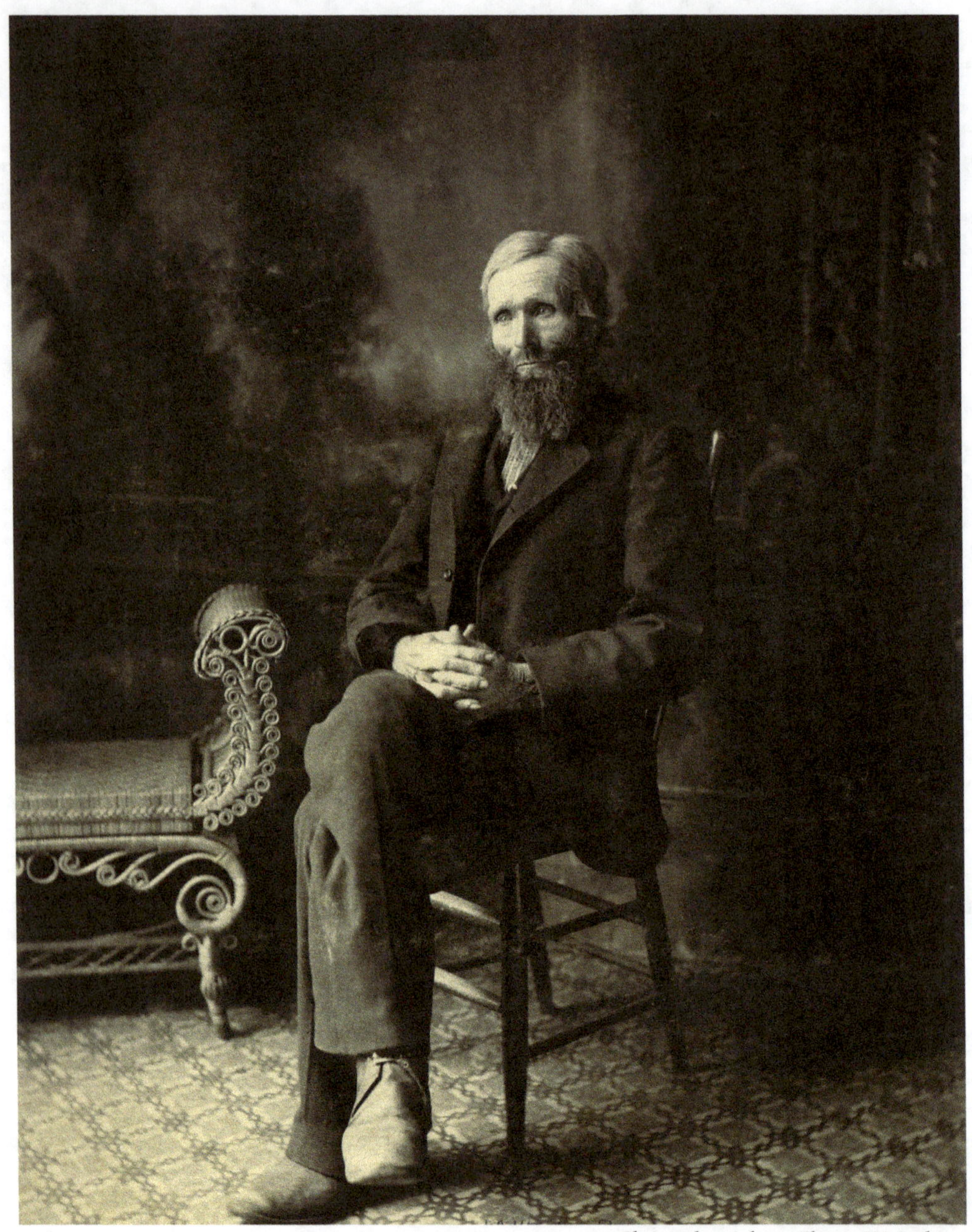

Christopher Aslesen Flaten, IU Archives

CHAPTER ONE

CHRISTOPHER ASLESEN FLATEN 1844-1911

MY GREAT-GRANDFATHER'S FAMILY CAME FROM THE SIGDAL area of Norway, located in the larger region of Buskerud, northwest of Oslo. They farmed the land in an area of mountains and dales, rushing waters, lakes and villages, a hilly, picturesque, cold and challenging setting.

Christopher's mother, Barbru Torsteinsdatter, had grown up there, as had many generations before her. Born in 1798 (one year before President George Washington died) she grew up and married my great-great grandfather Asle Bjornsen, on April 7, 1823, and this event was duly registered in the church book of the small nearby parish church in Eggedal. Asle (pronounced ASH-lee) was a husmann or a "cotter." He was a very hard-working man since he did not own property. Rather he had to lease small parcels from a local landowner so that he could provide for his large family. Several of those parcels he farmed were in the Sigdal parish, and one of which was called the "Frövold" farm. This land (which I have visited) is in a mountain clearing near a stream. Although their little stone house no longer stands, I could picture Asle and Barbru there, with their many children, foraging, fishing, milking a cow, tending sheep, planting crops. It took a tremendous amount of work and fortitude to make a living this way and Barbru and Asle's strength came from sheer will, but it also came from faith, family, friends and the traditions of life.

The grandparents were nearby: Barbru's mother, Turi Kristoffersdatter kept house for her husband, Torstein Pedersen, who was a furrier. His skills

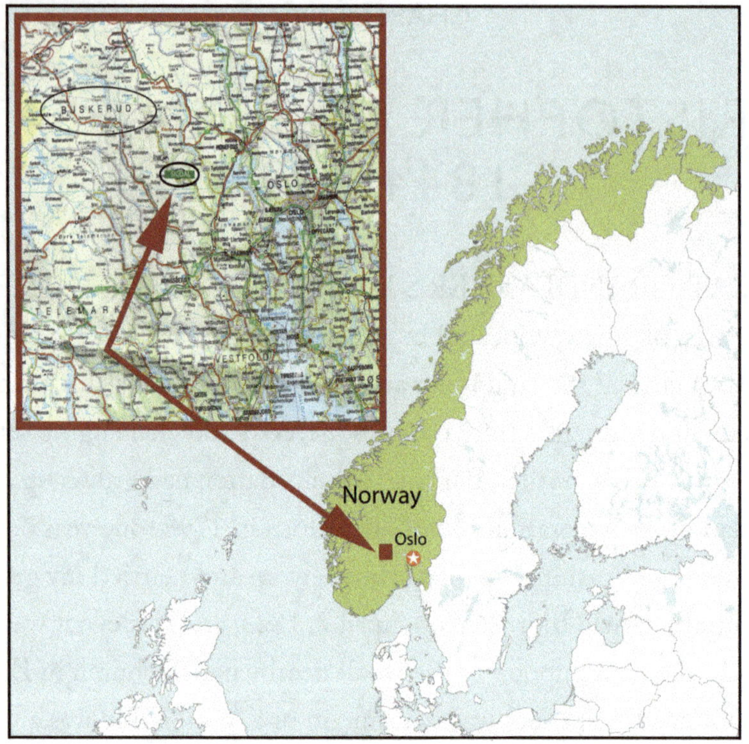

Top: map of Norway, with inset and red arrows pointing to Sigdal area.
Bottom: birth certificate for Kristoffer (Christopher) Aslesen.

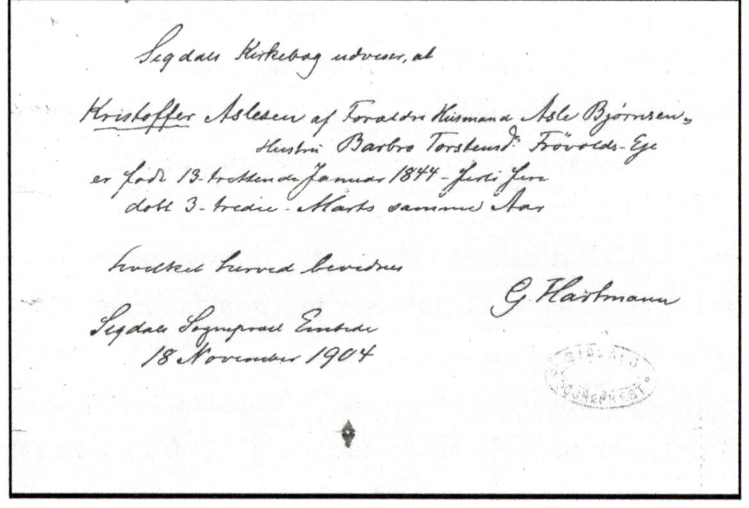

Sigdals Kirkebog udviser, at

Kristoffer Aslesen af Forældre Husmand Asle Björnsen,
Hustru Barbro Torsteinsd. Frövolds-Eje
er født 13-trettende Januar 1844 - [illegible]
døbt 3-tredie - Marts samme Aar

hvilket herved bevidnes

G. Hartmann

Sigdals Sogneprest Embede
18 November 1904

were much in demand in those frozen hills. His furs were essential to keeping warm in the cold houses of Norway, since down quilts were not common. He prepared sheep skins to make rugs and for use as covers in the horse-drawn sleighs in winter, and he sewed parts together to make big covers to use in beds. Their life on the Engen Nordre farm, which they leased, was modest and industrious and, I expect, filled with the love of family.

Asle and Barbru were blessed with many children; she gave birth to their eleventh and last child, the "baby of the family," who was my great-grandfather, **Christopher Aslesen**, on a cold winter day on January 13, 1844. He was swaddled in a warm fur blanket, and baptized shortly thereafter on March 3, 1844, while the family was living on the Frövold farm. His name in the Norwegian birth register was written thus: "Kristoffer Aslesen Frövoldeie."

You may have noticed that his last name at birth was not "Flaten." He adopted "Flaten" (pronounced FLAY-tn) later after he immigrated to America. His surname at birth was Aslesen. This is a "patronymic name" meaning he was named after his father's first name (Asle) with the suffix (son) added.

The final word "Frövoldeie" on his certificate indicates his birth place. In the Norwegian language, the "eie" suffix designates where a child is born. In his case, he was born on the farm property called Frövold and the "eie" translates to mean "at" that farm. The adopted name of Flaten was most likely taken from a nearby leased parcel called Frövolsflatin. Taking a last name from a countryside feature was called a "habitation name". In Norway, until the 18th century, only the nobility, civil servants and clergy had nonchanging last names. The adoption of a fixed last name was something all Norwegians did once they went to America.

CHRISTOPHER'S CHILDHOOD IN SIGDAL

It was in this mountain setting that he enjoyed his childhood. His family owned no land, and the land they leased was not choice land. As I have mentioned, this was a demanding life. Nonetheless, their lives and those of their neighbors were enlivened with troll tales and folk music from the hardanger fiddle. And what is childhood if not a time of play? For Christopher it was filled with the simple and cherished memories that are the sole purview of children around the world.

A fellow Norwegian, Anders Pedersen, writing in 1914, remembers his own childhood in Sigdal with this beautiful and nostalgic prose, giving us a very personal and poignant portrait to show what Christopher probably experienced as he grew up in the hills.

> "The land is small strips along the river where the woods do not prevail. There are hills all through Sigdal. As Nils Haugen said – the cows made the roads through Sigdal. In the old days in Norway the roads followed the high places over the whole land to get to the buildings of the larger farms, which were most often on the highest point of the farm. We traveled by cart but got off on the steep hills to make it easier for the horses. There were saw mills for meal, and fishing holes for trout during strong rain showers. The more it rained, the better the trout bit the hook, and it was only after the water became stirred with mud that they would bite. We used a hand cart in the summer and a sled in the winter to fetch our food (before we could afford a horse). I remember every hole and ridge in the yard and stone in the ground which lay in the same place as when I was a small boy. I climb the ridge and remember so many grand skiing competitions, and majestic snow angels. It is strange that the memories of our childhoods seem to be

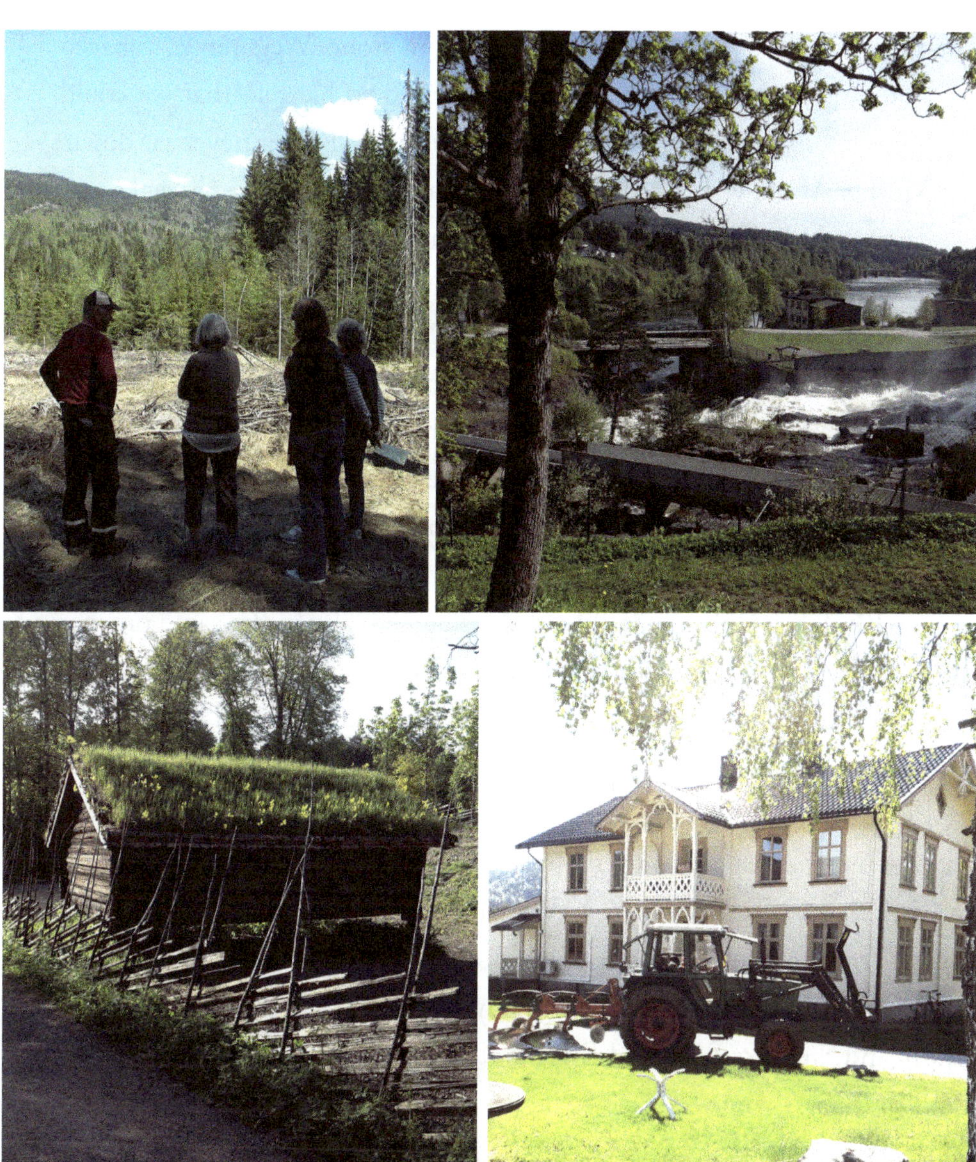

Clockwise from top left: Touring the original Aslesen land in Norway with Knut Båsen, Marianne Lauffer, Elizabeth Efroymson-Brooks, and our invaluable guide, Sigrid Kvisle. Landscape in Sigdal. Knut' s farmhouse in Frövold, likely standing during Christopher's life. The farm Flatin belonged to Frövolds earlier, but has since changed ownership. Today Frövold is split into two farms, and the owners of Frövold are Knut Båsen (who has turned the farm over to his daugher Gunn) and Nils Aasand. Knut's son, Bjørn lives at the farm and is a talented artist.) The small cottage would have housed sheep, goats and cows. Photos by author. 2014.

> the strongest. We made small houses from stone. We smoked tobacco from a pipe. My mother and father worked so hard so that we could present ourselves with honor in the community. Father never sat down. Mother would work in the fields, put leaves into large heavy sacks and carry them home, and mend clothes at night."

For Asle and Barbru, feeding their eleven children was a challenge but they managed. After all, the world around them had changed for the better. After the Napoleonic wars ended in 1815, they and everyone in Norway saw an improvement in living conditions. Hunger and epidemic were now solved with peace, potatoes, and the smallpox vaccine. Family sizes grew very large as a result.

But Christopher's family did not share equally in the same prosperity as the farmers who owned the large land tracts. Even though Christopher's family consumed herring and potatoes and may have received the smallpox vaccine, it was a hard struggle. Death was a frequent visitor.

Of the Aslesen's eleven children, two died in infancy (Bjorn b. 1823 and the first-named Christopher b. 1840). Three died quite young (Svanaug at 17, Liv at 19, Torsten at 25). Were their early deaths due to accidents, illness, or starvation? It is hard to know. Of the remaining six, two married and moved to a different area of Norway (Turi b. 1823 a twin to the earlier Bjorn; and the second-named Bjorn b. 1825) and the last four (Narve b. 1830, Berit b. 1833 -- who was Liv's twin, Barbro b. 1841 and Christopher b. 1844) emigrated to America. In 1852, there were five children at home: Bjorn (who would soon marry and move elsewhere in Norway) and the others who would soon leave for America: Narve, Berit, Barbro, and Christopher.

Their struggles could always be endured if there was hope. But given their perpetual landless status and the fact that land ownership was not only costly but unlikely given the inheritance laws, the lure of inexpensive American land was like a magnet to the young. The western territories of the U.S. were being conquered, divided, parceled, sold, and practically given away to those willing to not only stake a claim – but to also endure extreme hardship while doing so. And yet, to leave Norway meant to rip up roots that had been planted by many generations.

With lack of a future at home and with the promise of free land in America, and with the particular naive optimism that the young embrace, Narve left Norway in 1852, as the family's "pathfinder" and sailed to America, sending back advice and assistance to his sisters who followed and finally to his youngest brother, Christopher. Once the children left Norway, they most likely never returned. And once their father died in Norway in 1867, their mother followed them to America.

NARVE ASLESEN THE PATHFINDER GOES TO AMERICA

Narve arrived in America in 1852. What a spectacle greeted him! The panorama of America was much wilder than the one that would later lie before his brother Christopher's eyes only thirteen years later, in 1865. For in front of him lay few settlements west of the Mississippi, no trains and much unchartered territory. Here, it was exciting to feel the hope of new possibilities. Narve was a pioneer, a term little appreciated today since it takes time to digest exactly what type of desperation and hope fueled his ambitions.

More than just an immigrant knocking at the door of a nation, Narve was an immigrant hell-bent on a mission, that mission being land ownership. Tired, poor, wrecked refuse yearning to breathe free, homeless and tempest-tossed? No way! He was fueled with ambition, drive, determination and fire and this drive lasted a lifetime. He was unafraid to risk his life, sail rough waters and ride straight into the wild terrain of a nation soon at war with itself

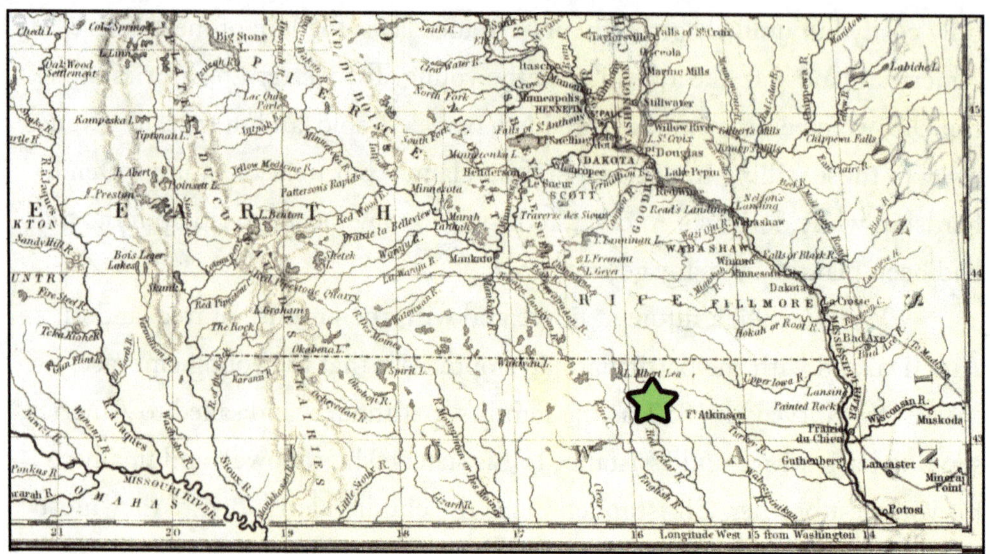

THE TERRITORY OF MINNESOTA: 1853. This Sectional Map shows the unsurveyed townships, undivided lands, roads, trails and Indian villages. The green dot marks the approximate location of Nunda near the settlement of Mansfield. Narve and Astri arrived there in 1858. When they arrived, the area had not been fully subdivided and much was still wild. Map: Hennepin Public Library.

and certainly at war with the indigenous people. With almost no safety nets or guarantees, no promise of protection from accidents, crime or death along the way, his trip is a marvelous adventure to contemplate.

But his risks were nothing compared to the yoke of poverty from which he was attempting to escape.

Although exaggeration makes for a good story, let me tell you that I do not exaggerate when I say that the prospect of owning land in America was such a grand opportunity that the miracle of it all is best understood by describing in more detail the system of land ownership that he sought to break free of in Norway.

There, land ownership was possible only for those who had been rich enough to purchase land from the Crown, church, or state, and once obtained, it became a generational guarantee of wealth and status. Indeed, there was (and still is today) an ancient "allodial right" to the land which means that any property sold must first be made available to a member of the family. This assures a very long-lasting agrarian society in Norway and means that land continues to stay in families for generation upon generation.

Land ownership meant that once a man owned his property, like the king, he owned it "by the Grace of God" and on it owed no rent, taxes, or even services (such as the obligation to fight in wars). The land itself created income from tenants, but more importantly, with it came absolute claim to the vital assets: hunting bases, areas for gathering eiderdown and eggs, fishing stations and more. This meant that cotters and tenants had to pay levies and tithes to hunt, fish, fell trees, and feed their families.

On this land, the farmlands were divided by "communal ownership" in an open field system. The landowner allowed two types of people to live on the land: a tenant (cotter) and a freeholder (a peasant with certain lease rights "bygselrett"). All yearly rents were calculated according to the size of one's accumulated goods (seed, butter, livestock, etc.) The cotters were stuck: the more success they had with farming, the higher the rate they paid in rent. Many freeholders leased multiple farms in order to try to prosper, but to no avail. Inheritance rules could make the transfers complicated or impossible, and any profits on the improvements on their leasehold farm might partly accrue to the landowner anyway. Later in the 1850s, something called the newer "cottager system" was added, which meant a large increase in the number of cottagers and a strict definition of their compulsory services on the farm. But these farms were ruled at times by little "barons" or "lords." Although the cottagers were connected to the transition from the old freeholder system to a newer freehold peasant ownership system, the Aslesens were cotters without money or prospects. It was a problem with only one possible solution: immigration.

So, once he reached the shores of America, Narve's strategy as an American pioneer was this: he spent the first six years of his life in Clinton, Rock County, Wisconsin in a community with other Norwegians. He took a job as a farm laborer in order to accumulate money. While there in 1856 he married young Astri Eriksdatter, also from Sigdal, a woman who had as much drive and ambition as he. And together, they and a group of Norwegians moved west to Freeborn County, Minnesota in a caravan following news from earlier Norwegian settlers in Winneshiek, Iowa (who had gone out to establish their claims in Freeborn County in 1854) that it was fertile and open land and much more affordable than land in Wisconsin! They hitched their covered wagons and set forward to the wide and marvelously open spaces of the new "Territory of Minnesota," so new that people voted for representatives even though it had not yet even been declared a State.

How I wish that I could have been sitting under the bow of their prairie schooner as they headed west. Narve and Astri stared out at a landscape of the pre-civil war era: the Dakota Sioux had been recently forced to cede nearly all of their land in the Minnesota Territory and homesteading had just opened up west of the Mississippi. Their wagon train drove through expanses with only military forts and few houses, but with lots of people living in their wagons. It was exhilarating beauty, tempered by terrible tales of great danger. They especially remembered one about an Iowa snowstorm so terrible it was dubbed the "Memorable Winter of 1856." But the land! It waited as a prize before their eyes. Narve and Astri were part of the onrush, the so-called "Western Fever," so crowded with wagons that it is hard to imagine today.

How was this land available to them at this time? The federal government had acquired this land through land cession treaties. Before the 1862 Homestead Act, which gave away free land to settlers, there was the Preemption Act. Under it, squatters were allowed to establish claims on surveyed (and later, unsurveyed) land and they paid a price for that land. Later, the railroads played the biggest part in determining land settlement out west.

Narve and Astri were headed to land which, one year earlier in 1857, had been granted to four railroad companies (including the Southern Minnesota Rail Road [SMRR] Company). This land was broken up into alternate sections (six miles in width on each side of the roads and their branches.) The railroads paid only 3 percent of their gross earnings in lieu of taxes, and were exempt from all taxation until sold. They were given 10 years to construct their roadbeds. There was quite a scandal in 1857 as these companies proved they had little money or knowledge to build a railroad. Since the state needed these lines so badly, however, a very controversial loan by the legislature quickly granting credit to these four railroad companies was referred to as the "Five Million Dollar Loan" was passed later in 1860. But these bonds were difficult for the railroads to sell, and, once again they were unable to pay their interest on the bonds. Since the railroads were in default, it was a good time to buy property. Quite a number of the Sections in Mansfield Township were owned by the SMRR which had received its land grant to build in 1857 but defaulted on payments in 1860.

Their ultimate destination, Freeborn County, Minnesota, was seeing plenty of traffic. A history of the time states that nearby residents of the town of Mansfield exclaimed, "incomers' attention is turned our way!" Mansfield, typical of the small farming communities of the area, was settled mostly by people from northern Germany, but they also had a then-called "littlement of Norwegians" who had grouped together in their own section. And although a few schools and churches were seen as signs of civilized and intelligent people, folks there also noted that "there is trouble getting legal documents signed, marriages legalized, and finding single women."

SETTLING DOWN ON SECTION 33 IN THE TERRITORY OF MINNESOTA

Finally, after six weeks by wagon on bumpy roads (barely more than paths which had been surveyed by early self-formed railroad companies), Narve and Astri arrived in Freeborn County, Minnesota in 1858, where they soon hurried to the Land Office to stake a claim on land in Section 33 in the nearby township of Nunda, land which had been subdivided as an original settlement by the Southern Minnesota Rail Road (SMRR) Company.

Early family documents of this period are few, but there is a written reference to Narve in "Early Settlements of Nunda," a history of Freeborn County, as remembered in 1882 by the original settlers:

> "The early or earliest settlement of Nunda dates back to 1856 and was rapid and constant until all of the vacant land was secured and occupied. Amongst, if not the first settlers in the township, were James

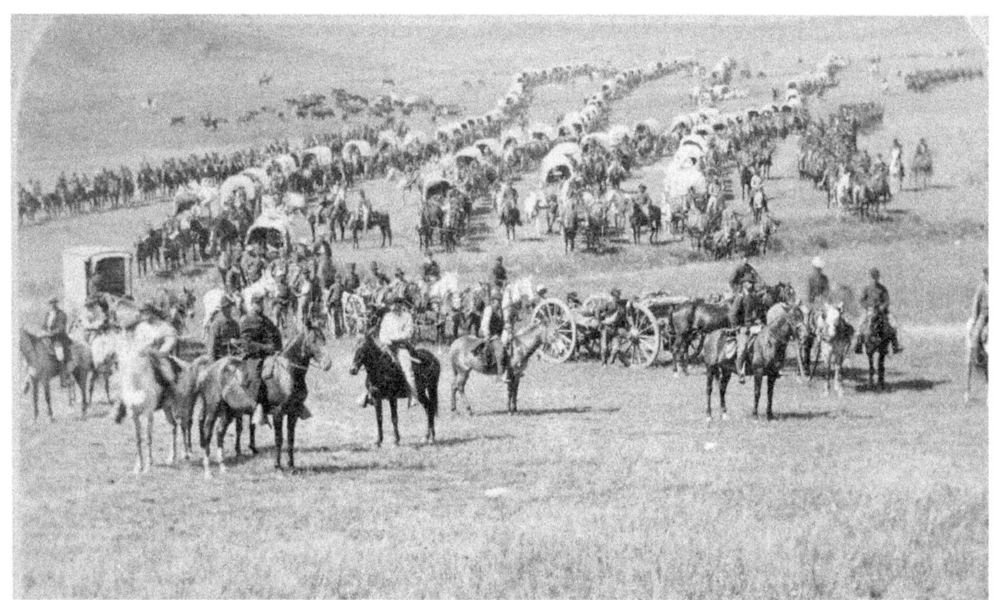

Above: A column of cavalry, artillery, and wagons, commanded by Gen. George A. Custer, crossing the plains of Dakota Territory. By W. H. Illingworth, 1874 Black Hills expedition. Although this is a military group, one can see a good view of the open territory and the spectacle of a wagon train. Photo NARA 77-HQ-264-854.

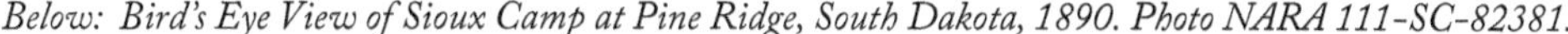

Below: Bird's Eye View of Sioux Camp at Pine Ridge, South Dakota, 1890. Photo NARA 111-SC-82381.

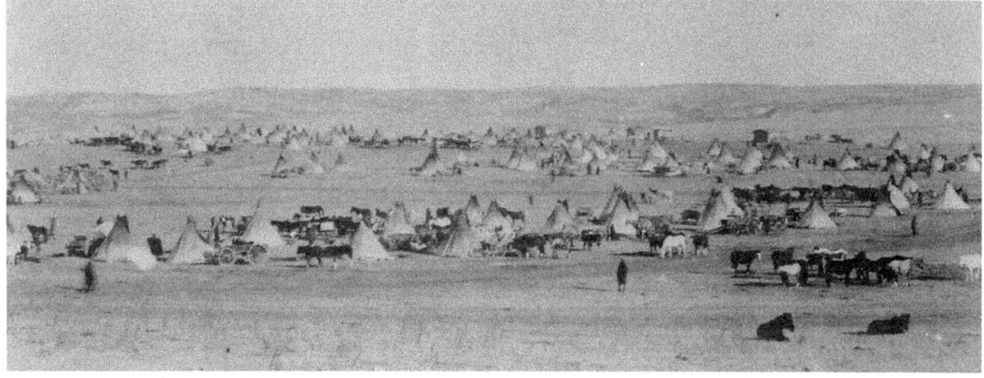

> Wright and Anthony Bright, who came in the winter of 1855-56 and commenced what was known as the Bear Lake settlement. … The year 1857 marked a large influx in population. [Settlers were from Ireland, Norway via Winneshiek County, Iowa, New York, Vermont, Germany, etc.] … In 1858, Narve Esleson, of Norway, lost no time in securing a habitation in section thirty-three where he now lives. Knudt Oleson in 1861 had also secured land and has since been joined by others of his countrymen. … Narve Flaaten, Peter Larson, Tosten Nelson, Stenger Jellum, Hogan Rasmusson and others also came in 1858. Politically speaking, the residents of Nunda first came together in 1857….a blacksmith shop was opened in the spring of 1866…a general merchandise store in 1880 … a sorghum mill in 1873."
> (Narve Flaaten was not, as far as I can determine, related.)

Happy as new landowners, the residents of Freeborn County soon realized that purchasing land also meant putting up with problems caused by the railroad. Specifically, taxing and collecting revenue for upkeep of roads was the major issue and continued to be the bane of their existence throughout everyone's lifetime. The railroad did not have funds to build roads (although part of its grant obligated it to provide roads) and the towns did not want to subsidize the railroad. There was a deep distrust between the railroad companies and the citizens which was traced back to "The Panic of 1857" when railroad companies could not fulfill the terms of their land grants, so the Minnesota State Legislature issued illegal bonds to the tune of 5 million dollars to bail them out. No one ever forgot about it, especially at town hall meetings. At one Mansfield Town Council meeting, they proudly declared, the town is "out of debt and has never voted any railroad bonds to beggar the people and enrich monopolists."

But in spite of the obstacles, Narve and Astri treasured their new home. There were signs that their land had been previously worked; there were already a few structures on the land. Narve was interested in education from the start and soon hosted the first school—the school in District No. 44 was taught in a vacant house on his property by Miss Sarah Emery. The Aslesens had only a baby at the time but there would soon be more pupils on the way.

STILL WILD TERRITORY: A BROADER HISTORY OF MINNESOTA

Narve and Astri settled into their cabin in Nunda. Meanwhile, America was in a state of extreme crisis.

All of this wild and unsettled land was available because the Minnesota Territory legislature had just sent a representative to Washington armed with a big check for $50,000 in order to purchase a land grant. The Land Grant passed Congress on March 4, 1857, as one of last bills signed by President Pierce. Two months later, Minnesota was admitted into the Union on May 11, 1858. (Slavery was specifically ruled illegal in their new state.)

Narve and Astri had so much determination to survive and build that they absolutely could not be deterred from day-to-day struggles by the wider issues, but their "littlement of Norway" could not have foreseen the next events in American history which put their efforts into perspective: their lives became truly imperiled, for up to this point the challenges had been like trying to remain afloat in a canoe on a rushing stream. But what came next had the force of Niagara Falls, and over they went.

On April 12, 1861, the U.S. Civil War was declared. By March 1862, Minnesota mustered a full infantry regiment and sent companies south to Mississippi, Tennessee, and Alabama while others stayed to defend nearby Fort Ridgely. And while there is no evidence that Narve fought in the Civil

War, many residents of Freeborn County participated as soldiers of a regiment.

A short while later, on August 17, 1862, "The Indian Outbreak of 1862" began. This extremely violent event took many lives and represented the last efforts of the Dakota Sioux people to hold on to their hunting rights in Minnesota. Most likely, Astri and the children fled to the safety of Fort Ridgely about 100 miles northwest of their home, as about 800 settlers were killed by some of the Dakota Sioux. The following text is intended as general information about this uprising and is taken from a Wiki page. While I have read contemporary accounts of this incident and encourage you to do the same, I won't diverge from the family history in order to elaborate on this subject, so I respectfully provide only this basic information.

The Dakota Sioux had been removed to a reservation in Minnesota in 1851 and hunting buffalo was their chief means of subsistence. The government had signed to buy property from the Sioux and to make annuity payments, so the Sioux came to the Government Agency to collect the agreed-upon money and goods, most of which were late or never made available. There was unfair dealing between the agents and the traders to the exclusion of the Sioux. The Indians incurred debt while realizing they were being rapidly pushed off of their ancestral lands of choice agricultural soil, streams, forests, and stone quarries. Some, but certainly not all, of the Sioux were hostile, but they were all literally starving. It came to a head on August 17, 1862, when a party of Sioux approached a home, an argument ensued over a borrowed wagon and food, and the residents were shot. The Sioux traveled on to several other homesteads, shooting more residents. As soon as the tribe learned of these murders, some in the council declared war on all settlers. The Sioux decided to attack the Government Agency the next morning and to kill all traders. The Agency was attacked, and settlers ran to Fort Ridgely.

Many settlements were attacked and extensive killing began. An estimated 800 settlers were killed. In response, soldiers captured hundreds of Dakota men and interred their families. Surrender finally took place in December 1862. A military tribunal sentenced 303 Indians to death, but President Lincoln commuted the sentence of 264. On the day after Christmas, December 26, 1862, after trials and sentencing by a military court, 38 Dakota men were hanged (one commutation) in Mankato in the largest one-day mass execution in American history. The next year, the rest of the Dakota were expelled from Minnesota to Nebraska and South Dakota. The United States Congress abolished their reservations. Their defeat meant the end of any payment of further annuities, all discontinued by an Act of Congress.

At the same time, Congress was busy appropriating more land. Land mapping and distribution was happening in the midst of Civil War. Like a prairie fire, the flames of Western migration were fully conflagrated by the time of the passing of the historic "Homestead Act" on May 20, 1862, granting 160 acres without cost to any settler who promised to cultivate the land for five years. The Civil War ended April 9, 1865, and the men from Freeborn County, Minnesota returned home to continue with farming. And as a final reminder of federal power, on November 10, 1865, Sioux Chief, Shakpedan, and another man named Medicine Bottle were executed at Fort Snelling, Minnesota, 100 miles due north of Narve and Astri's home.

CHRISTOPHER ASLESEN LEAVES NORWAY and HIS ARRIVAL IN AMERICA

BY SHIP

Meanwhile, Christopher prepared to meet Narve and Astri in Minnesota, excited that free land was now to be had through the Homestead Act. He was living alone with his father and mother, 72 and 67, but since he

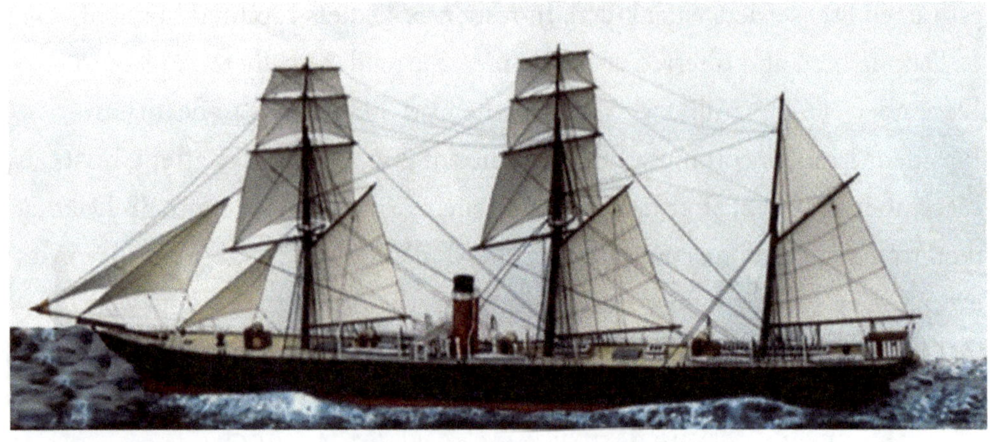

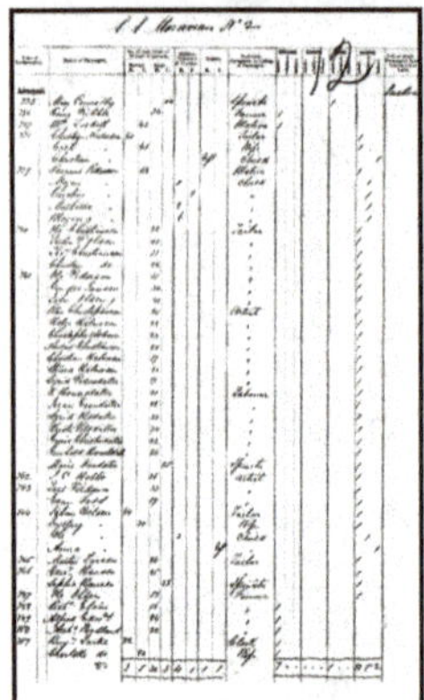

Above: A model of the S.S. Moravian created by "Bob" (no last name provided). Art: 2020 Caledonian Maritime Research Trust.

Left: the Captain's ship log. Christopher is listed as a passenger. The ship sailed from Liverpool to Quebec in 1865. Freeborn Co. Historical Society.

Christopher's actual itinery is unknown. However, based on information about trips taken at the time by other immigrants, the itinerary I describe is likely. Below: an 1885 map for Christopher's hypothetical train journey from Quebec to Milwaukee. This assumes he ended in Milwaukee. This was a common route for Norwegian immigrants and would have put him closer to Rock County, Wisconsin. The train route is speculative, and is based on the supposition that his brother, Narve, met him and escorted him back to the settlement in Minnesota. Map: David Rumsey.

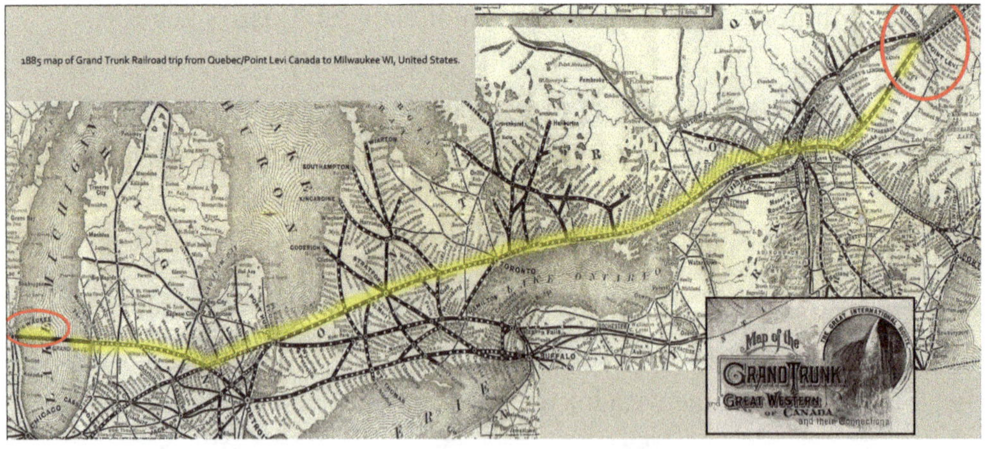

was now 21, he was legally able to emigrate. To do so, he received his papers from the Minister in Sigdal on April 18, 1865, and immediately began to make preparations to go to America.

He traveled by steamship on the *S.S. Moravian*; that much is documented. As to his actual itinerary and experiences during the trip, I have reconstructed, based on contemporaneous trips, what his trip to America would have likely been like. His journey might have begun at the farm in Sigdal, continued by wagon to the fiord of Christiana (Oslo), then by sail to where he would set foot on deck of a new steamship waiting in port in Liverpool, then by this steamship to Quebec, the port of entry to America.

Based on information of the time, in preparation, a few years earlier, Christopher would have had to have carefully packed his own food for the long journey: dried meats, herring, peas, potatoes and flatbread, flour, butter, whey, beer and sour milk to last at least three weeks aboard a sailing ship. What a packing list! But fortunately for him, sailing to America was easier due to the new steam engine technology. Christopher's steamship, the *S.S. Moravian,* was known for accommodating the immigration trade and they boasted supplying "plentiful provisions ... with as much food as they can eat, all of the best quality and cooked and served out by the company's servants." And the journey would not last three weeks but now only twelve days.

Since he probably chose to travel steerage class, the ship informed him that he would still need to furnish his own bedding and utensils. So, he packed sheepskin coverlets, a plate, mug, knife, fork, spoon, and water can, all of which (along with farm implements) he packed into carefully labeled trunks. The trunks were then loaded onto a cart, then later hoisted onto a boat sitting in the harbor in Christiania, soon to set sail for the huge port of emigration, Liverpool, now swelling with thousands bound for America. Once arriving in Liverpool, he purchased his ticket from the steamship company. Instead of carrying ready cash, he tucked a draft from the steamship company into his coat pocket to exchange for American money in Milwaukee.

While waiting to board in Liverpool, he admired the *S.S. Moravian*, an iron single-screw steamship, in all her magnificence. She was a British passenger/cargo ship, part of the Allan Line, built in 1864 on the Clyde River in Scotland by Robert Steele and Company, a company known for excellence in ship building. Propulsion was to be by sail and steam: one screw (propeller) and three masts, attaining a speed of 11 knots per hour with 500 hp and a weight of 2,600 tons. She was a thing of beauty on the sea.

But it may not have been a smooth voyage. Sea sickness was inevitable. He may have found sleeping in the narrow berth challenging, as the salon and staterooms were all in the extreme after-part near the noisy screw engine. There were no electric lights or opening portholes. Even a bath was very scarce. If dressed properly he could get a hosing off early in the morning by the boatswain. However, the accommodations were still considered very good by standards of the day. He was able to walk about the entire deck of the ship, as ventilation and safety were very important features. The captains and officers displayed gentlemanly bearing and earned praise and admiration. And the food provided was superior. There was much to be commended. Yes, gone were the days of miserable, long and dangerous voyages. It was comfortable enough that even British author Frances Hodgson Burnett (author of *The Secret Garden)* and her family had emigrated on that very same ship one month earlier in June 1865. (The Burnetts settled in Tennessee.)

Once settled onboard, Christopher most likely befriended other Norwegians, including Guri Kristensdatter Råmanset, from Buskerud, accompanied by her brother, Anders Kristensen Råmanset. They became acquainted and all registered on the Captain's Log as members of "Group 741." (Strangely, both Christopher and Anders specified their occupation as "artist" while other choices on the log were tailor, musician, matchmaker, laborer, spinster, farmer, clerk, matron, child, mason, miner, carpenter. Why did they choose "artist"? A careless bookkeeping entry perhaps? A problem with English literacy?)

Probably the voyage was rather crowded, yet they passed the time pleasantly by sharing tales of Sigdal and Eggedal, farms and families, and listening to music-makers aboard ship. Was it over the advertised breakfast of coffee, sugar, fresh bread, oatmeal porridge, and molasses that Christopher determined to marry Guri? Perhaps during that supper of fish and potatoes with pudding for dessert?

After twelve days at sea, Christopher Aslesen, Guri and Anders, and their fellow passengers sailed past Belle Isle, up the St. Lawrence River, and straight into Quebec, Canada on June 22, 1865, and all were most eager for the next leg of the journey, to finally step foot on American soil. Fortunately, the Allan Line made the process easier than it had been for earlier immigrants.

BY TRAIN

Once they landed at the Quebec port and had their papers stamped "approved" for entry into the United States via Canada, they were loaded onto a steamer and shuttled to the south shore of the St. Lawrence River to the "New Liverpool Cove" and nearby Pointe-Lévy Railroad Station. The steamer had been provided by the railroad company, making their transition as smooth as possible from sea to rail. Once docked at the cove, they were loaded directly into the waiting train, thus avoiding being taken advantage of (as one contemporary guidebook cautioned) "by the intrigues of designing lodging-housekeepers and others," a notorious problem for tired and gullible travelers.

I personally visited this very same train station at Pointe-Lévy while on a trip to Quebec in 2015. With the help of a friendly Canadian cyclist, my husband Pat and I were escorted to the village of New Liverpool, where we saw photographs of the old wharf and ships surrounded by thousands of floating logs, ready for transport to England. It was a reminder of how industrial this port used to look, but also how wooded the surrounding countryside was, too.

The train, the *Grand Trunk Railroad,* into which Christopher, Guri and Anders, and the other passengers safely boarded, had recently been established in Pointe-Lévy, making rail travel now possible from Maine to the whole United States. But riding the Grand Trunk could be a mixed bag. Sometimes immigrants who had been given a special low rate were crowded into trains with uncomfortable seats and lost bags. And which class or section of the train did Christopher choose to take? For his comfort, I shall kindly place him in a comfortable car and assume Narve had sent him at least enough money to afford it. Perhaps Guri and Anders were seated nearby? After all, they would all end up, eventually, in the same town of Mansfield.

Now comfortably seated, Christopher stared out the window at vast forestland as the train rattled west, first to Detroit, then to Grand Haven, Michigan, then via steamer across Lake Michigan to Milwaukee. Only four weeks earlier he had been in the hills of Sigdal. Now he marveled at this foreign land and at the vast expanse of flat terrain. As he pictured the land he would own he felt the narcotic pull of permanence and the elixir of hope. Here, finally, was opportunity, and he could accomplish anything with the strength of his own hands. Opportunity was soon to present itself.

THE FINAL LEG: BY WAGON

When his train finally pulled into the Milwaukee station on May 9, 1865 (one month after the final day of the end of the Civil War) Christopher stepped off the train onto the wooden platform, strode through the board-

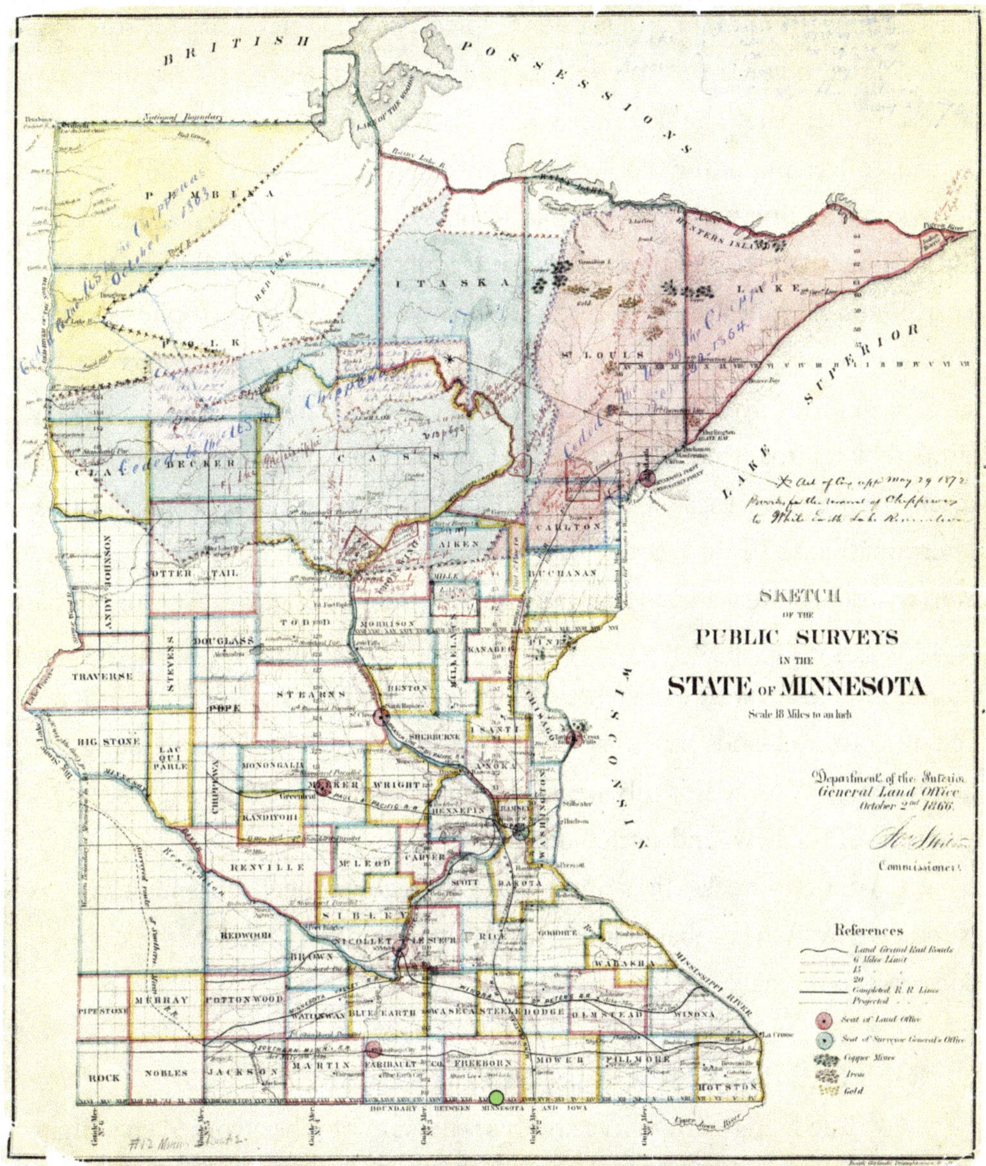

THE STATE OF MINNESOTA: 1866. This map reflects the surveyed subdivions of townships, railroad lines, land offices, and mines (iron and gold) in place at the time Christopher arrived here in 1865. Freeborn County is located at the bottom edge of the state, in the middle where the green dot is. Map: NARA 6039426.

and-batten waiting room and suddenly spied Narve. What a site for sore eyes he was! "Hei! Hvordan har du det?" It had been thirteen years since they last saw each other. They shook hands while Christopher described the details of his trip, conversing in the old Norwegian tongue.

Continuing with this possible scenario, once outside, Narve hoisted Christopher's trunks and boxes onto his wagon, slapped the oxen, and off they set overland 80 miles south to Rock County, Wisconsin. Christopher shared news from home. Fatigue began to prevail, but he was intensely overcome by his surroundings. They passed soldiers on foot and families in covered wagons camped by the roadside. Once at Rock County, Christopher was welcomed by others from Sigdal. These were the earlier settlers who shared his unshakable determination to begin a new life. They rested briefly and he shared news from the old country and took in news about the farming, weather, and details about the new Homestead Act. After resting several days, they finally set out another 300 miles west to Freeborn County in the new state of Minnesota. The uncultivated lands passed slowly by, as their wagon meandered along the rough dirt trail in the hot July weather. Christopher inhaled the new scents, as the spirit of the new land settled deeply into his soul.

After two weeks, they drove into the rustic pioneer settlement of Nunda where Astri probably greeted them with a hearty meal of pork, potatoes, apple cake, and black coffee.

CHRISTOPHER CHOOSES HIS LAND: SECTION 14

While living with Narve and his wife, Christopher worked steadily to improve Narve's property, and a year later he looked to purchase his own. He attended a public meeting in the nearby new town of Mansfield and applied for a grant for farmland by paying a small filing fee at the Land Office. He then sat down, carefully unrolled a map of Mansfield Township and began studying it, looking for natural assets and prime farmland. As he considered each alternating, odd-numbered section which had been subdivided by the SMRR, he pointed to Section 14. On it was a small patch of oak to the north, an essential fuel to survive the brutal winters. This property in Section 14 looked very attractive to him.

He chose well. It was only ten miles from his brother Narve, and there was a large lake to the north and the state of Iowa to the south. It was very much a "full prairie" township, described at the time by surveyors as ideal farmland with these words: " … the soil is dark loam, underlaid with sand and gravel. ... there is Bear Lake to the north in Nunda, and a small creek, Lime Creek, in the southeast with its outlet emptying into the Shell Rock River on a southwesterly course."

Some might say this land came with a special pedigree. Only 21 years earlier, in June 1835, Capt. Nathan Boone, youngest son of the famed explorer Daniel Boone, had walked through these very same fields. Boone, acting as guide for Capt. Albert Lea and his three detachments of 60 men, was doing surveying along the Des Moines and Mississippi Rivers.

So here, on Section 14, Christopher Aslesen set down his roots in America, establishing himself on 160 acres that returned to him with pride of ownership what he put into it with devotion, constant toil, and determination despite the extreme hardships which he was to see. There it was! The guarantee that finally he was to be a landowner with rights and an inheritance to pass to his children. Nevermore a cotter. The shackles of poverty loosened its hold.

CHRISTOPHER BUILDS HIS FARM IN MANSFIELD

FIRST MARRIAGE

Shortly after he filed on his claim he proposed to and married the young girl that he had met on the voyage over, Guri Christensdatter Råmanset. This happy event took place on January 6, 1866, in the parlor of the nearby house of Eric Ellingson in Silver Lake, Iowa. Narve served as a witness and later the new couple registered their marriage at Silver Lake Lime Creek Church.

One year after marriage Guri was pregnant, but their daughter, Gunhild, died a year after birth. Their next child, Asle Christopherson ("A.C."), was born on a cold day in January 1869, and grew up a strong, healthy lad, eventually spending almost his whole life on the farm. They worshipped at Silver Lake Lime Creek Church and relied on family and neighbors who came together to collectively build and share practical information. Guri's brother Anders and their mother Barbro lived nearby, and so they were also there to help.

Then suddenly Guri died, and all records of the date and reason are lost. Thus, Christopher became a widower with one child. Fortunately, Christopher's mother Barbru, who had immigrated to Minnesota by this time, lived with Narve and Astri. Perhaps he sent little A.C. to live with them and the cousins while he continued to farm. But he forged ahead because time does not stand still, especially for Minnesota farmers. Change meant progress. The nation continued to expand. Newspapers announced the completion of the mighty Transcontinental Railroad in Utah on May 10, 1869. And the pioneers continued to arrive.

Townsfolk later recorded that in this year "the tide of emigration in May was at its flood. Prairie schooners by the score were passing through town and day after day the white canvas might be seen surrounded by herds of cattle as they wended their way westward." County Council notes from this year also record everything of concern, from intoxicated citizens, to land swindles, to suicides, gales, church bell installations, and accidents with gruesome details which were not uncommon: "Joseph Schorbeck, fourteen years of age, was killed by a runaway accident early in January. His body was dragged three miles and mangled beyond all recognition."

SECOND MARRIAGE

In 1871, Christopher obtained his U.S. citizenship, a milestone. Here, it is most important to note that he listed his last name on his citizenship papers as "Flaten." He used this new last name when he married a second time, at age 28, to my great-grandmother, Margaret ("Margit") Taralsdatter, age 21, on May 26, 1872. Margaret's family had immigrated to the area the same year as Christopher, in 1865. Her father owned a farm nearby on Section 2, Mansfield Township. He may have been introduced to her through his next-door neighbor, farmer Kittel Taralson Olsen, who was Margaret's youngest brother.

Very soon thereafter, on September 30, 1872, the birth of my grandfather **Gunerius Aslesen Flaten** occurred in Alden, Freeborn County, Minnesota. He was baptized, according to Silver Lake Church records on November 10, 1872. (His middle name on the birth certificate was Aslesen, but he used the middle name "Christopher" throughout his life.) The witnesses were, once again, Narve and Astri, as well as Margit's sisters Ingrid and Birgit Taralsdatter. The families enjoyed a small church celebration.

But as soon as the new year began, the deadly forces of nature suddenly arose and stunned Christopher with fierce force. He could not have imagined his close call with death in what old-timers would forever recall as "The Blizzard of 1873." Here is an account from the local Manchester newspaper:

> "On January 7th, the thermometer dropped some thirty or forty degrees in one minute and in as brief a time the worst blizzard

Certificate of Baptism

He that believeth and is baptized shall be saved. Mark 16:16

This Certifies

That Gunerius Aslesen Flaten a Son

of Kristoffer Aslesen Flaten and his wife

Margit born on the 30 day of

September in the Year of our Lord, One Thousand ~~Nine~~ Eight Hundred

and 72, at Freeborn County, Minnesota

Received
Holy Christian Baptism

on the 10 day of November in the Year of our Lord,

One Thousand ~~Nine~~ Eight Hundred and 72.

Almighty God, the Father of our Lord Jesus Christ, who hath begotten thee again of water and the Holy Ghost, and hath forgiven thee all thy sins, strengthen thee with His grace unto life everlasting.

Sponsors: Narve A. Flaten, Astrid E. Flaten

Ingrid Taralson, Birgit Taralson

B.B. Gjeldaker, Pastor 1870-1876

Silver Lake Church Records- Book 1, Page 254

In Witness Whereof, I have this 18 day of May in the Year of our Lord 1938 hereunto set my hand and the seal of Silver Lake Norwegian Evangelical Lutheran Congregation of Worth County, Iowa.

Casper T. Hjelstad Pastor

> known to the white settlers of Minnesota took the place on a mild and pleasant January day. The wind from the northwest attained a velocity of some forty miles an hour, and within sixty minutes the mercury touched thirty degrees below zero. After raging for fifty-two hours, the blizzard passed away as rapidly as it came. Several people in the county perished. One woman lost her way between her house and her barn and was found frozen to death fully two miles away. In some places in the state people perished in their beds."

Christopher, living near Bear Lake, had gone to haul firewood from the nearby woods but had gotten completely lost in the whiteout conditions and only survived by sheer chance when he stumbled upon safe refuge for shelter where he was able to wait it out. He could have easily been one who did not survive. In Minnesota, 70 people died of exposure and many were maimed for life in this infamous polar wave. Now, if this were a single catastrophe it might be put into perspective in time.

However, in September of the same year, much worse was yet to come. The entire state began to suffer an unrelenting onslaught of grasshoppers. The notorious "Grasshopper Raids" began and endured for five seasons, systematically stripping bare vast fields of wheat, oat, corn, and barley. There was devastation and countless, hopeless mitigation attempts.

Minnesota farmers tried many things to get rid of the grasshoppers. They beat the grasshoppers with flails. They dragged heavy ropes through their fields, and plowed and burned their fields. They raised birds and chickens to eat the grasshoppers. They dug ditches that they hoped the grasshoppers would be unable to jump over. They filled these ditches with coal tar and set them on fire, thinking that the smoke might drive away the hoppers if the ditches did not. In later years, farmers made "hopper dozers," which consisted of sheet metal covered in coal tar or molasses. They dragged the hopper dozers through their fields, catching grasshoppers in pans and then emptying the pans into fires. None of these efforts were successful. Eventually, in the summer of 1877, the grasshoppers vanished just as quickly as they had arrived. An April snowstorm damaged many of their eggs which encouraged farmers to redouble their efforts to destroy the grasshoppers. The surviving grasshopper eggs hatched, but by August the grasshoppers had flown away.

And as if those catastrophes were not enough, bad news came in three: the underpinning of the financial structure of the entire community buckled when the "Jay Cooke Failure" touched off a financial panic with widespread bankruptcies. (The Jay Cooke Bank financed the Civil War, but became overextended with building the Northern Pacific Railway. This panic triggered the Economic Depression of 1873-1877.)

What were the Flatens to do but to continue on and remain determined to survive to the next year and to return to the fields. If they knew how to do anything, they knew how to do much with little. Despite the loss of their wheat, Christopher and Margaret had a small income from honey and apples and they added a precious daughter, Anne Marie, in 1874 to their family. They undoubtedly got their strength from their church, their community, and their families.

In any case, Christopher had enough optimism to purchase adjacent land in 1872. In June, he purchased an additional 21 and 92/100 acres from Horace and Martha Robinson for the price of $150.00.

HE RECEIVES HIS LAND GRANT in 1874

Finally, the most important day in his life arrived, the turning point in his life, the achievement of all of his hopes and dreams. Christopher received

33

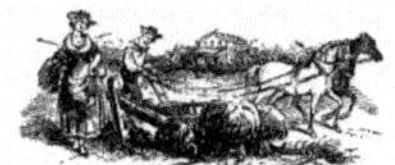

The United States of America,

TO ALL TO WHOM THESE PRESENTS SHALL COME, GREETING:

Homestead Certificate No. 3167
Application 5336

Whereas, there has been deposited in the **General Land Office** of the United States, a CERTIFICATE of the Register of the Land Office at Worthington Minnesota, whereby it appears that pursuant to the Act of Congress approved 20th May, 1862, "To secure Homesteads to actual settlers on the public domain," and the acts supplemental thereto, the claim of Christopher Aslesen has been established and duly consummated in conformity to law for the South west quarter of Section fourteen in Township one hundred and one, of Range twenty three in the district of Lands subject to Sale at Worthington Minnesota containing one hundred and sixty acres.

according to the Official Plat of the Survey of the said Land returned to the **General Land Office** by the SURVEYOR GENERAL.

Now know ye, That there is therefore granted by the UNITED STATES unto the said Christopher Aslesen the tract of Land above described: **To Have and to Hold** the said tract of Land, with the appurtenances thereof, unto the said Christopher Aslesen and to his heirs and assigns forever.

In Testimony whereof, Ulysses S. Grant, PRESIDENT OF THE UNITED STATES OF AMERICA, have caused these letters to be made Patent, and the **Seal of the General Land Office** to be hereunto affixed.

Given under my hand, at the CITY OF WASHINGTON, the fifth day of November, in the year of Our Lord one thousand eight hundred and Seventy four and of the Independence of the United States the Ninety Ninth

By the President: U. S. Grant

By S. D. Williamson, Sec'y.

L. K. Lippincott, Recorder of the General Land Office.

his land grant, signed by President Ulysses S. Grant on November 5, 1874. This meant that the land was his free and clear without mortgage. (Of course, he was still obligated to pay property taxes.) Here is, verbatim, that certificate: (see previous page)

Homestead Certificate No.: 3167. Application 5446.

The United States of America, to all to whom these presents shall come, greeting:

Whereas, there has been deposited in the General Land Office of the United States, a certificate of the Register of the Land Office at Worthington, Minnesota, whereby it appears that pursuant to the Act of Congress approved 20th May, 1862, "To secure Homesteads to actual settlers on the public domain," and the acts supplemental thereto, the claim of Christopher Asleson has been established and duly consummated in conformity to law for the South West quarter of section fourteen in Township one hundred and one of Range twenty-three in the district of Lands, subject to sale at Worthington, Minnesota containing one hundred and sixty acres according to the Official Plat of the Survey of the said Land returned to the General Land Office by the Surveyor General.

Now Know Ye, That there is therefore granted by the UNITED STATES unto the said Christopher Asleson the tract of Land above described: To Have and to Hold the said tract of Land, with the appurtenances thereof, unto the said Christopher Asleson and to his heirs and assigns forever.

In Testimony whereof, I, Ulysses S. Grant, PRESIDENT OF THE UNITED STATES OF AMERICA, have caused these letters to be made Patent, and the Seal of the General Land Office to be hereunto affixed. Given under my hand, at the CITY OF WASHINGTON, the fifth day of November, in the year of Our Lord, one thousand eight hundred and seventy-four and of the Independence of the United States the Ninety Ninth. [then signed by Grant, and two officials.] (Reproduction on page 43).

I assume that he applied for this land with the last name Asleson, and his land grant was titled with the same name even though his last name on his citizenship paper was Flaten. What last name did he go by in his community? A search through the local newspaper, the *Freeborn County Standard,* suggests that he went by Christopher Asleson and that his children consistently used the last name Flaten.

They very likely framed and hung this document and gave it a prominent place on the wall of their front parlor. But land ownership came with nonstop worries as they continued the battle against the Rocky Mountain locusts (1872-1877) which were still devouring crops. Throughout the county he found brotherhood with other farmers as they helped each other fight the locusts and replant fields, and found solace as they worshipped at church, and found a few hours in between for their continued petition to the county board to vote against the railroad's never-ending attempts to press for bonds to finance roadwork. Although few bonds were ever issued in Freeborn County, it makes for interesting and dusty reading to revisit the extremely heated objections brought forth from villagers and farmers whose property taxes were raised without proper notice. Many a railroad bond was contested and ended

A Horrible Accident

It is with sorrow that we record the horrible and heart-rending accident that occurred in the town of Mansfield, on last Tuesday, the 4th inst., in which a woman was burned to death.

Mr. Christopher Aslesen and family, living near the Mansfield postoffice, were the great suffers, and we give the details as our informant furnished them to us.

All the family had retired except Mrs. Aslickson, who was finishing up some of her household duties. Of a sudden, the husband was awakened by her cries and found her lying under the table with her clothes on fire. She said, "The lamp has burst," when she fainted and expired immediately. He carried her body to the door and rushed back into the flames to save the children, whom he succeeded in getting out safe, except one little boy whose hands are so badly burned that it is uncertain about saving either of them. Mr. Asleson was burned so badly that his life is in danger.

The body of Mrs. A. was nearly consumed. She leaves a husband and three children to mourn her loss. Dr. Rowland was called to attend them, and reports their condition critical. The house and contents were totally destroyed.

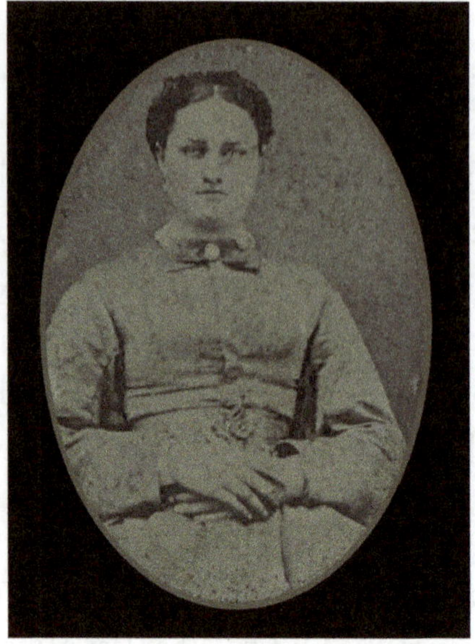

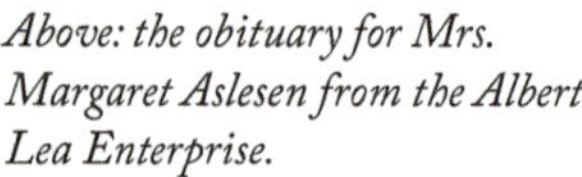

Above: the obituary for Mrs. Margaret Aslesen from the Albert Lea Enterprise.

Top right: an unverified photo which the author believes may be Margaret. Photo: IU Archives.

Below: photo labeled "mother". The author believes this to be Susana Gunhild Jacobsdatter, fourth wife of Christopher Aslesen. Photo: Collection of Margaret Daisley.

up in court. The county of Albert Lea had voted almost unanimously against the railroad bond question. But they did vote for buying coronets for the band and for fire extinguishers.

Amid the bonds and the bankruptcies, the bailouts and battles with bugs, the town's priorities lay with education, something Christopher willingly made an investment in. In 1875, just a few fields away, School No. 92 was built; he and Margaret's children did, indeed, walk to this school as soon as they were old enough. (I am sure they did not walk barefoot!) And a fine school it was. Built in 1875, a one-room schoolhouse, 18 x 24 feet, with fine high ceilings. The teacher was Mr. Ambrus Morey and that year he taught 21 scholars. Also in that same year, a post office was established at the postmaster's home, right next to the school. Considered a real luxury, it was a new way to get information quickly – seed catalogs, H.J. Ward Catalogs, and postcards.

But the very worst tragedy Christopher would ever know in his lifetime was to strike this year. In 1875, Christopher's wife Margaret (my great-grandmother) unexpectedly died in a fire when a hanging lamp exploded above her. Here is a transcription of the grim account from the local newspaper.

A Horrible Accident

It is with sorrow that we record the horrible and heart-rending accident that occurred in the town of Mansfield, on last Tuesday, the 4th inst., in which a woman was burned to death. Mr. Christopher Asleson and family, living near the Mansfield post office, were the great suffers [sic], and we give the details as our informant furnished them to us.

All the family had retired except Mrs. Aslickson, [sic] who

> was finishing up some of her household duties. Of a sudden, the husband was awakened by her cries and found her lying under the table with her clothes on fire. She said, "The lamp has burst," when she fainted and expired immediately. He carried her body to the door and rushed back into the flames to save the children whom he succeeded in getting out safe except one little boy whose hands are so badly burned that it is uncertain about savings either of them. Mr. Asleson was burned so badly that his life is in danger.
>
> The body of Mrs. A. was nearly consumed. She leaves a husband and three children to mourn her loss. Dr. Rowland was called to attend them and reports their condition critical. The house and contents were totally destroyed. *(Albert Lea Enterprise, Thurs March 11, 1875, p6)*

It is impossible to imagine how Christopher was able to recover, let alone go on, after having been burned so badly, but he somehow gathered strength from his community and his church to face life and loss. How did he protect his children and nurse them back to health, grieve the loss of his wife, rebuild his home and contents? He turned to Narve and Astrid, then to the Lime Creek Church parish for help to build once more from the ground up, surely, as he had helped others when they themselves needed it. His friend Ole Knudson built a coffin and the County Council covered the costs for the burial. But the amount of strength it must have taken to endure these hardships is beyond my understanding. Did he have what I observed in my own father, Clarence—a very stoic demeanor, a seemingly unshakable strength? Was there no time for grief?

And all the while, he and all of the farmers continued to fight against the grasshoppers. The grasshoppers continued until 1877, which was the same year Christopher married again for a third time.

THIRD MARRIAGE

Although his obituary lists only three marriages, records confirm there was a brief and tragic marriage in 1877. Records show that Christopher Aslesen married Ingebord Larson (of Tynes, Norway) on March 1, 1877, in Freeborn County. But again, sorrow struck soon thereafter: a year later, her infant daughter died after childbirth and she herself passed away one month later in 1878 from consumption (tuberculosis).

FOURTH MARRIAGE

Christopher continued to farm the land. He remarried for the final time, at age 35. On May 18, 1880, he married a widow from Sello, Norway, Susana Gunhild Jacobsdatter, age 41, at the Lime Creek Lutheran Church. She had three sons from a previous marriage: Johanne Aletta Simonsdatter, Jacob Johannes Simonson, and Soren Mathias Iva Simonson, all born in Norway. Her first husband, Simon Simonsen, had died in Norway. Two of the sons, Soren and Matthias, came to live with the Aslesen/Flatens.

He and Susana had a beautiful daughter together, Sena, born in 1881. Their life in Freeborn County continued on in their small community, always surrounded by the possibility of dangers like prairie fires. My, they were brave people. By 1882, their farm produced wheat, oats, corn, barley, potatoes, hay, and plenty of apples, dairy cows and sheep, and honey and bees. Although there were five railroad companies whose routes crossed Freeborn County, when Christopher wanted to bring his farm produce to ship, he used the new SMRR Alden station, to the north.

Yet, the black hand of death continued to knock on their door, and to their deep sorrow, their precious 10-year-old daughter Marie was taken away

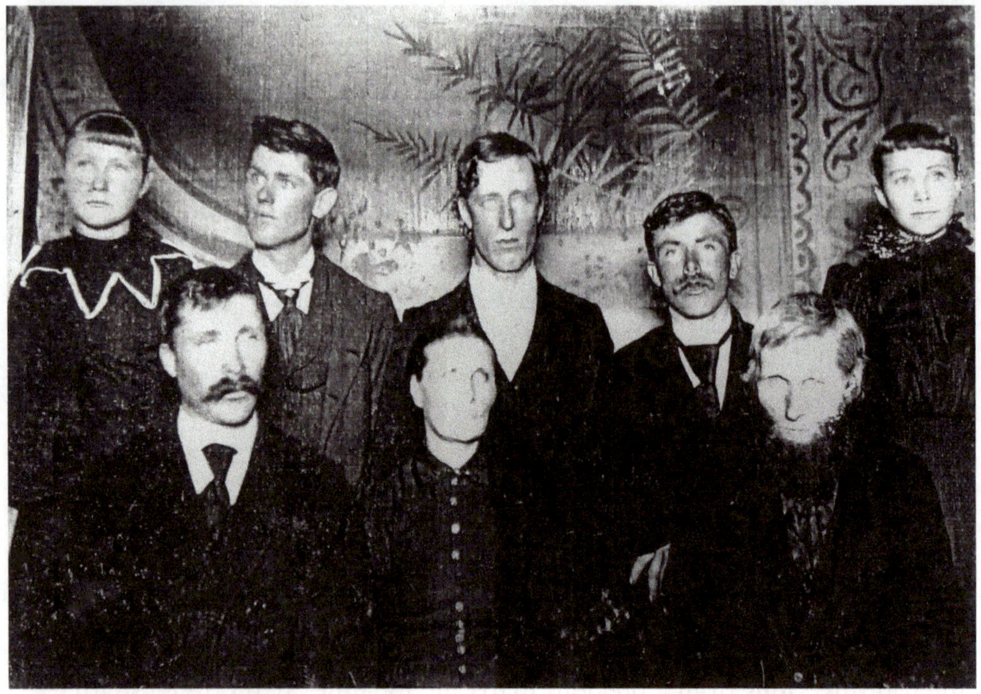

The Aslesen Flaten family. Ca. 1893. Gunerius is in the back row, second from the left. The author believes the others to be as follows: FRONT ROW: Jakob Simonsen (27), mother Susana (52); father Christopher (49). BACK ROW: Sena (12), Gunerius (21), Asle (24), Soren Matthias Simonsen (22) and Marie (10). Photo: Collection of Bill Flaten.

Right: the 1878 map of the Mansfield Township. The Aselsen/ Flaten family lived in Section 14 (above the "E" and "L" in MANSFIELD in red square. The children attended the school in the next section catty-corner to their property, in section 10. Map: Freeborn County Archives.

Plat of Mansfield: 1878

Township 101 North. Range 23 West. of the 5th Principal Meridian

Freeborn County. Section 14 C. Asleson

in 1884. The cause of this tragedy is unknown to me and the records are not clear on even this date.

Amid destruction, and against the odds, order prevailed. The community continued to grow. Out of toil came 160-acre farms with huge, gambrel-roofed barns for hay, each farm an independent operation, with hogs, chickens, ducks, sheep, goats, cattle, a large garden and fruit trees. You could see neighbors who were extremely important come to help at threshing time. In Nunda, huge creameries, a newspaper, general stores, bank and schoolhouse, churches, and of course roadwork, and new, more convenient railroad track laid. In Alden, a City Hall was erected in 1891, housing a fire department and council chambers, and featuring a fine hall for entertainment and lectures. This was an extremely fine accomplishment by the settlers, evidence of their communal desire to build a new society with rights and responsibilities for all.

The older Flaten children were now attending the old one-room schoolhouse nearby. In 1882, when Gunerius (G.C.) was 10 years old, there were 25 students in the classroom, there were 100 days in the school year, and the teacher was Miss Annie Fitsgerald. These early days suited young G.C., who was to grow up and become a teacher in nearby Alden. He enjoyed reading very much. Christopher was involved in education decisions, too, and attended County Board of Commissioners Annual Meetings in 1885, petitioning for a change in the boundaries of school districts. Meanwhile, Narve, in 1877, was still involved in road problems. The county board appointed a committee to examine and report on the validity of claims for road damages filed by Henry G. Emmons and Narve Asleson.

But Narve got tired of fighting about roads, and decided to move 275 miles north of Nunda, away from Freeborn County, to Grant County, close to Elbow Lake. And so, he obtained a land grant on this new property on June 30, 1883. His son Asle Narveson ("A.N.") remained close to Christopher and stayed on Narve's original farmland near Nunda, and he was well-liked in the community when he decided to open up a popular general mercantile and hardware store in Emmons. (Later, in 1886, he sold Narve's Nunda property in March 1895 to B.H. Larson, and moved to property he owned at Pickerel Lake, still not too far from Christopher. However, A.N. and his family eventually moved to Canada.)

Christopher's farm was large and productive and his life in Norway now seemed very distant. How fine it was to own his own land, his farm, to see his children baptized, confirmed, educated, and married (Gunerius), and to learn the business of farming, to celebrate holidays, to attend church, to finally own what he had worked for, claim it and pass it along to his children. Christopher had known tremendous challenges, many more than most people meet in a single lifetime, and yet he stood up to them. He earned his freedom in America. His brother Narve had prospered also, being described in an 1894 news article as a "well-to-do" farmer who was erecting a new, large barn.

But their toils had an end. Narve passed away in 1897 at the relatively young age of 67, and two years later Christopher's dear Susana passed away at the age 58. He continued farming for nine more years, and in 1902 he even had a new windmill erected. But the added wind could not do enough. The physical labor became too great. In July 1907, he developed chronic bronchitis and became too ill to farm.

So, in December 1907, rather than pass his farmland on to his children, he sold his entire estate (181 and 92/100 acres) to Bennett N. Bergerson for a price of $5,500.00. He put the amount in the bank. And then his family dispersed: A.C. moved to Washburn in North Dakota (and later to Pine County, Minnesota). Sena moved to Waterloo, Iowa. And at the age of 64, Christopher went to live first with his son G.C. and wife Ollie in Hettinger, North Dakota, in their very modest homestead, and for a short while in their larger "golden oak" home, where Ollie nursed him. He decided to return to his beloved Minnesota for the last six weeks of his life, staying with his nephew A.N. at Pickerel Lake, until he passed away October 12, 1911, age 67, and was then buried in Lime Creek Cemetery, Emmons, Freeborn County, Minnesota.

Christopher was known throughout his community as a man who went out of his way to help others. While he did not attain a formal education, hold any office, or claim fame in any way, his is the story of the ordinary man, the immigrant with a dream built on opportunity and hard work; a man who came with little, helped to build a community from the ground up, weathered the elements, pulled his way through tragedy, never quit and never sat to rest. For he was a farmer, and farmers can never rest. He and the "littlement of Norwegians" did what we all now take for granted. Together, he and his family and neighbors built society from nothing but their bare hands. They are the quiet heroes.

OBITUARY: CHRISTOPHER FLATEN, 1911

Christopher Flaten, one of the first settlers in Mansfield, died Thursday evening at 6 o'clock at the home of his nephew A.N. Flaten near Albert Lea. Deceased was born in Norway Jan. 13, 1884. He has endured all kind of hardships. In the 70-ties he was caught in an awful blizzard while hauling wood from near Bear Lake, but fortunately he struck the house of a settler where he remained until the storm ceased. Later his house burned down and his wife was killed, he himself escaped with terrible burns from which he lay senseless for several days. He has been married three times. His last wife died in the fall 1899. He has resided in this township up to 1908, when he sold his farm afterwards he stayed with his son G.C. Flaten the last year, about six weeks ago he returned. When he was taken sick they immediately sent word for his sons and daughter. G.C. Flaten of Hettinger, N. Dak., and Miss Sena Flaten of Waterloo, Ia., came to see him alive, Asle C. Flaten did not get the telegram in time, he got here about one hour late for the funeral. The deceased is survived by the above named children and a large host of relatives all of whom will have our sincerest sympathy in their bereavement. The deceased was a kind-hearted man and was always willing to help those that was sick or needed help, the memory of his good deeds will not be forgotten.

Freeborn County Standard, Albert Lea, MN. (10/18/1911, p. 8)

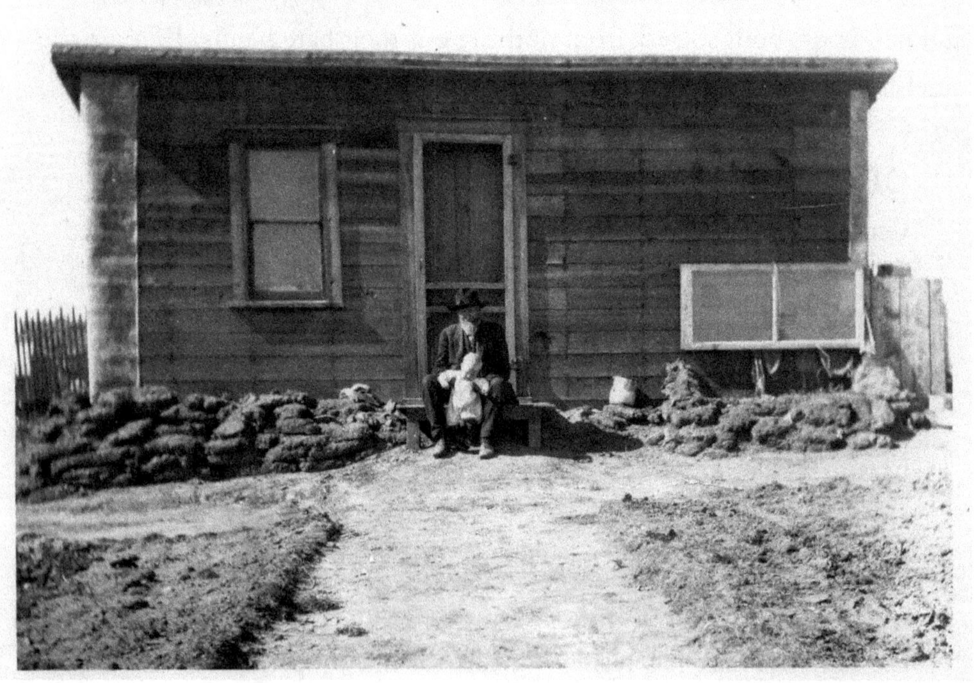

Christopher sits on the front stoop with his grandson, Clarence. Location is Hettinger, North Dakota, the first home of his son Gunerius and wife Ollie. 1911. Photo: GC Flaten, Collection of Margaret Daisley.

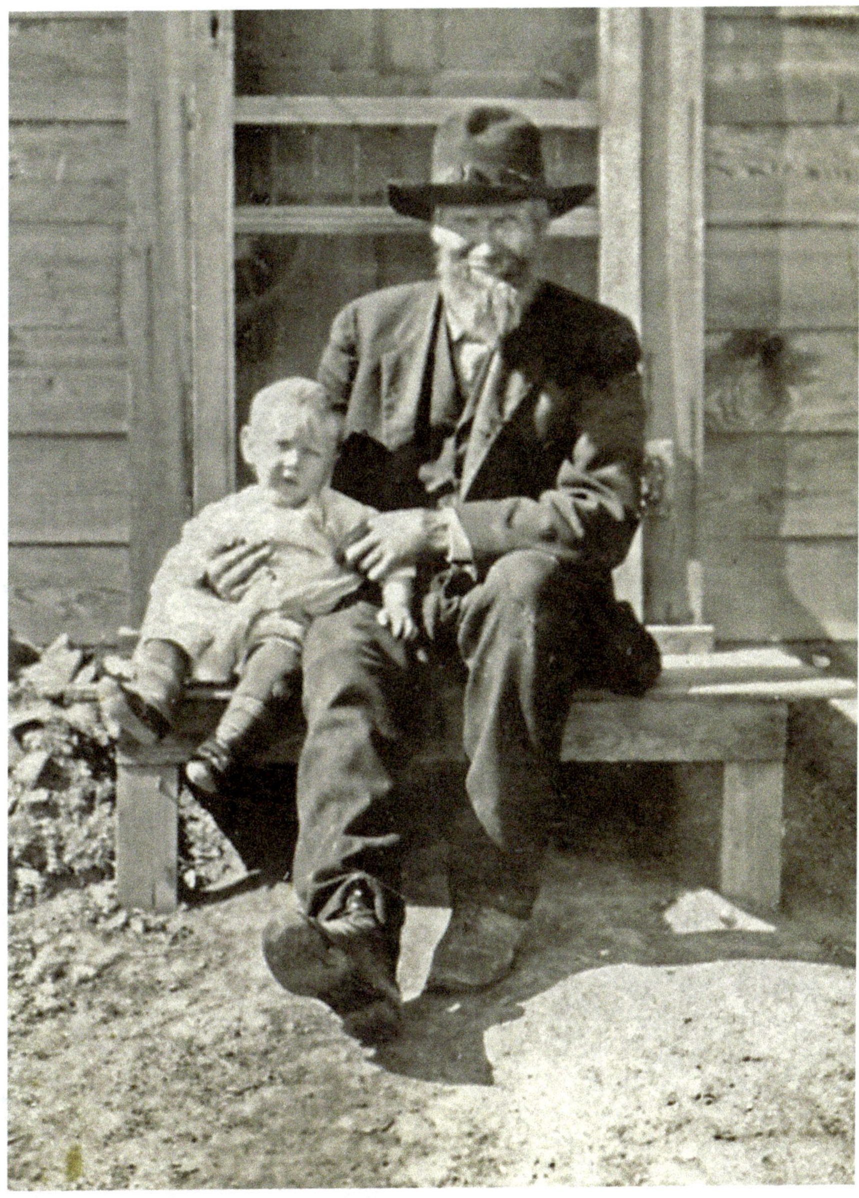

Christopher Aslesen Flaten with his grandson, Clarence Flaten. Photo: GC Flaten, Collection of Margaret Daisley.

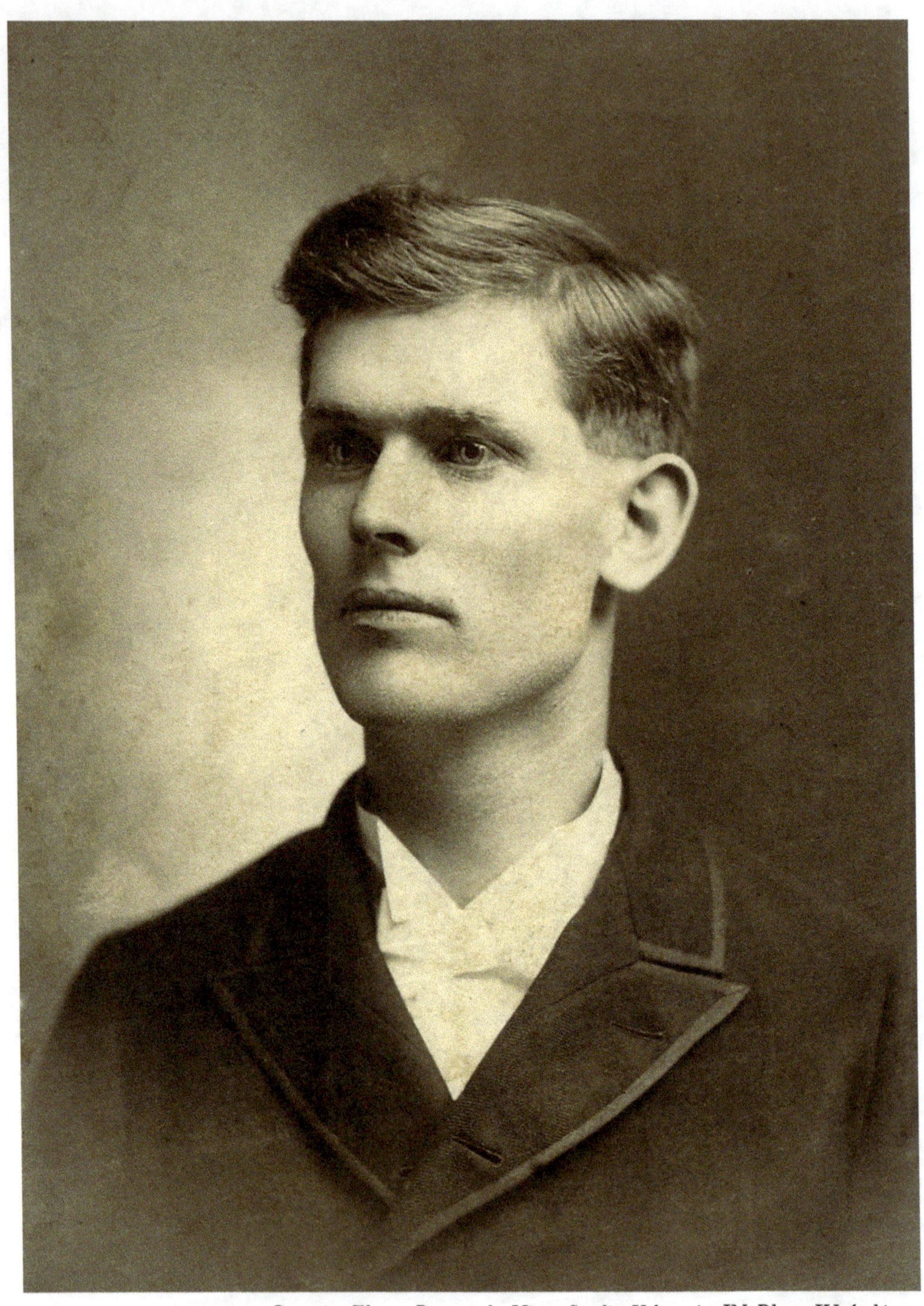

Gunerius Flaten. Portrait by Hinea Studio, Valparaiso IN. Photo: IU Archives.

CHAPTER TWO

GUNERIUS FLATEN 1872-1954

CHRISTOPHER'S SON, GUNERIUS ("G.C.") GREW UP ON THE farm. He and his step-brothers, Jakob and Soren, helped with the animals and crops while his little sister Sena tended to housework. But they all walked to school nearby to learn to read and write in English, and to memorize geography and arithmetic. According to his daughter, Alpha, G.C. had a very good memory. "He knew his bible real well and history, including what dates things happened." Young G.C.'s expectations of life were quite different from those of his father and mother. He was a first-generation American who took for granted his established roots in the community. His cousin A.N. (fourteen years his senior and newly married) welcomed him to hang out at his popular mercantile and hardware store in Emmons. They were both outgoing and friendly, both first-generation Americans with aspirations, but they both knew the practical hardships of life on the farm, too.

Because he was bright, G.C.'s ambitions lay in a wider world beyond barns, barley, and hay bales. He may have picked up a copy of the *Freeborn County Standard* in A.N.'s store one day, and there he would have seen an article about the World's Columbian Exposition in Chicago. He may have heard about it from others. But soon enough he decided to attend the "Chicago Day" event, October 9, 1893. He was 21 years old, and the event changed his life. Or at least opened his eyes to many new possibilities. And although I have no evidence for it, I am guessing that the family photo on page 50 may have been taken at the Exposition.

THE MARVELOUS EXPOSITION

He enthusiastically boarded the train and joined millions of people at the Exposition. Vast in scope, it introduced them to the Pledge of Allegiance and the Ferris Wheel, Scott Joplin playing ragtime, the novel "Juicy Fruit Gum" was introduced, as were moving walkways, and the great Buffalo Bill's Wild West Show. He saw the latest technology in the Electricity Building, such as Thomas Edison's kinetoscope, search lights, a Morse Code telegraph, a seismograph, and even electric incubators for chicken eggs (something they could certainly use on the farm!)

In the Zoopraxographical Hall, he listened to Eadweard Muybridge give a series of lectures on the "Science of Animal Locomotion" and with a zoopraxiscope machine Muybridge showed his moving pictures in the first commercial movie theater. The electrotachyscope of Ottomar Anschütz (which used a Geissler tube to project the illusion of moving images) was demonstrated. All of this undoubtedly sparked an interest in photography and the art and science of photo in motion. Surely it was there that G.C. observed and became captivated by the magic of the camera.

The Exposition revealed extraordinary machines of progress, promoted undoubtable optimism about the future and it showcased plans for the "City Beautiful" movement, with its new and improved cities and skyscrapers. He and 26 million visitors were awed and dazzled by modernity.

G.C. returned home, filled with ideas. Three years passed on the farm, but his bright mind looked past the furrows. In January 1897, age 25, he enrolled at the Northern Indiana Normal School and Business College, the largest teacher training school in the U.S. He chose this school in Valparaiso, Indiana because it offered room, board and training at an affordable rate, and it also allowed him to test into some credits to be applied toward his degree. He enrolled as a student in the Scientific Department. There, he relished coursework and, because he was outgoing, he joined the Star Literary Society, attended lectures, debates, and classical music concerts. One year and six months went by too rapidly. At age 26, he graduated on June 2, 1898, with the Scientific Class and a degree in teaching. But he left Valparaiso with more than the degree. There were many photography studios in Valparaiso, and he soon became captured by the magic.

The day he picked up a camera (probably a Kodak box with 5x7 glass plates) was to be a turning point in his life. He practiced his skills intensely by taking photos of campus friends, and he also learned how to create motion pictures using a "stereopticon" which was like a slide projector (popularly known as a "magic lantern") that had two stacked lenses. When operated, it produced the illusion of a motion picture. It was a precursor to the motion picture camera. It is safe to say that he discovered his true interest in life.

When he returned home, he jumped right into the life of the community. He joined the Mansfield Literary Society which met at the local schoolhouse monthly on Friday evenings, and he was soon elected President. There, he found welcomed company with others interested in knowledge and discussion. The society would chose interesting topics to debate, for example, "Resolved, that overproduction of wheat is the cause of its current low price," and "Resolved, the U.S. should increase its army and navy." He was elected to run for office as Public Surveyor on the People's Party (a populist, agrarian party) in 1898. He very much loved meeting with, and talking with, people.

He found a home in Emmons, and with his teaching degree, began to teach at the elementary school in Alden, District No. 70, but he discovered that teaching was not to be his calling. He once told his daughter Alpha that he had 75 pupils in his class and that it was too many. He also said that a number of the students could only attend part-time because they had to work on the farm and that teaching those older students could be near impossible.

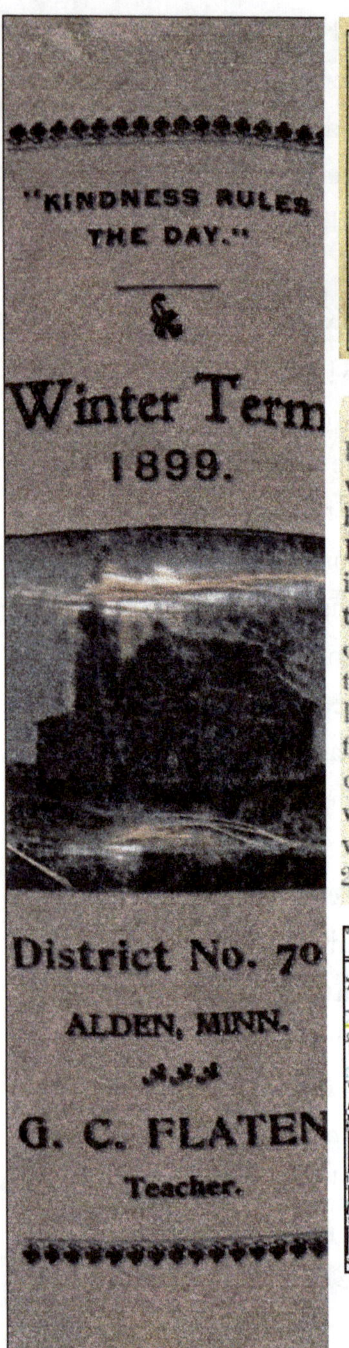

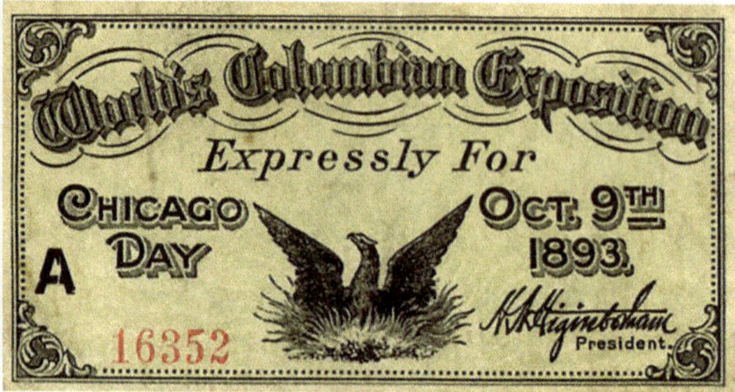

Marie Antoinette—a thrilling lecture on the French Revolution, will be the attraction at the opera house, Bricelyn, on the night of Friday, March 31st. The lecturer is Mr. G. C. Flaten, our former townsman, who is well known to our people as an orator and entertainer of considerable ability. His lecture is illustrated by means of a fine stereopticon, showing the life of the ill-fated Queen together with sixty other magnificent views. The price of admission is 25c and 35c. 30-

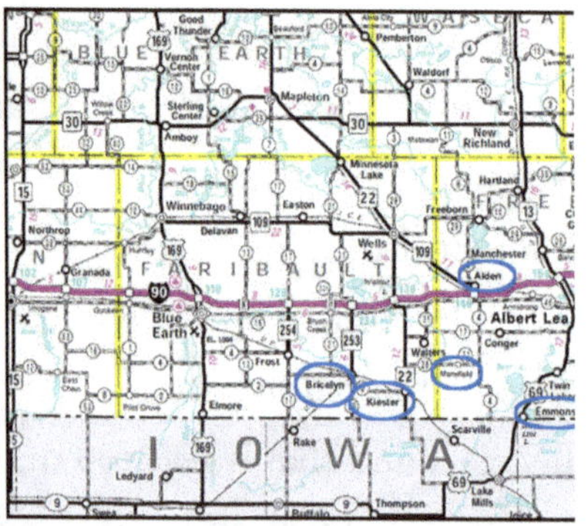

Far left: Silk bookmark from G.C. Flaten's classroom.

Top: copy of G.C.'s ticket to the 1893 Exposition in Chicago.

Left: clip from newspaper article, part of a review of one of G.C.'s lectures using the stereopticon.

Bottom: map showing location of towns in which the Simonsen & Flaten Photo Studio did business.

Bookmark and ticket: IU Archives.

Although he had purchased a home in Alden, nearby Bricelyn caught his attention and he soon went into the photography business there.

The City Directory shows that the very first photograph gallery in town was run by John Simonson, photographer. During the building boom of 1899, a small building was erected to house a new photo studio, now called Simonson & Flaten. G.C. put teaching aside and now set up the photography studio with Simonson; he was the junior member of the firm, and they became known as photographers of Bricelyn, Kiester, and Emmons, Minnesota. Their work captured the changing landscapes and somber portraits of local citizens.

BRICELYN BRIDE

It was very exciting for him to be in this modernizing town. Bricelyn was expanding. In Bricelyn, lives were getting brighter, thanks to the new contract the village council entered into with the Lockband Gas and Fuel Company to construct a municipal gas light plant for the village. "On Monday evening, Dec. 24, [1902], gas from our light plants was turned into the mains, and Marshal Foster had turned on the lamps, the street was light as day. People could see the brilliancy of the illuminations for miles around Bricelyn, and wondered if the town was on fire."

And the city fathers rightfully bragged about being progressive. They boasted about being the first town in the County to install a municipal water plant, a municipal gas light plant, a high school, and a newspaper "second to none in Minnesota" (The Bricelyn Sentinel), the earliest hospital, and the first movie theater, a sewage disposal system, and paved and surfaced streets. And a train to ship "sleek beevs and grunting swine" to Chicago.

Gone were things the old-timers used to live with: wooden sidewalks, warming pans, spinning wheels, the "Jew Peddler," "Rushing the Growler," revival meetings, hair watch chains, grasshopper invasions, mattresses filled

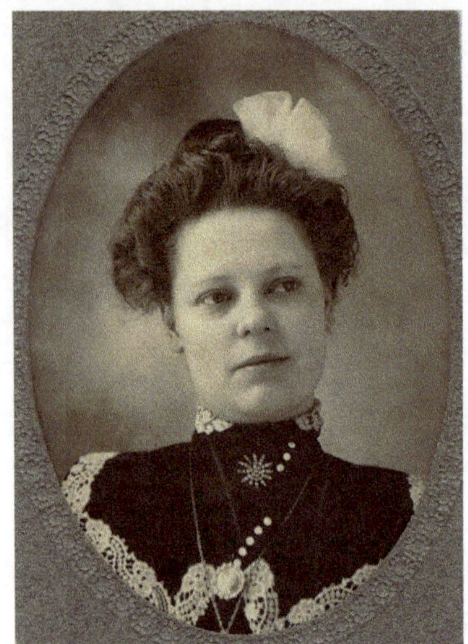

Left: Mary Christensen. Photo: Collection of Patricia Burke.

Below: Mary (second from left) and two friends join G.C. (far right) for an evening of book reading. G.C. was President of the Mansfield Literary Society which met at the local schoolhouse. The photo location is unknown although it looks to be a well-appointed parlor. Photo: IU Archives.

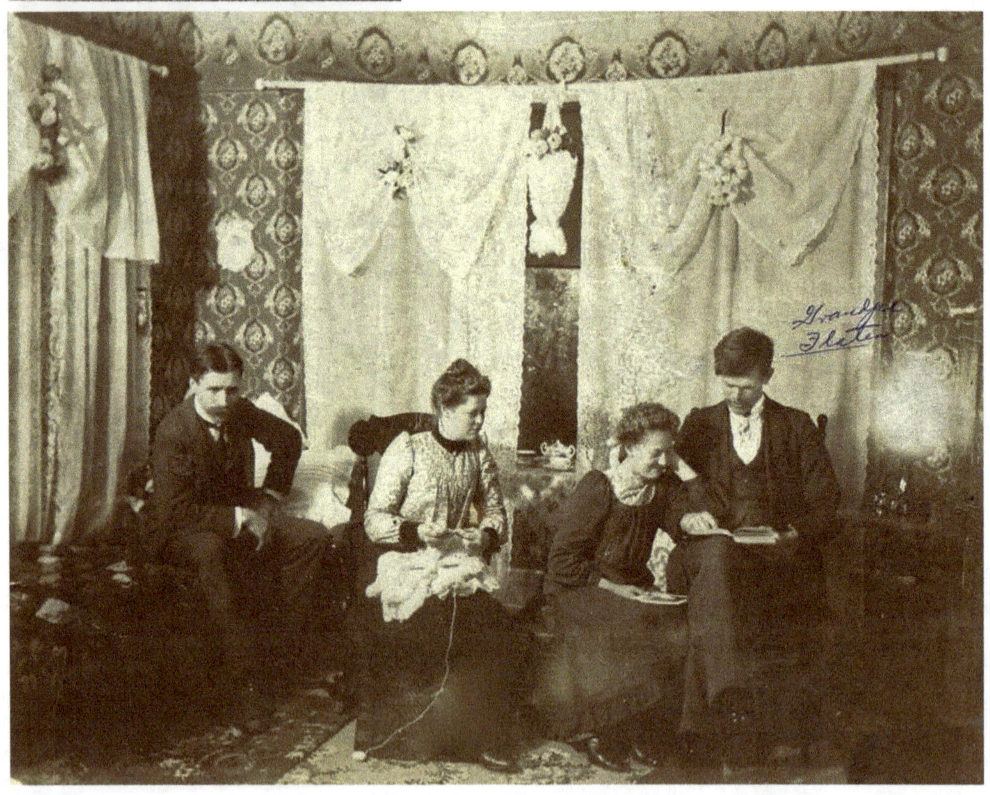

with corncobs, and standing around Carl Peterson's livery stable on Sunday to hear the elders exchange whoppers.

G.C. was quite busy practicing photography. Bricelyn's local newspaper, *The Sentinel* ("All The News All The Time") required photographs. Many townsfolk wandered into the studio for their portraits. Photography was much in demand, so much so that in addition to the studio in Bricelyn, Simonsen & Flaten also purchased land in Keister for additional studio space, October 22, 1901: Lot 13, block 13, from the Iowa & Minnesota Town Site Company. In the evening, G.C. entertained crowds by putting on magic lantern shows in town halls and country schoolhouses and got good reviews as "an orator and entertainer of considerable ability." Perhaps this is where he first set eyes on his lovely Mary.

Mary Christensen was a bright, young teacher in the Glenville public schools, an "estimable young lady of good character and great ability" according to their wedding announcement in the *Freeborn County Standard.* Mary ("Marie") was a vibrant person who shared G.C.'s interest in higher education, having herself attended school 50 miles away, the Mankato Normal. Taking a certificate to teach at an early age, she dedicated herself to the public schools for six years.

They were married on September 3, 1902. G.C. and Mary, age 24, celebrated in a small ceremony which took place in Mary's parent's home near Alden. Laura Christensen and Sena Flaten were bridesmaids, and his business partner, J. Simonson, and Mary's brother Henry Christenson were groomsmen. A newspaper announcement noted that the groom is "a man of ability and exceptional character....and will succeed." And so, with great happiness in their hearts, they set up a nice home in Alden, and G.C. joined the Modern Brotherhood of America in 1903, took out an ad in the City Directory for his services as a photographer, and their prospects looked favorable. He and

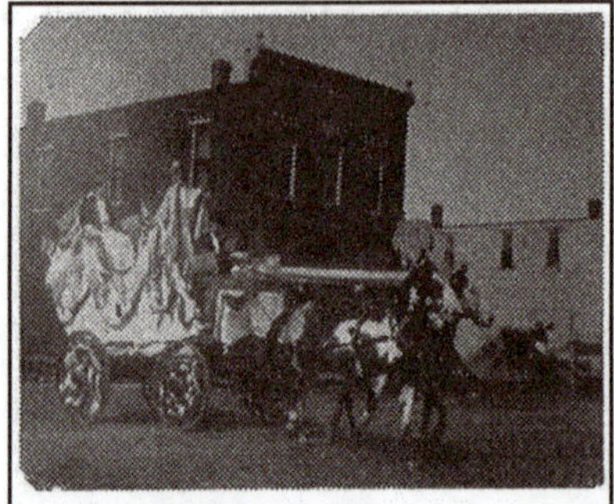
Arvilla Noakes, attendant, Mrs. Flaten, 1903 celebration queen.

Above: newspaper story of the parade. The Freeborn Sentinel.

Right: G.C. and Mary's wedding portrait. Photo: Collection of Patricia Burke.

Below: Assumed to be the wedding gathering after the ceremony. At center, the bride and groom. To G.C.'s left is his sister Sena with J. Simonsen. To the bride's right is her sister, Laura and brother Henry. The author also believes that the following persons can be identified: G.C.'s mother, Susana, two persons to the right of the bride, and perhaps Christopher, next to Susana in the back rwo. The newpaper announcement stated that the ceremony was small. Perhaps this was a reception after the ceremony. Photo: Collection of Patricia Burke.

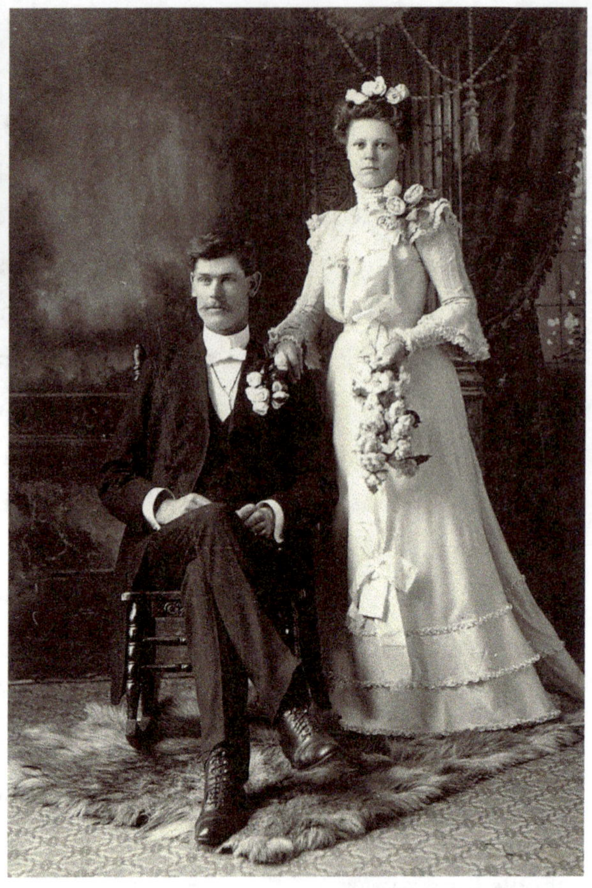

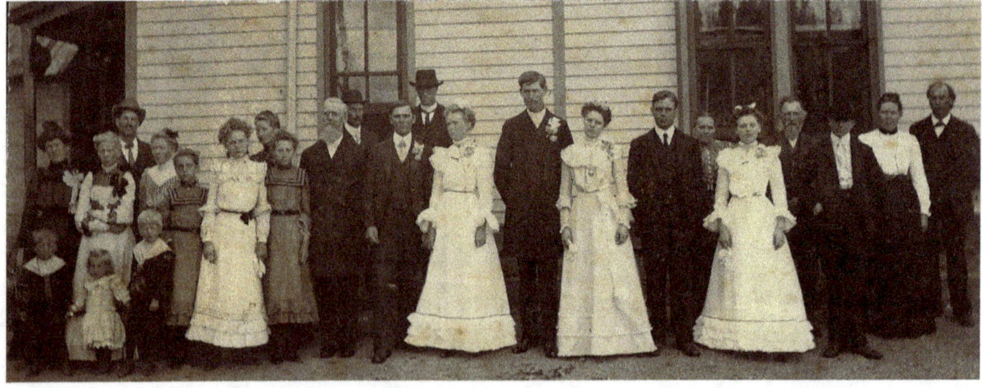

Mary purchased hardware and furniture at Fink & Lindeman in Bricelyn and together they created a new life.

Mrs. G.C. Flaten was so beautiful and popular that her friends elected her Queen of Bricelyn's 1903 Carnival that summer. This parade was part of a spectacular town Celebration of 1903 (one so grand that a local historian still noted it while writing in 1949). The town was celebrating its rise out of a muddy field to a modern assemblage of banks, halls, barns, watering troughs, schoolhouse, railroad elevators, churches, and a new opera house, and its fervor was powered by an intensely patriotic optimism.

G.C. and Marie threw themselves into the three-day whirlwind event, listening to seven brass bands, one of which featured negro minstrels with a 15-piece brass band show, playing all day and night on the streets. There was dancing, too, all day and night, even in the opera house, and there were tent shows with vaudeville and "girl shows" and shell games (impossible to stop by the ladies of the town), and a newly built grandstand seating 2,000 to host senators and congressmen, whose oratorical skills stoked everyone's pride. And of course, the Grand Parade. As Queen, Mary rode on the lead float and waved at her admirers.

Their married life was filled with rich promise, and great happiness, as they were surrounded by friends and family. Life was so happy, that it made the sudden sorry turn of events all the more painful. They had only been married a year and a half, when fate delivered the worst possible blow: Mary suddenly died April 28, 1904.

The consoling tone of the *Freeborn County Times* obituary explains that she passed away peacefully after an illness of "several months duration of a nervous malady. ... Her pleasant personality and beautiful Christian life won for her friends everywhere and it was with deepest grief that her failing health and ultimate death was learned." And from a notice in the *Minneapolis Star*,

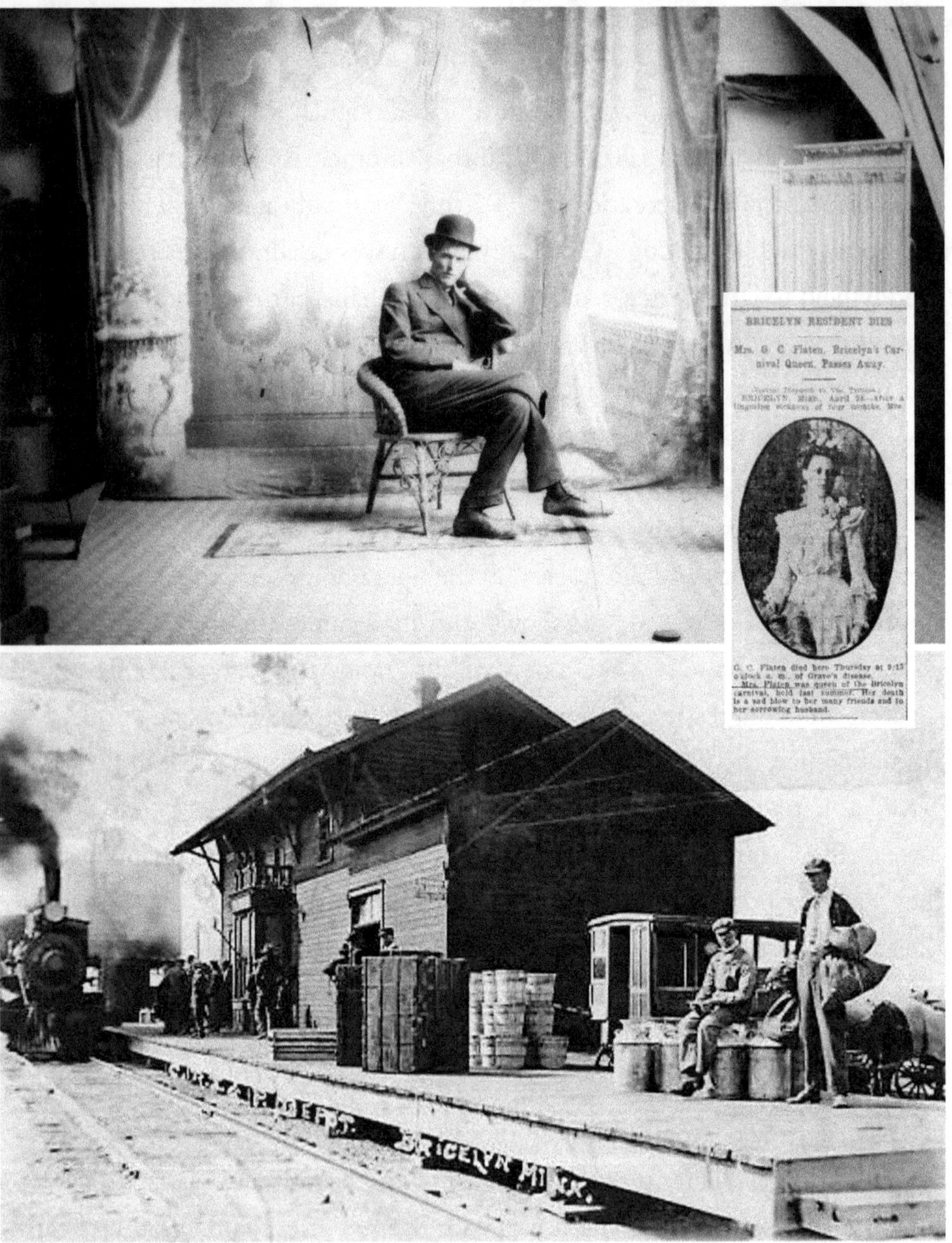

BRICELYN RESIDENT DIES

Mrs. G. C. Flaten, Bricelyn's Carnival Queen, Passes Away.

Special Dispatch to The Tribune.
BRICELYN, Minn., April [illegible].—After a lingering sickness of four months, Mrs. G. C. Flaten died here Thursday at 9:15 o'clock a. m., of Grave's disease.

Mrs. Flaten was queen of the Bricelyn carnival, held last summer. Her death is a sad blow to her many friends and to her sorrowing husband.

Top: G.C. perhaps in his studio. IU archives. Mary's Obituary, Minneapolis Star Tribune. Bottom: The Bricelyn train station, photographer unknown. Lakenwoods.com.

further details: her "lingering illness of four months" was diagnosed as Grave's disease.

G.C. was never the same after that. Rather than summoning resilience, he reeled. He remained in Alden and struggled to continue on. Perhaps he found work to be a distraction from his grieving process. He rented a hall in Bricelyn in 1905 and continued to deliver lectures with his stereopticon, sharing images that enlarged happier moments. The March 29, 1905, issue of the *Freeborn County Standard* gave another great review:

> "G.C. Flaten delivered an able lecture at McCall's hall, Emmons, on 'Marie Antoinette' of the French revolution. His lecture, illustrated with many choice stereopticon views both stationary and moving, was much enjoyed by all. Mr. Flaten has a first-class instrument and exhibited considerable ability as a public speaker. He speaks this week in a neighboring village in Iowa. We wish him abundant success."

He continued to tour local towns to give stereopticon shows. Several newspaper accounts in 1905 state that he traveled extensively through the western states on business. And he kept up on property taxes on his home in Alden in July 1906. But with a final, deep sadness, he contracted with H.C. Hanson Burial works for a beautiful marble memorial marker for his departed wife and had it erected at Alden Cemetery in Freeborn County, Minnesota in 1906. He decided to put his grief behind him. Everything around him reminded him of what he had lost. Going forward, whenever the U.S. Census listed "Education" he would put "none." He looked to reinvention.

In July 1906, he purchased 200 shares of Kansas Cooperative Refining Company at 10 cents per share, the first of four "installments" for 500 shares. Being a man of his times, he may have felt it was a forward-thinking investment since the company processed illuminating oil (for all of the lamp posts in towns) and naphtha (kerosene for stoves and lanterns and a diluting agent for heavy oil transport) which were in very high demand, and also small amounts of gas and fuel oil for heating, and gasoline and lubricating oils for transport. With the coming age of the automobile, he knew there would be more demand. He may have read this full page ad in the local magazine *Vick's*:

> "No one ever got RICH working for WAGES. This is the way nearly all the great wealth in the world has been gained in the past. No other business in the world shows such enormous profits and at the same time such almost absolutely safety and absence of speculation, as the Oil Refining business. The Kansas Co-operative Refining Company's property consists of more than twenty-five acres adjoining Chanute, Kan., in the very heart of the oil district. Your chances are good to make a profit of at least 50 to 100 percent in a short amount of time. Sold by the Union Security Co, in Chicago IL. fiscal agents."

The Kansas Coop was one of many such small refineries cropping up at the time in Kansas and Oklahoma in an area known as the Mid-Continent Field. The company was refining oil from local fields and supplying local needs. But Standard Oil was supplying the east coast with crude oil, monopolizing major pipelines and vast refineries, and unfairly controlling the rails, making it impossible for smaller companies to afford to ship. The Kansas Cooperative could not compete with Standard Oil and went out of business. Luck was not with him. G.C.'s shares were now worthless.

He kept searching to find new beginnings that did not include reminders of tragedy. He needed to forget. There was a sure path to the future: follow the railroad tracks. It would, at least, keep his mind busy.

Around 1906, age 34, "he went to work for the railroad in Bricelyn and ended up in Hettinger," his daughter Alpha recalled. What called him West? What exactly did he do for the raiload? The Chicago, Milwaukee & St. Paul Railroad was extending their line from Bricelyn as part of the transcontinental push west of the Missouri River. The railroad's line snaked westward to build more towns, part of the process historian Ray Billington describes nicely as "the repeated rebirth of civilization along the western edge of settlement during the three centuries required to occupy the continent." G.C. continued to take photographs, and he traveled widely according to newspaper clips. Perhaps the railroad used some of his photographs as promotions for the towns which they developed along the rail. Perhaps he worked on the crew and took and sold photos at the same time.

But why did he finally choose Hettinger, North Dakota as his new home? The new town of Hettinger, 560 miles northwest of Bricelyn, was to hear the sound of the railroad's whistle soon enough.

DESTINATION: HETTINGER

In that town, G.C. was to meet and make lifelong friends with a giant of a man, a man remembered in his lifetime and beyond as an endearing and enduring founder and friend, a leader and man who seized opportunity while it was fresh. This man, Paul W. Boehm, was the key influence determining the course of G.C.'s new start in life, and later, that of G.C.'s son, Clarence.

Paul Waldemar Boehm, Esq., fresh out of law school in Michigan (class of 1905) with a practice in North Dakota, soon made his first trip to the tent village of Hettinger with his partner Mr. Gunberg, where they founded the Boehm-Gunberg Land & Loan Co. with several men and women. He was prepared for business as a pioneer Land Office lawyer specializing in locating homesteads. Town lots in Hettinger officially went for sale on October 1, 1907, the day the railroad first entered town (the typical method for selling property owned by the railroad). Ads touted Adams County as a place of rich prairie "where every farmer is prosperous and as independent as a king," and where land from $12.50 to $20.00 per acre was available on easy terms. The land business kept Boehm very busy with deeds and loans.

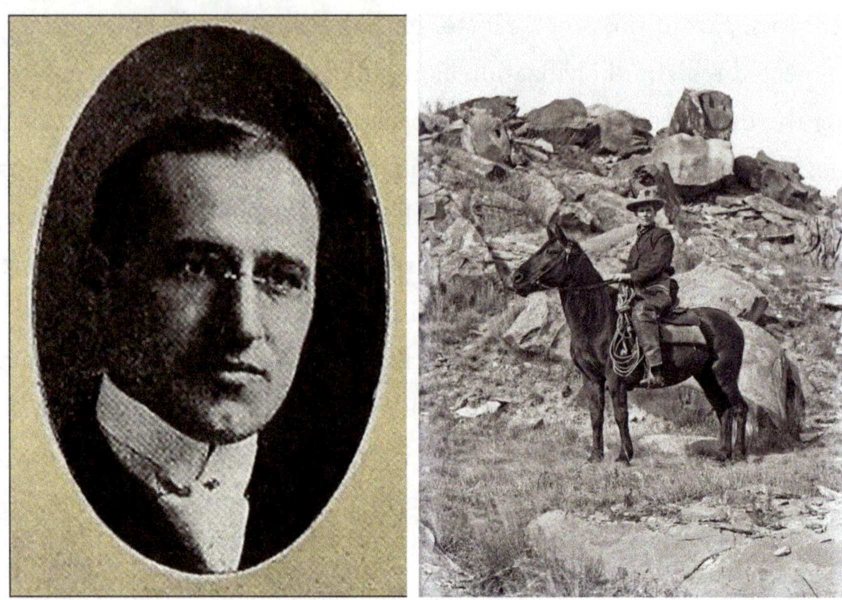

Left: Paul Waldemer Boehm. Right, G.C. Flaten on horseback. Photo on right: IU Archives.

Below: original settlement structures were physically moved by horses to their new location once the town was platted by the railroad. This may be in Hettinger. Photo: GC Flaten, IU Archives.

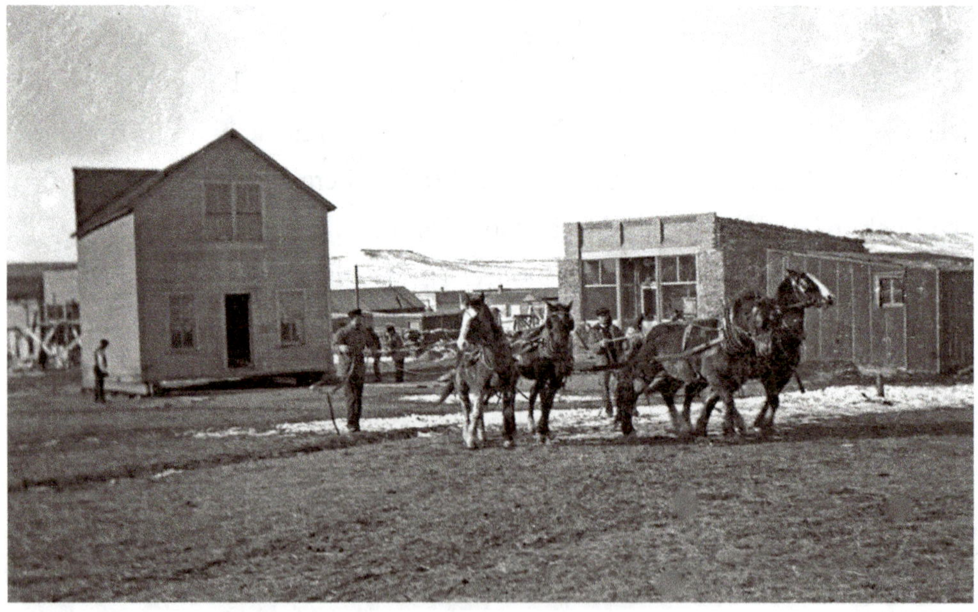

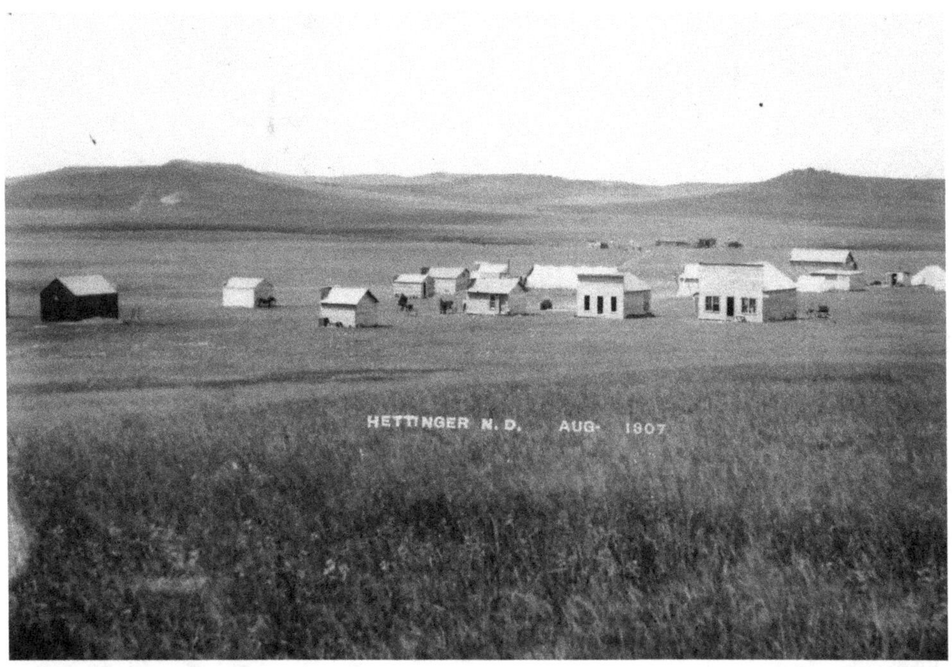

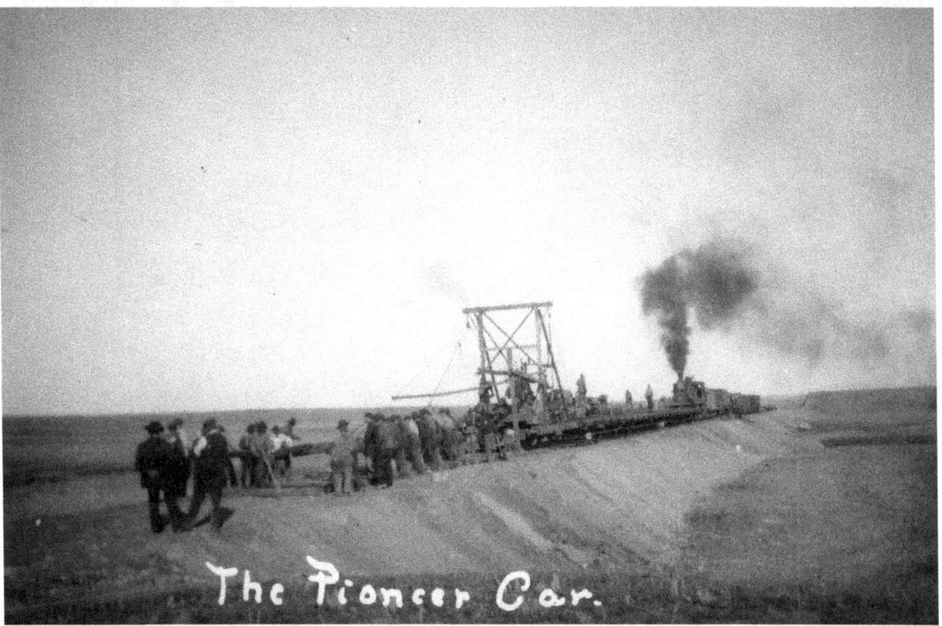

Top: Hettinger, 1907. Bottom: "The Pioneer Car". Crew appear to be laying new track. Ca. 1907. Photos: GC Flaten, IU Archives

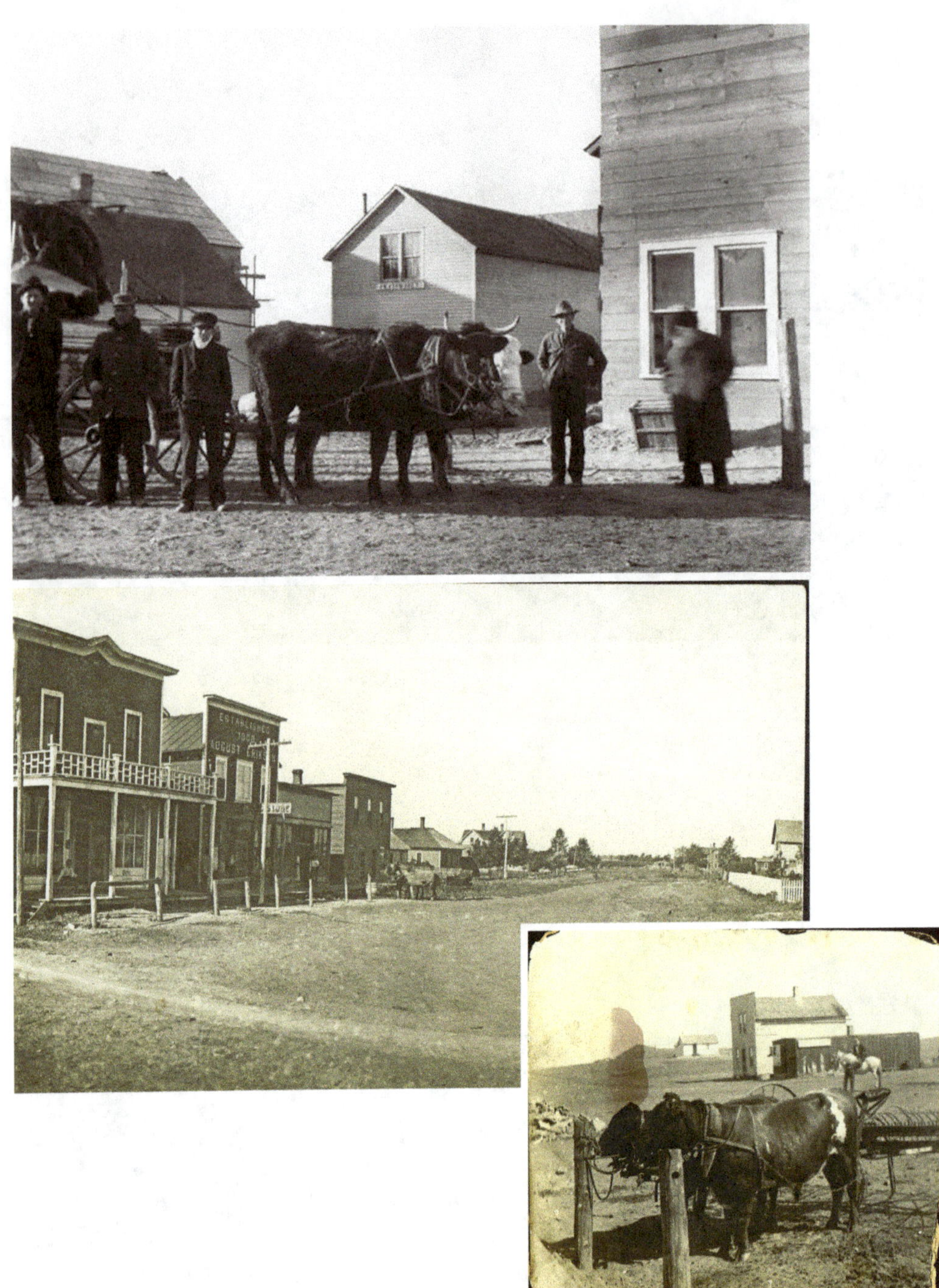

Left page: early towns were dependent on horse and ox. These photographs taken by G.C. show early towns and frontier. According to Hettinger historian, Loren Luckow, Gunerius rode on trains to local towns (especially Bowman) and took photos of their buildings. He was known for climbing water towers to get a good vantage point. At this time, he traveled around North and South Dakota.

Right: the stage coash may be the one from Lemon, SD.

Below: the cold winters required a wagon sled for hauling.

Photos: GC Flaten, IU Archives.

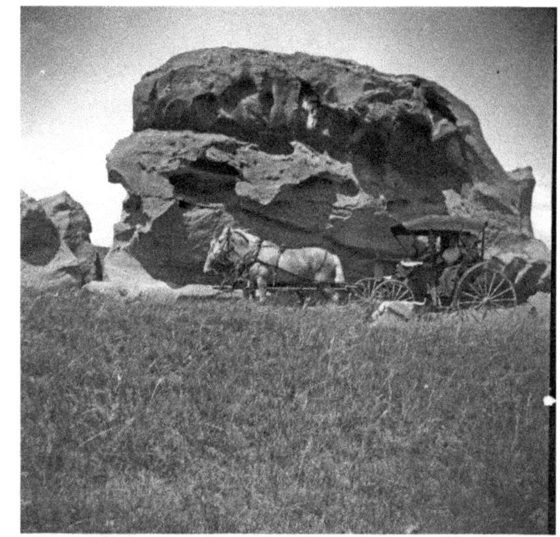

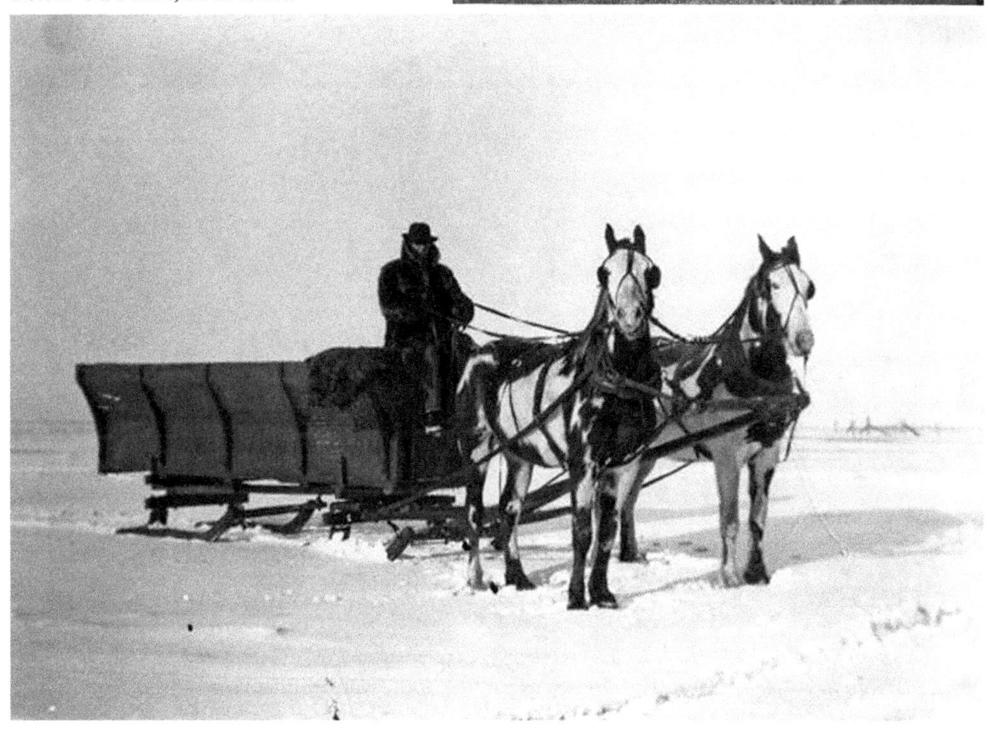

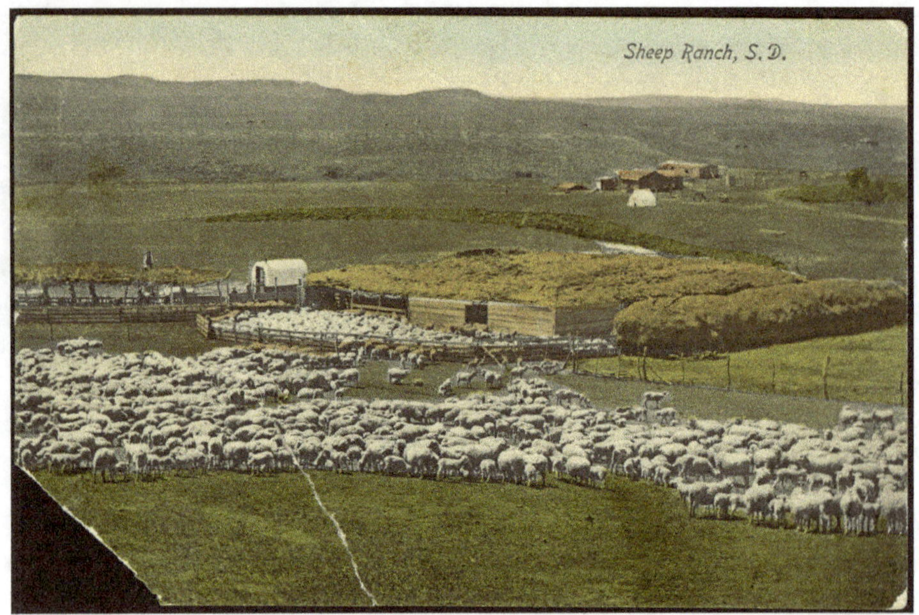

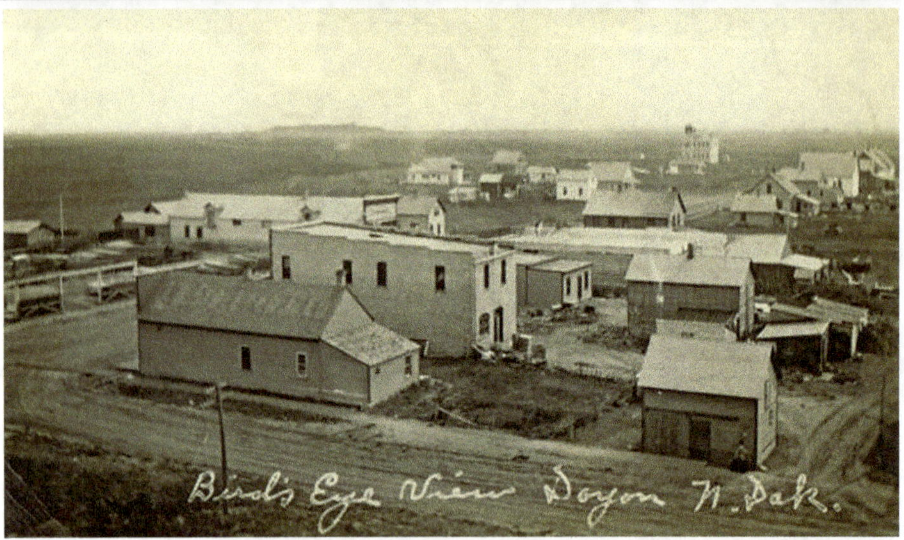

Top: "Sheep Ranch near Hettinger N.D." This image was printed on POSTCARD stock, suitable for correspondence through the U.S. mail. Printed on the back: Pub. by Bloom Bros., Minneapolis, Minn, for G.C. Flaten. Made in Germany. On G.C.'s original print of this image, handwritten on the back: "Jessfield's Sheep Ranch near the Grand River". Ca. 1905.

Bottom, a bird'seye view of Doyon, North Dakota. Ca. 1911. Photos: GC Flaten, IU Archives.

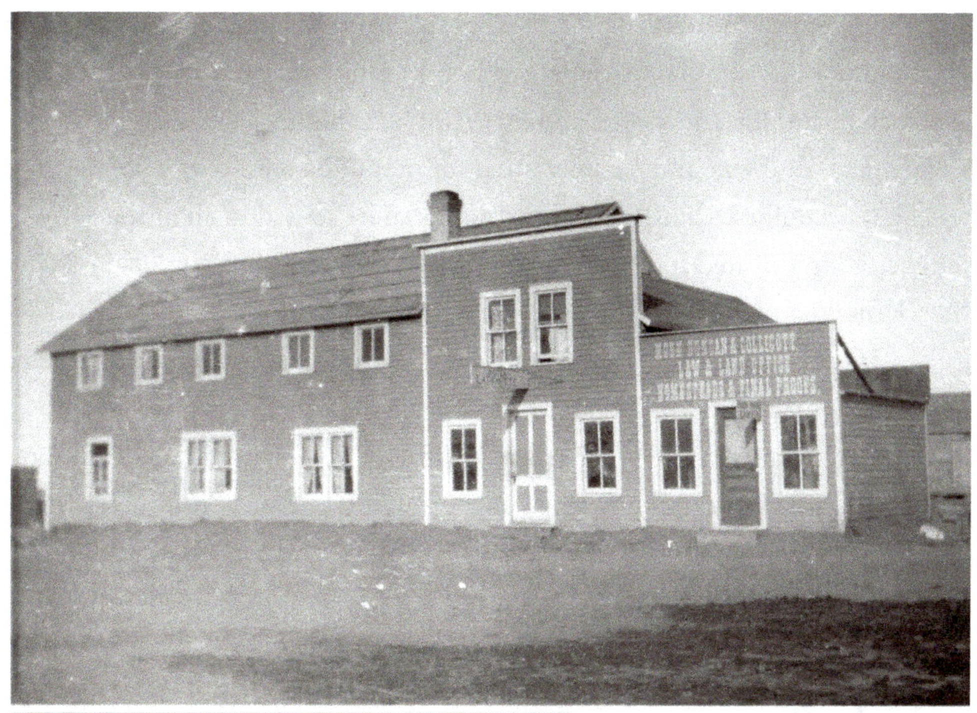

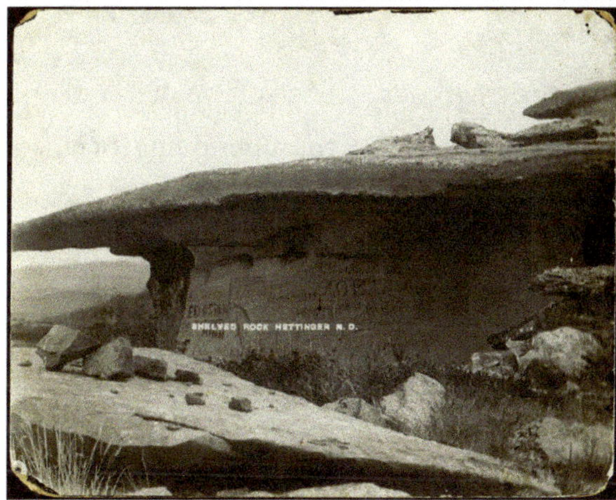

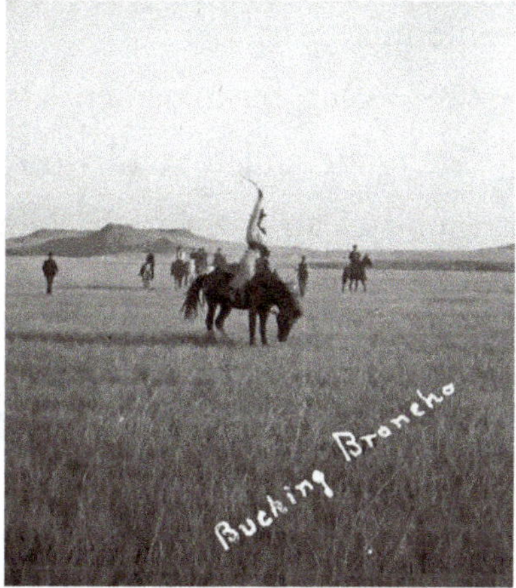

Top, next door to the original Lafayette Hotel in Hettinger, the law and land office of Moen, Duncan & Collicott, offering homesteads and final proofs. Ca. 1906.
Above left, "Shelved Rock", a typical butte formation in Hettinger. Right, a bucking bronco, probably part of the entertainment at a tent event. Photos: GC Flaten, IU Archives.

The 1862 Homestead Act rules kept changing, and the new variations, such as "commuting," "tree claim," "enlarged homesteads," and "residence change" and such meant his knowledge and expertise were highly valued for the new landowners. Paul was immediately hired for new and contested cases. But it was Paul's genuine enthusiasm for the potential he sensed in all of the early settlers that motivated him to dedicate his efforts to building the "Eldorado of the Plains."

If ever there were a town promoter, Paul was it. He was quickly elected to a leading position as President of the village, then as the first Trustee of the City government (1908-1909), and continued to practice law as County Attorney. Aside from his knowledge of the law, it was Paul's enthusiasm for joining with his neighbors that endeared him to everyone in the community. He joined the Lions Club and the Masonic Lodge, ensuring a connection with most of the townspeople.

Here's a short quote from Paul, from a history written for Hettinger's centennial year:

> "Our businessmen are enterprising, our citizens hopeful and energetic and that all work to a common end – the upbuilding of a good clean town with a fine moral atmosphere ... we are proud to emphasize, Adams County may well be proud of its Metropolis, and this great Eldorado of the Dakotas may well point to Hettinger as the best example of city buildings within its vast confines."

Soon, Paul and G.C. crossed paths. And here is a quote recorded in the town's history mentioning Paul and G.C.'s their early friendship:
"In April 1908 the village men met and elected Paul Boehm president. Trustees were Frank Rhoda and J.S. Green. Fred Davis was village clerk. The committee was responsible for the railroad company creating 'Mirror

Lake' so named by G.C. Flaten the photographer, as we stood after a big rain contemplating the result of The Record's plan to provide fresh water for the railroad and as we hoped to secure the division point for Hettinger." (Being declared a "division point" for a steam railroad meant that the trains must stop at that station point in order to reswitch and change engines. It made a station stop a strategic point along any route and would give the town status and jobs. It is a designation that Hettinger town founders continued to desire for many years.)

Probably it was at an early tent meeting that G.C. and Paul originally met. They were both outgoing. But it is certain that both men knew each other early on and that each continued to play important roles in the community and eventually in each other's personal lives. They would even become brothers-in-law. (Paul married Bessie, sister of G.C.'s future wife, Ollie.)

Paul's enthusiasm met with G.C.'s desire to find new meaning in life. G.C. decided to rebuild his life in Hettinger. He threw everything into it. Once the town lots opened for sale on Lot Sale Day, G.C. selected land south of the village of Hettinger: 80 acres of U.S. government land in Adams County, Hettinger Township, Section 35. Then he went to work building a very modest house while traveling the area as a photographer. He enjoyed this new challenge.

Very quickly, by late 1908, the town was busy with stores, a hotel, attorneys, newspapers, a physician and dentist, a courthouse, an opera house, a tailor, blacksmith, and telegraph shop—but no saloons, which was a deliberate preference by the founders who warned that "none will be tolerated."

G.C.'S FUTURE WIFE: OLLIE EVANS

Parallel to G.C.'s life, there lived a young woman in Minnesota who had grown up in Rock County, only 150 miles west of the Flaten farm in

Freeborn County.

Olia "Ollie" Evans grew up on a farm just outside the village of Steen, in Rock County, Minnesota, in a large family: she had six brothers and four sisters. Her conservative father, the imposing Benedict Evanson, was a fire-and-brimstone preacher in the Evangelical Lutheran Church in Rock County who had immigrated in 1857 from Norway. "Han Bendik," as he was known ("Han" being a title showing respect), was good at warning his congregants of the perils of demon rum and the need for strict moral codes and was quite a success in the pulpit as well as on the farm. He formed the Evans Company in Steen. Ollie's mother, Anna Moe, also an immigrant (1863), had come from a family with property in Norway and she carried a certain gentility about her. Their lives were prosperous.

Around 1890, Han Bendik decided to buy enough land to give each of his sons a farm, so he began to purchase farms in Logan Township, Minnehaha County, South Dakota. That is how the Evans family established roots in South Dakota.

Ollie, like G.C., was a confident first-generation American, raised on the farm. She was independent-minded, very capable and strong, able to make hard decisions. She was practical-minded, determined, and had that spirit that G.C. would need to move forward. Unlike G.C., she did not have a formal education. Norwegian was spoken at home. Her English was elementary. When I was very young, she occasionally wrote to me on lined paper in shaky cursive. How I treasured those letters because I felt a connection with her as my eyes traced her handwriting.

OLLIE'S SECTION 4 in the BLACK HILLS MERIDIAN

Although the Evans boys would eventually inherit farmland in South Dakota when Han Bendik died, five of his children (Hans, Abe, Ollie, Bessie,

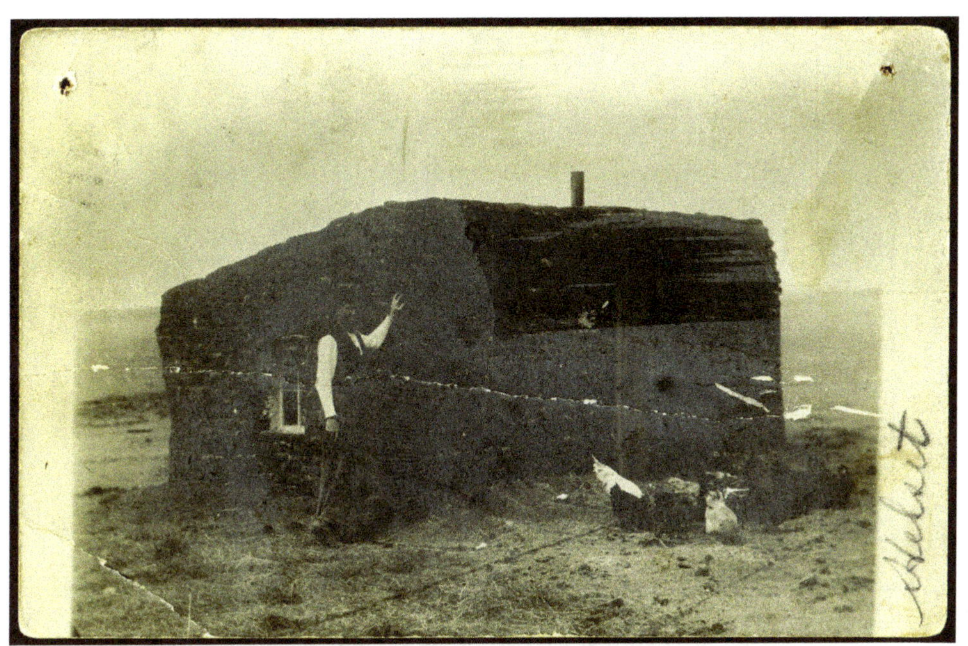

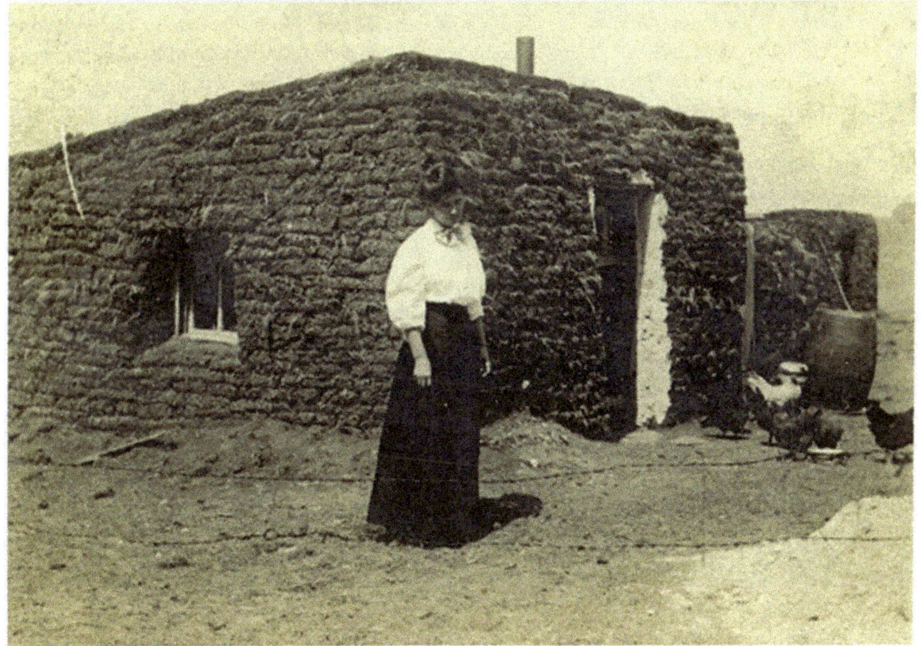

Hans (or brother Abe) above, and sister Ollie Evans below, standing in front of their sod huts on their claims near Strool, North Dakota. Ca. 1908. Photos GC Flaten, IU Archives.

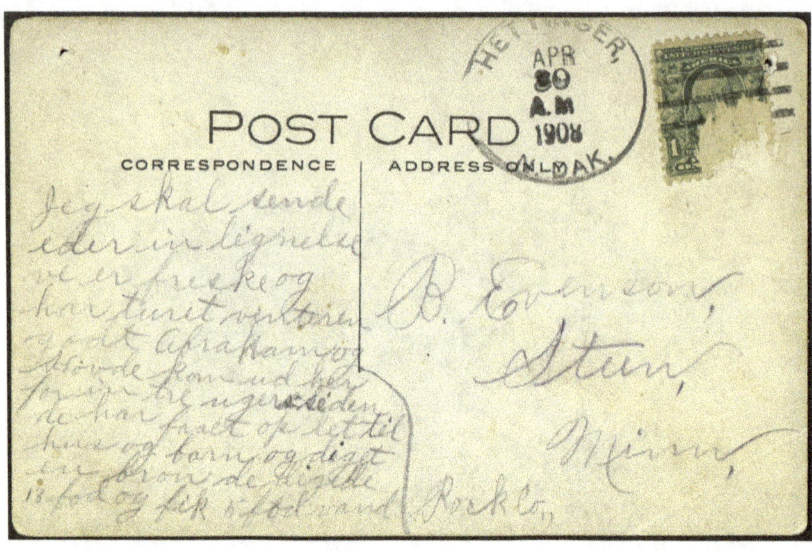

Ollie's image was printed on "Postcard" stock which was suitable for correspondence through the U.S. mail. Handwritten in pencil on the postcard (above) in Norwegian, reads, in part: "April 23 1908 Ja nu Skal de Joa si met fine Lus og der staas en madam poa din un sinfen ud-han de haft regen i dagdet regnenhis lit nu Haften ? barn og ond Abe ...?" Addressed to her mother Mrs. Annie Evans, Steen, Minn. Postmarked Hettinger April 30 1908. N Dak.". TRANSLATION: "I will send you some words that we are healthy and have managed the winter quite well. Abraham and Hovde came out here about three weeks ago. They have raised something easy for a house and barn, and dug a well, they dug 13 feet and got soil and water."

Below, women were a part of the settlement process. Some owned their own claims and were known as bachelor farmer girls. Some of the images were printed on "Postcard" stock which was suitable for correspondence through the U.S. mail. Photos: GC Flaten, IU Archives.

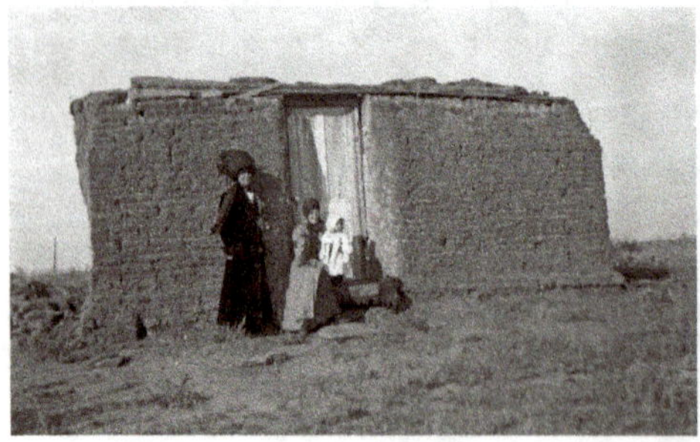

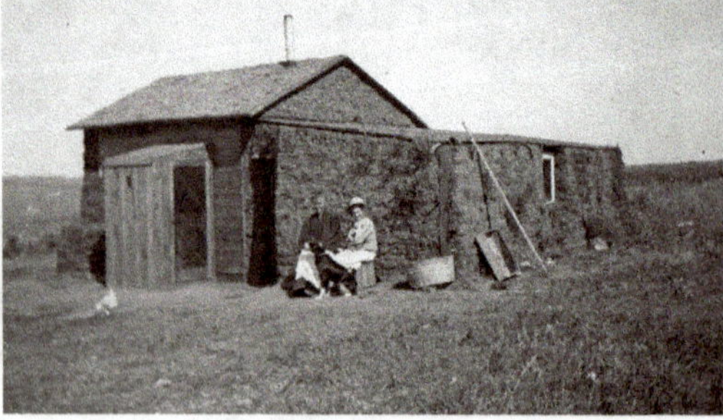

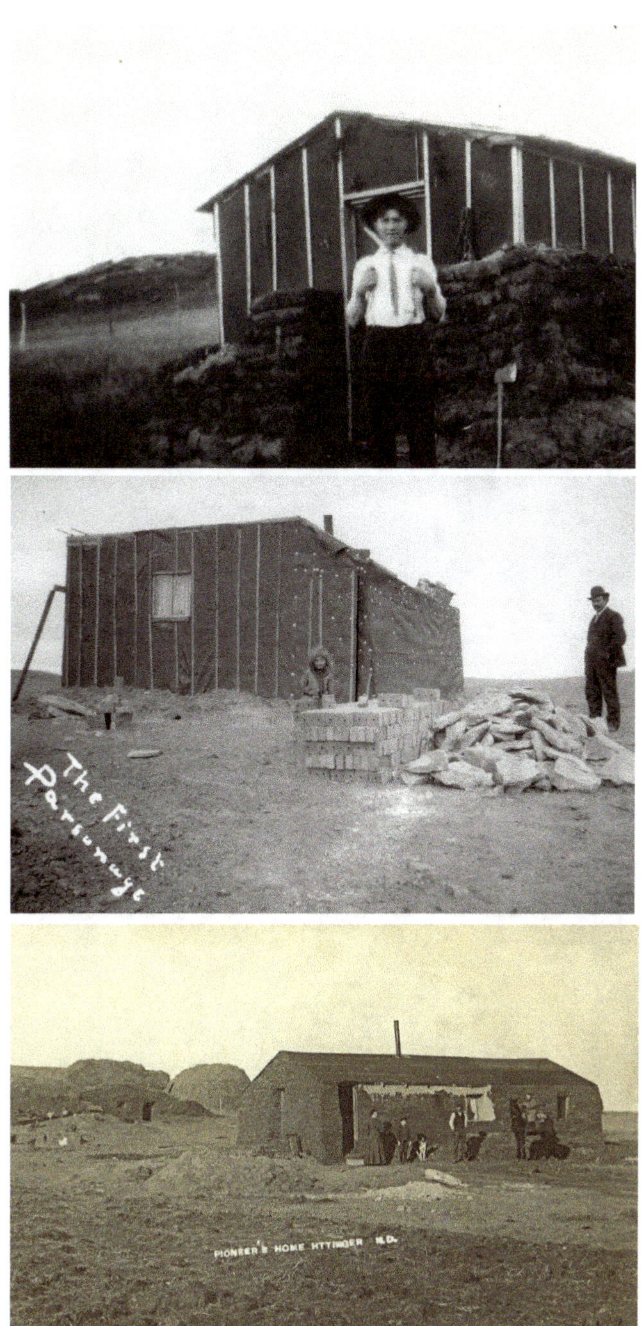

Photos of early pioneer homes. Ca. 1905? Photos: G.C. Flaten. IU Archives.

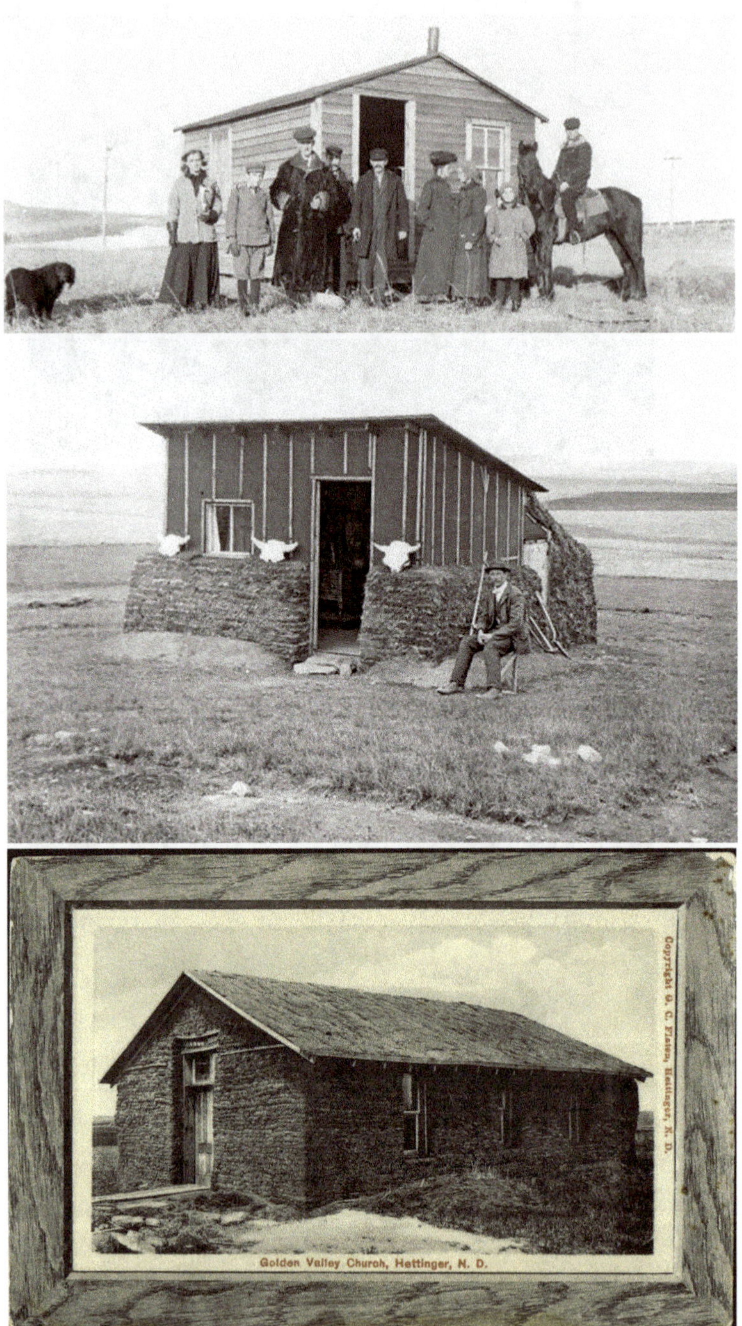

Photos of early pioneer homes and church. Ca. 1905? Photos: GC Flaten, IU Archives.

and Mary and her husband Haftor) went seeking their own property in 1907. Like many at that time, they heard about the public land being offered in the Black Hills Meridian of northwest South Dakota. It had opened due to the Sioux Agreement of 1889, but now new railroad lines opened up, making transportation links to these new properties possible for many. So, with the multitudes, Ollie, Hans, and Abe left Steen and headed to northwest South Dakota. According to her daughter Alpha, Ollie left to "keep home" for her brothers Han and Abe. But Ollie, too, bought property which directly abutted Hans' land.

THE PROCEDURES FOR HOMESTEADING:

1--SUBMIT A "LAND ENTRY APPLICATION." In this application, swear that you will acquire title to the lands by payment of cash or its equivalent and/or by entering upon and improving the lands. Swear that you are a citizen, not already property owner, this is your exclusive home, the land is for actual cultivation and settlement, that you are not working for a corporation, you do not intend to speculate, have personally examined the land and are acquainted with it, and that there are no minerals on it.

2--FILE A "COMMUTED HOMESTEAD ENTRY:" For land not exceeding 160 acres, Section 8 of the Homestead Act of 1862 allows you (if you do not want to wait five years to complete your entry) to "commute" it after 14 months by paying $1.25 per acre. To do so, you also have to make proof of settlement and cultivation. (This is what Ollie -- and perhaps her brothers -- did.)

3--FILE A FINAL CERTIFICATE: A document that evidences that you, the homesteader, are entitled to a patent provided that no irregularities are found in connection with your entry.

4--PROVIDE FINAL PROOF: A detailed statement by you, the

homesteader, and your witnesses purporting to prove that you have fully complied with the public-land laws relating to your entry. Done at the General Land Office, register and receiver determine proof sufficient, homesteaders receive a final certificate.

5--RECEIPT OF FINAL PATENT (Deed). Upon final adjudication, you, the homesteader are issued a patent for the lands you had entered. Ollie filed for her "proof" (also known as "proving up your claim") and was issued her "Patent." Hans and Ollie filed for their patents from the government in June of 1909. This land conveyance was called a Patent because when someone buys land from the government it is either called a grant or a patent. Thereafter, if the land is sold to an individual it is called a Deed.

So, in the Fall of 1907, Ollie and Hans drove their wagon north from Steen, Minnesota to Strool, North Dakota (443 miles), crossing the Great Plains and skirting the Indian Reservations of Standing Rock and Cheyenne River to the northeast. Their destination, Strool, North Dakota, was so new it barely had a few buildings, but what a history. Although today it is not even a ghost town but only a bump in the turf, Strool was originally founded by a Jewish Latvian, Bernhard Stroohe (later changed to Ben Strool), who was on the run after aiding in an attempted overthrow of Czar Nicholas II. Narrowly escaping capture, he immigrated in 1906 and headed to Hettinger (of all places) where he obtained his citizenship in 1908. He then headed west, filed on a claim, called it Strool, brought provisions, and started a store there. Eventually he ran the whole town. Most likely, Ollie and Han did business with him.

Before Ollie and Han stopped in Strool, they first headed to the General Land Office in nearby Lemmon, to look at the tract book and examine which properties were available. Ollie's eyes landed on a section of land in Hardings County, in the northwest section of South Dakota, north of Big Nasty Creek, and in between the North and South Forks of the Grand River. Hans chose adjacent land. Leaving Lemmon, they drove the 42-mile, day-long ride to Strool. After they stayed overnight in Strool, they drove their team out due west to locate the landmarkers in Perkins County. Later, after they visited the property, they filed a Land Entry Application. This application began the clock: it was up to them now to improve the land so that they could make a "HOMESTEAD PATENT FILE" to hold title to the land in 14 months.

Abe and Ollie came prepared with a wagonload: a washboard, lumber, pigs and chickens, seeds, a tent, biscuits, provisions, warm clothes, sheepskins and blankets. They needed cows, and to break the earth they needed at least a single plow and a horse. They brought wood for fuel. And, of course, Ollie relied on her chickens for eggs. They built a sod hut, and inside Ollie carefully tacked her dry goods box onto the wall to store her sugar, tea, syrup, salt and pepper, and coffee. She nailed together boards for a bed with great efficiency, and made a mattress by stuffing ticking with buffalo grass. She had brought a laundry stove with a drum where bread could be baked. There! The flour sack became empty as the long cold winter days went by.

Ollie wrote a postcard to her father on April 30, 1908, and mailed it from Hettinger, to "B Evenson" in Steen: her handwriting is difficult to make out. But she was describing the efforts of her brother Abe, and brother-in-law, Haftor Hovde, to drill a well on one of their claims..

It was not an easy area to settle. Ollie and Hans wondered about the wisdom of their choice. Soil in their area was Pierre shale, sticky clay, which is rock hard when dry and there was typically little rainfall and drying winds. In fact, in 1910 and 1911, there was a drought; the Spring of 1911 was particularly dry and hot. Many left the area, already mortgaged, and simply walked away from their properties. The local newspaper, the Perkins County Leader, whose bread-and-butter income was the printing of legally required notifications of "proving up" a claim, folded. Things only finally turned around in 1915. But the Evans children held on to their properties.

G.C.'s NEW LIFE

At that same time, and not very far away in Hettinger (only 25 miles from Lemmon on the railroad line), G.C. was establishing his new life. The surrounding was topographically quirky and prospects for a grand new beginning and the right direction looked bright. Because G.C. was a very genial and gregarious man, he became known to the locals as a community promoter. The landscape was beautiful, rolling, fertile, with wind-formed buttes. His skills as a photographer captured the birth of surrounding towns, but also recorded important historical data. The pioneers who were homesteading to the west of Hettinger treasured his photographs as proof that they had, indeed, completed their requirements for building a home and improving ("proving up") the property; they were eager to be immortalized on film, or at least, to send their postcard to relatives. He took photos of all of the important milestones: weddings, births, and formal portraits. He also traveled to all of the railroad towns to record the development of the surrounding area with its multiplying towns. He was well known for climbing up tall water towers in order to get just the right bird's eye view.

Although I do not know the story of my grandparents' first meeting, I have imagined the following scene as a possibility.

G.C. may have been driving a new 1908 Model T out to take photographs of the buttes and the growing settlements. Destiny was at the steering wheel when he drove into the Black Hills Meridian area in Harding County, North Dakota, up to the claim owned by Miss Ollie Evans.

Ollie looked off into the distance to see his automobile approaching. She welcomed visitors, so when she saw the tall gentleman step out of the car and walk toward her small shack, she shooed the chickens out of the way and stood ready to determine just what might be his business. G.C. looked at Ollie and saw a small and determined woman with a friendly and beautiful smile, and as they both conversed in Norwegian, he gladly asked her to pose in front of her sod hut.

"*Jeg er Gunerius Flaten. Hva heter du?*" And, continuing in Norwegian, he said finally, "Do stop by the studio next time you are in Hettinger. Your photo made up as a 'PENNY POSTCARD' will be ready for you. I have to send it to Kodak to be processed, but it should only take about one week," G.C. suggested. Ollie wondered, "Can you get one of my brother Hans's shack, too? It's the next property over." Certainly, he replied, no problem, and that will be ready for you in Hettinger at the same time. G.C. hopped back in the car, continuing on, looking forward to his next visit with her. His eyes scanned the horizon.

Ollie, of course, came to Hettinger and bought two postcards from G.C. and mailed them to her mother Anna and to her sister, Bessie. She spent the afternoon talking with G.C. about homesteading with siblings near Strool.

Later, G.C. introduced Paul Boehm to Ollie's younger sister Bessie. They were all young and ambitious and busy. At the time, Bessie Evans, 14 years younger than Ollie, was homesteading with their sister Mary Hovde. There were social events for the young "bachelor farm girls." Might they have attended the town dances?

As a so-called "bachelor farm girl," Ollie worked hard, but may have taken time to socialize. There were occasional dances in Strool. Sometimes Mrs. George Lemmons (whose husband was a well-known rancher) would organize the 42-mile ride to Hettinger on the Lemmon Stage Line stagecoach. At these big tent events there were games and dances—one lady for every ten men. For example, the first "real dance" was in the old Security Bank building, where cramped quarters meant taking your dance partners outside for a cool stroll. Both ranchmen and settlers mixed, and there was plenty of six-shooter shots and "squirrel whiskey" (moonshine) later in the night brought in by a "blind pigger" (an operator of a speakeasy). (Hettinger founders seemed to have found a way around the no-saloon rule. Alcohol was illegal in North Dakota from 1889 until 1932 when the State abolished its prohibition laws.) But from what I have learned of Ollie, it is most unlikely she participated in the dances and definitely not the moonshine, since her family members were very strict Lutherans.

Ollie was all about business. On June 14, 1909, she "commuted" her homestead by paying $1.25 per acre of land to own the property. Since Ollie owned 160 acres, she paid $200 in order to prove up. I am unsure where her money came from. Perhaps she took out a loan.

Around the same time, G.C. proposed marriage to Ollie—perhaps as they sat in a rowboat, overlooking beautiful Mirror Lake. At least, I like to think so.

1909. MARRIAGE: GUNERIUS AND OLLIE

G.C.'s second marriage, at age 36, to Miss Ollie Evans, 28, in Hettinger, at the Adams County Courthouse, on September 30, 1909, was a low-key ceremony. They were married by Judge Sonderal and no witnesses are noted on their certificate. After many years of searching for direction, G.C. found in Ollie a resourceful woman who embraced challenges, who was extremely practical and wanted the same things he did: a family and a home. She moved into G.C.'s very modest house in Section 35 and soon became pregnant. The small house was crowded.

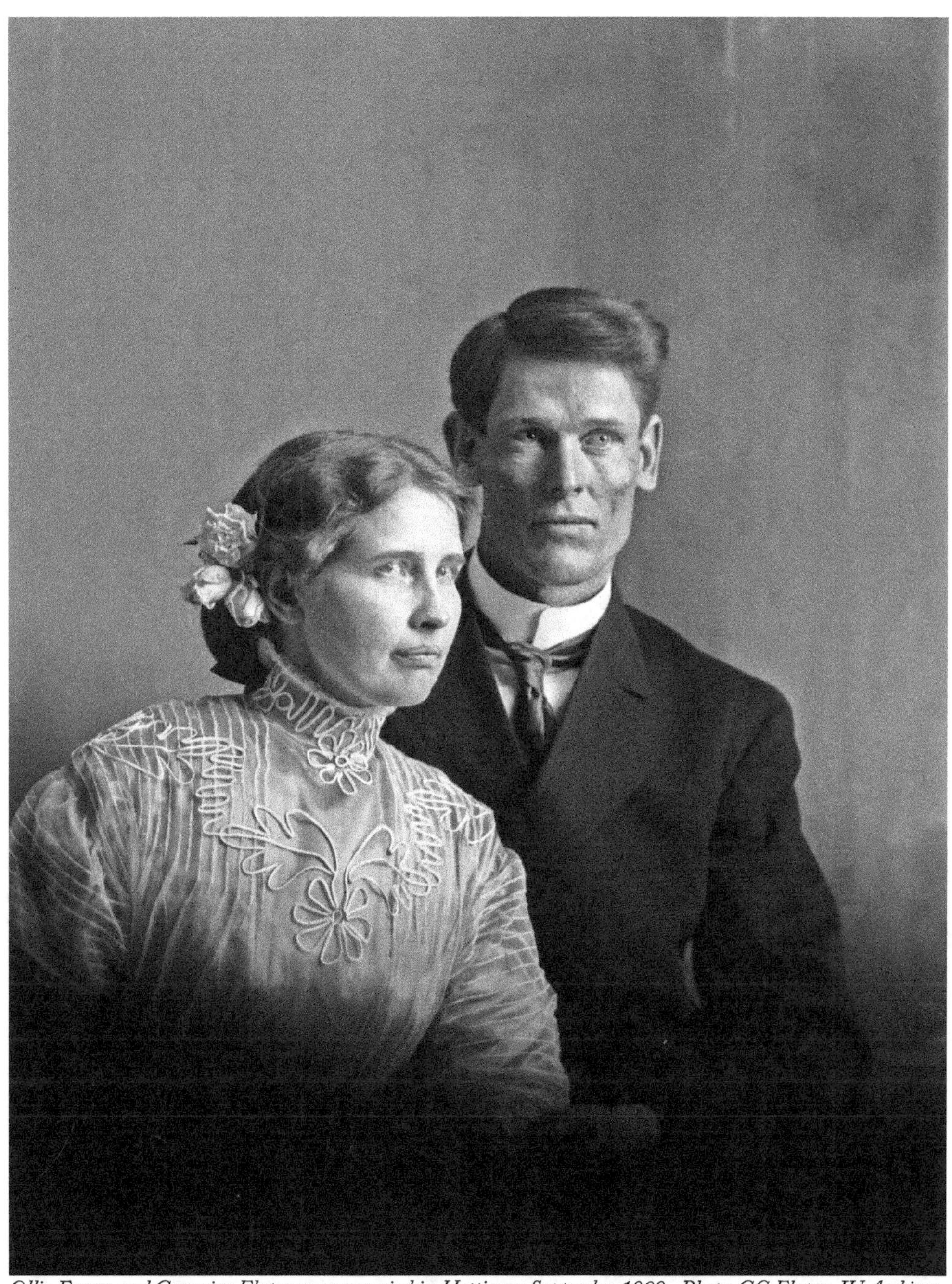

Ollie Evans and Gunerius Flaten were married in Hettinger September 1909. Photo: GC Flaten, IU Archives.

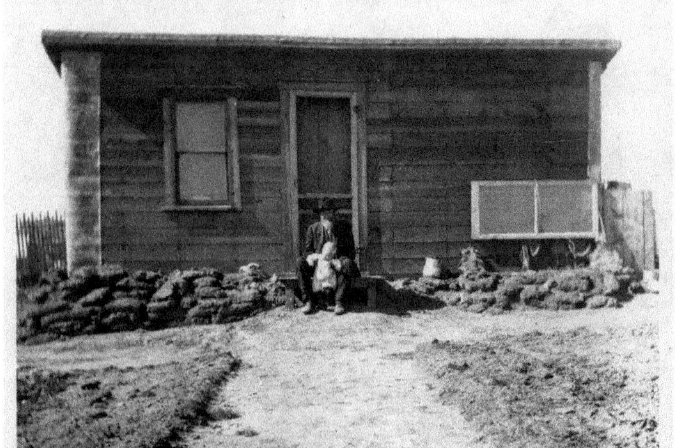

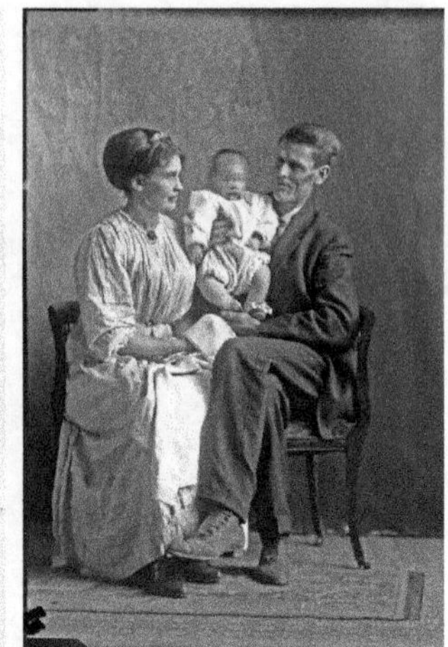

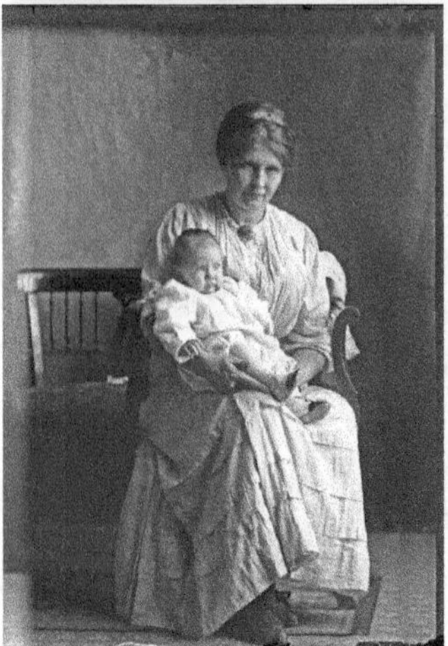

1911. The small house (top left) was the first home which G.C. built south of town. After Ollie and G.C. were married and had their first child, five people lived there including Christopher and Ollie's brother Hans. The plat below shows it was located south of town. Top right, Ollie and Gunerius with Clarence. Middle left, Ollie and Clarence. Right, man with the hat has been cautiously identified as Han Bendict Evans. Bottom left, G.C. drives a Model T. Photos by GC Flaten, IU Archives.

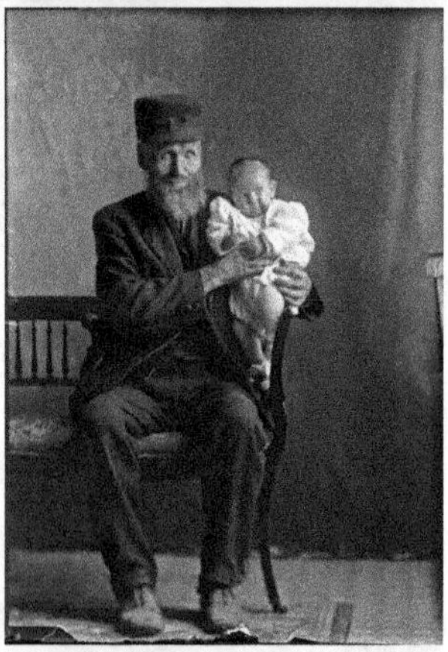

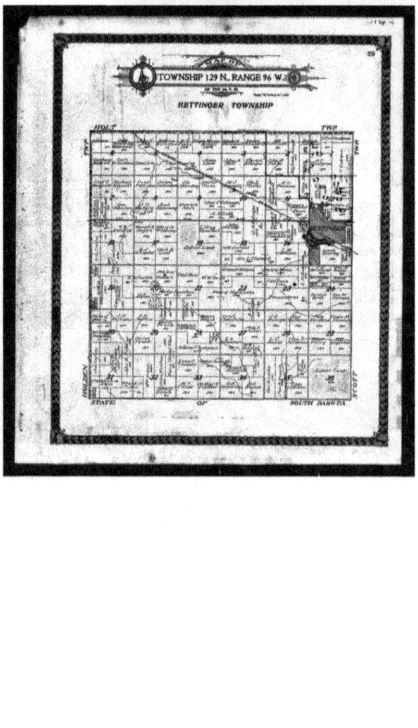

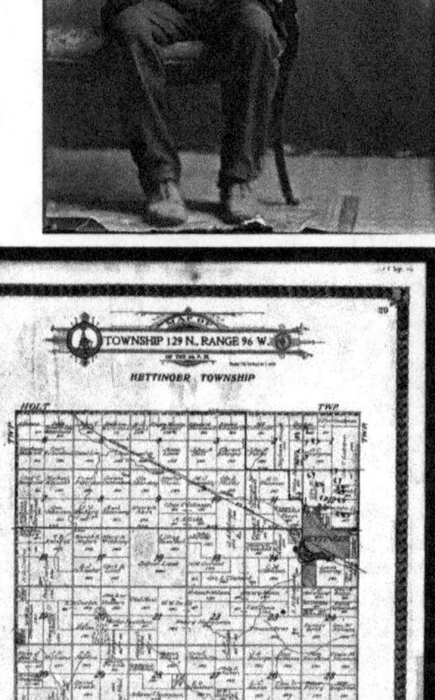

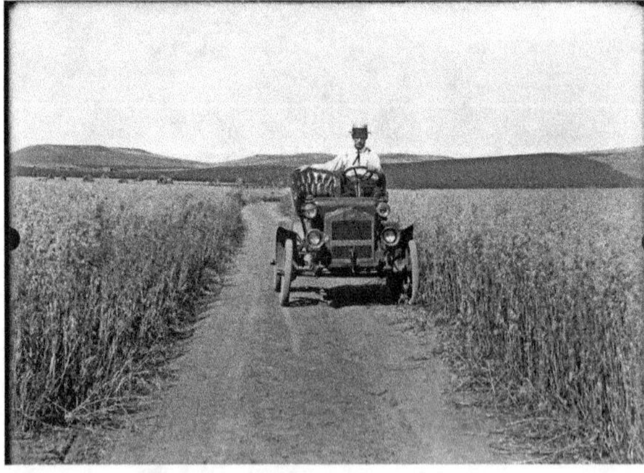

G.C.'s father, old Christopher Aslesen Flaten, who had sold his beloved farm in Minnesota, had come to live with Gunerius around 1908. He was ill with bronchitis and required nursing. And Ollie's brother Hans Evans came to live with them in 1910, listing his occupation as "photographer" in the census. Ollie, who was busy creating a new home with G.C., Christopher, and Hans in residence, soon added a fourth: August 27, 1910, she gave birth to their first son, my father, **Clarence Malven Flaten**. Soon after that, Ollie returned to the Black Hills in Harding County, with toddler Clarence in arms, to help her sister Bessie who had decided to file her own claim, one which Bessie would soon prove up in 1913.

1911. HAN BENDIK DIES | OLLIE SELLS HER SECTION 4 CLAIM

At this time, in 1910, Ollie's father, Han Bendik, dying from cancer, summoned his sons to his home so that he could distribute his property, but one of his sons refused to come (according to family lore) and was struck from the will. Ollie's daughter Alpha wrote in a letter:

> "Her father wanted to buy a farm for each of his sons and got five up close to the one Ebon lived on. [Ebon was Ollie's son who eventually farmed the property in Sherman, South Dakota]. Only one son didn't get one because he refused to come home when Grandpa Benedict was sick with cancer.".

When he finally passed away in 1911, Han Bendick's will gave the farms to the boys (he may have also given one to Mary Hovde), and to the girls he gave an equivalent sum in cash. He followed the Norwegian tradition of "Equal Compensation" for all of his children. Ollie inherited a good sum.

THE MAGICAL GOLDEN OAK YEARS

When Ollie finished homesteading with Bessie and returned to Hettinger, she and G.C. decided to move to a finer, grander home in town. G.C. sold the small home in Section 35, and Ollie used her inheritance. G.C.'s father Christopher Aslesen was still living with them at this time and may have lived in the new house for a short while before returning to Minnesota in the Fall of 1911. But he did contribute to the expenses for his nursing care.

The Flaten's beautiful, two-story white frame house, within walking distance of the town, mirrored the feelings of promise and prosperity that were rising all around them. It was the beginning of a wonderful, happy, idyllic life in Hettinger. The distinguished home had already been built in 1910 before they signed the paperwork to purchase the lot from the Milwaukee Land Company for $250, so they moved right in.

Because the interior was finished with polished oak, and because the home was large and grand, Alpha called this the "house with the golden oak" and added that "there was a beautiful fireplace, 5 bedrooms, bath and all." It featured two stories, with a large front porch. It was a popular gathering place, and many happy memories were made there with friends and members of the town.

In addition to the home, G.C. also had a bill of sale written on June 30, 1910, for a photography store located in town, 100 South Main Street, purchased from the same Milwaukee Land Company. It was located very near the train station and other shops. Being one of the first storefronts that visitors approached after they stepped off the train upon arrival in Hettinger, it was in a prime location, clearly marked "FLATEN'S STUDIO," ready for business. And he was. His photography studio also included framing services and Ollie may have helped at the studio, too.

G.C. was an extremely productive and artistic photographer, with a wide array of subjects: portraits and landscapes, and social history, like the building of the railroad, transportation, local figures, and holiday events. When he traveled in the surrounding area, he used to climb up to the top of the water towers and take panoramic shots of the surrounding countryside. And he also enjoyed shooting lakes, waterfalls and the intriguing natural shapes of the buttes. He often used his family to practice portraiture. His work magically captured a panorama of endeavors. He hastened to record construction and development of the early towns and the labor of his fellow Americans. Although I do not have a record of his photographs being used in advertisements and promotional pieces of the era, the content of his work was similar to other photos used to sell farmland and promote towns and growth. His photography was both journalistic and poetic. His photos were carefully staged and well lit. The skill needed to compose a good shot required much practice, as these were taken on glass plates, which meant he usually got only a few shots at taking a lasting impression.

Given his productivity, it is unfortunate that more of his works do not survive today. As his daughter Alpha writes, "My Dad used to send used negatives back to Eastman Kodak and they would remove film and recoat them so they could be used again." In this way, many of his original images were wiped away. Also, there are family tales of glass negatives being thrown away while cleaning out an old shed. Nonetheless, many of his images do survive and are housed both at Indiana University Archives Photograph Collection (accessible online at https://webapp1.dlib.indiana.edu/archivesphotos/index.jsp) and the Dakota Buttes Museum in Hettinger and more are in the private collections of family members. Some may have also been donated to the University of South Dakota.

Meanwhile, after Ollie finished proving up her Section 4 claim in 1909, she paid the property taxes on February 21, 1911, in Harding County

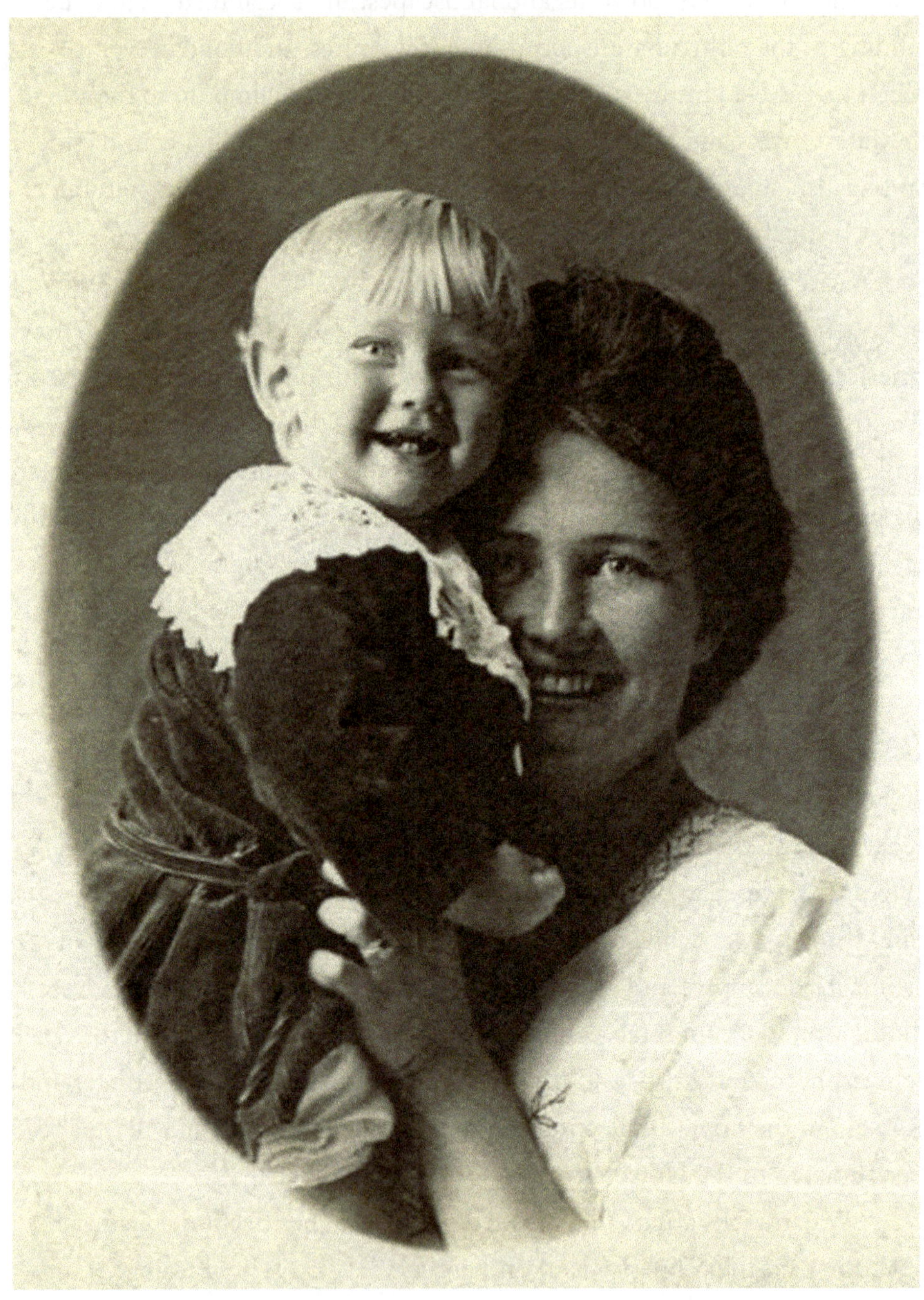

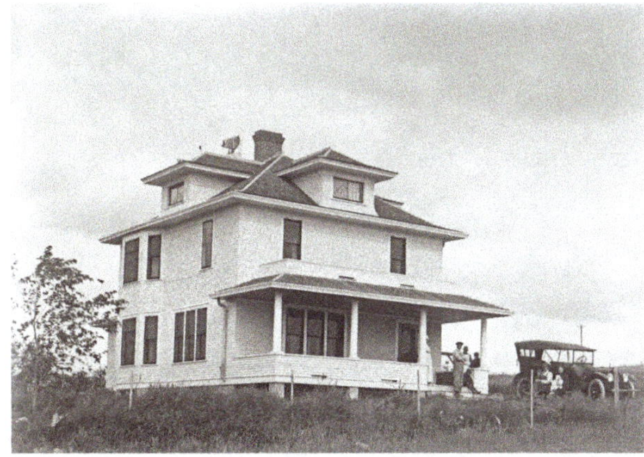

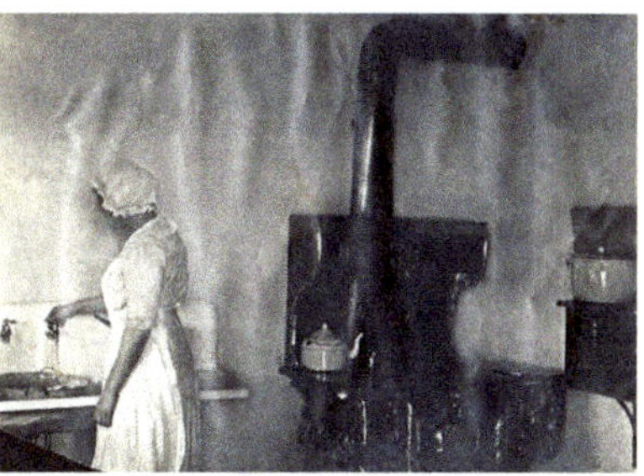

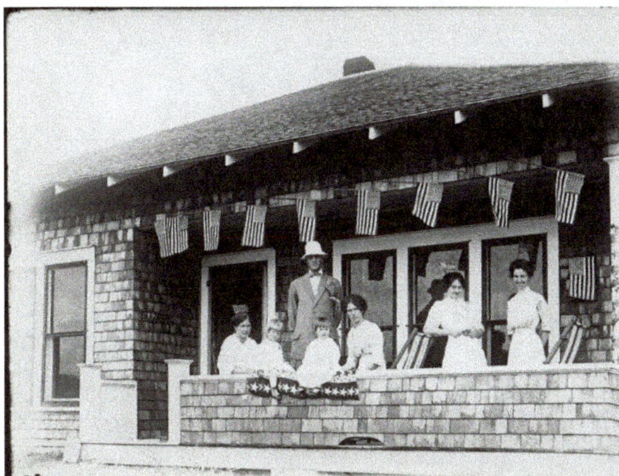

Opposite page: Clarence and Ollie. 1911.

This page top left: the Golden Oak house. Top right, probably Ollie in her new kitchen.

Left middle: Fourth of July, Ca. 1913. On the porch, Ollie and Clarence left. Standing is Paul Boehm and seated next to him is Bessie Boehm. The two ladies to the right are unidentified.

Below: The ladies are wearing large "peach basket" hats which were introduced in 1908. Ollie Flaten is in the center. With her are most likely her brother and sisters.

Photos GC Flaten, IU Archives.

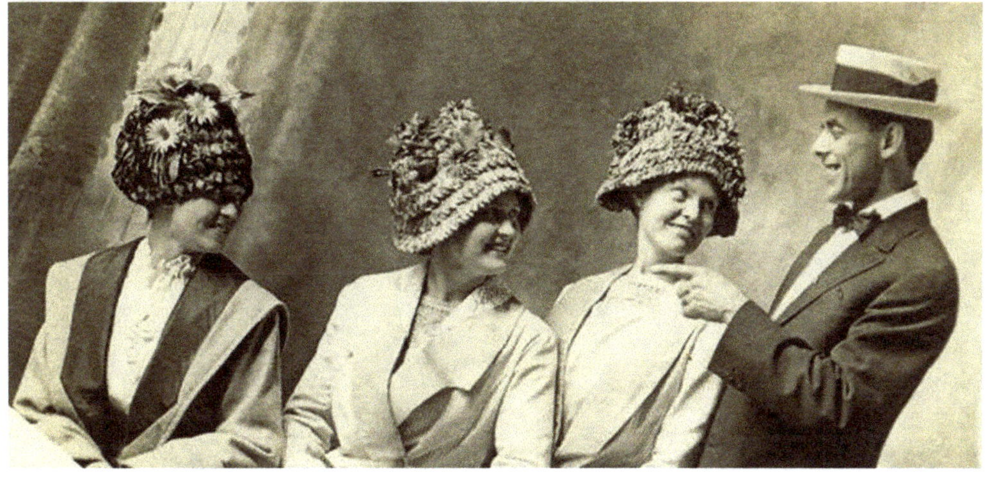

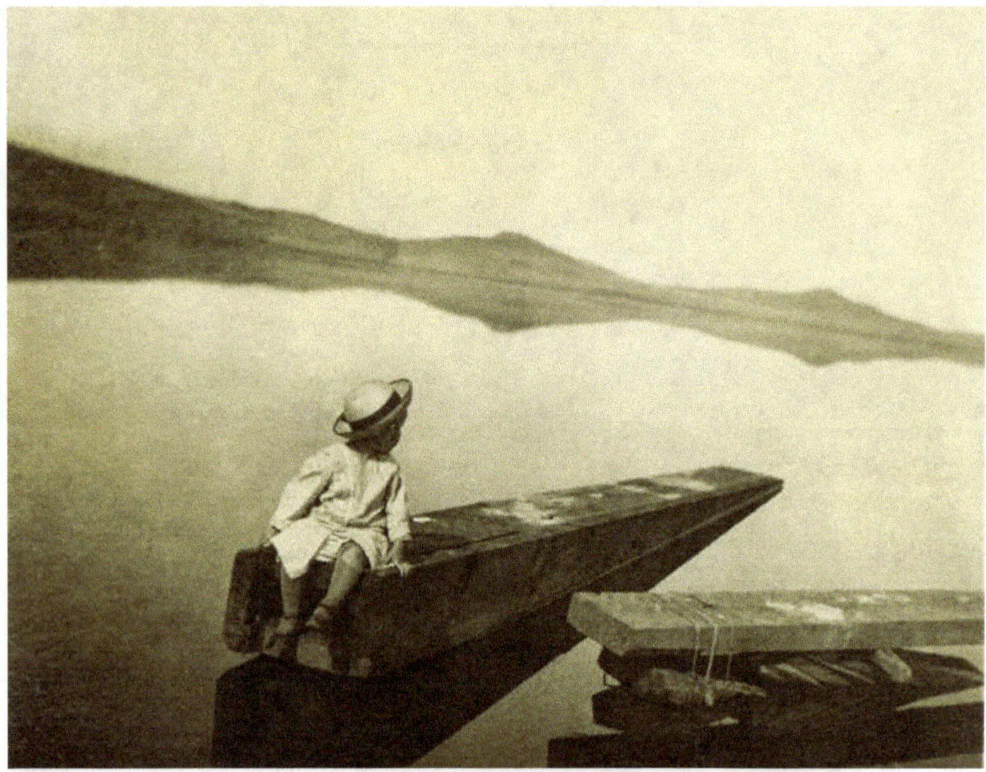

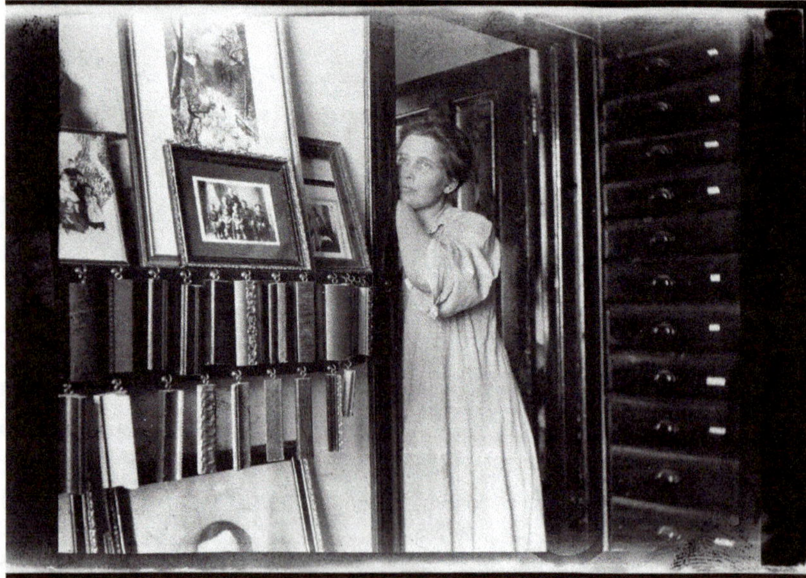

Top: young Clarence overlooks what is undoubetdly Mirror Lake in Hettinger, a lake named by his father.

Left: Ollie Flaten poses in the Flaten Studio.

Photos: GC Flaten, IU Archives.

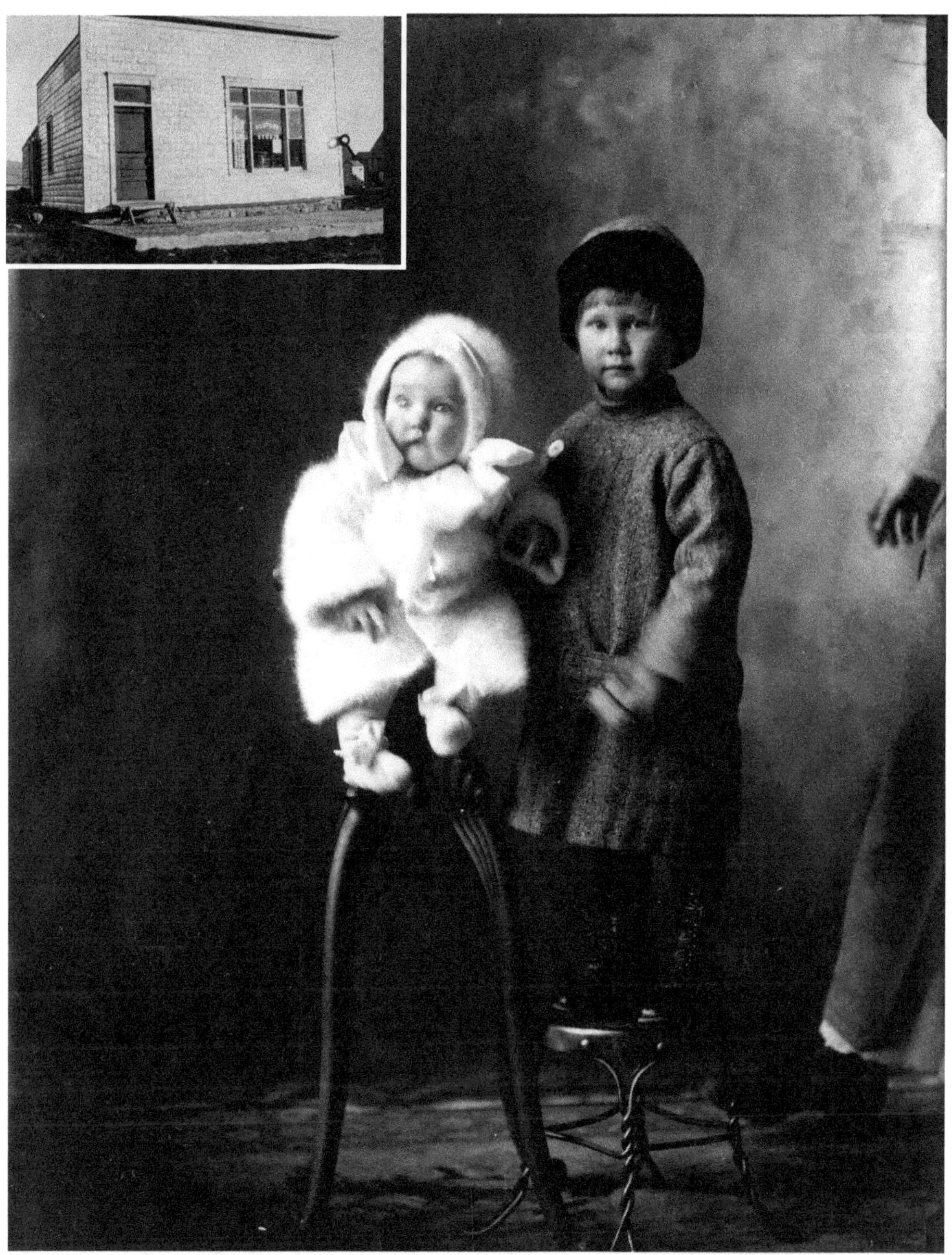

Inset: The Flaten Studio on Main Street. Portrait of Baby Alpha and Clarence. Ca. 1913. Photos: GC Flaten., Top: IU Archives. Bottom: Collection of Flaten family.

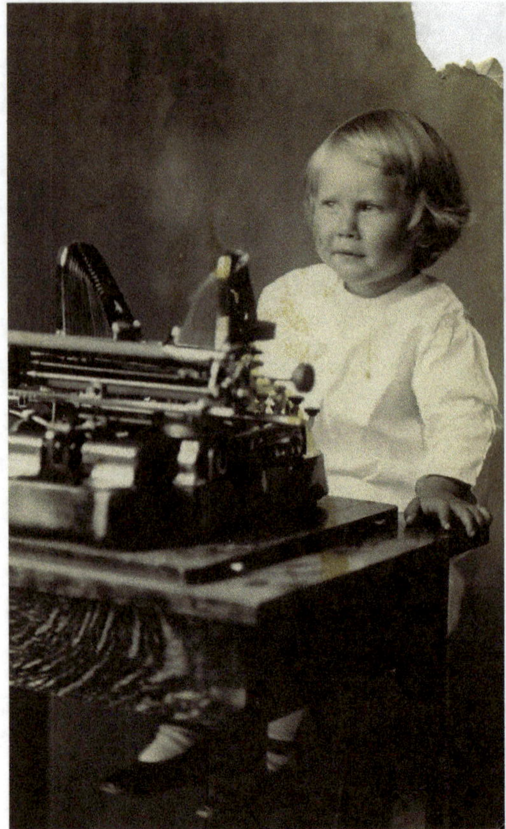

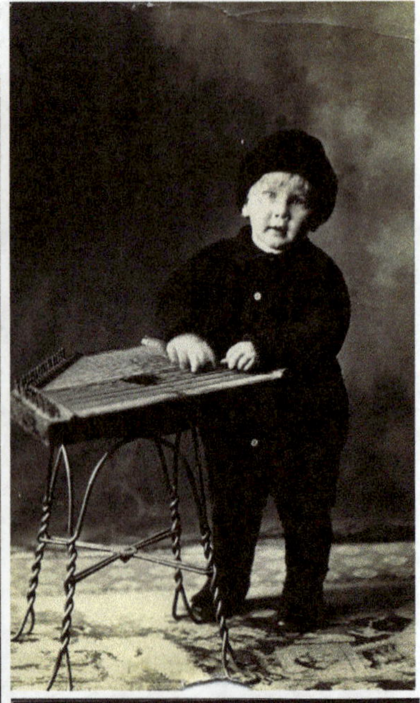

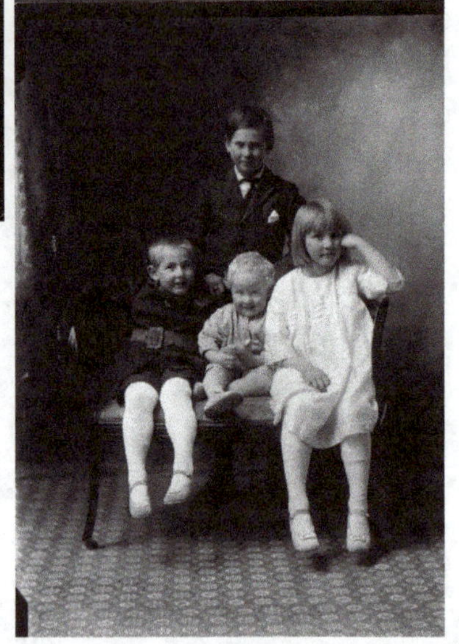

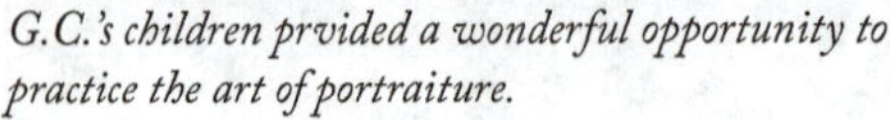

G.C.'s children prvided a wonderful opportunity to practice the art of portraiture.

Top left and right: Clarence. Ca. 1912. Photos: CM Flaten, IU Archive

Right: Bert, Clarence, Ebon and Alpha Flaten. Photo: GC Flaten, Collection of Flaten family. 1918.

Facing page: Clarence Flaten in a costume. Ca. 1915. Photos: CM Flaten, IU Archives.

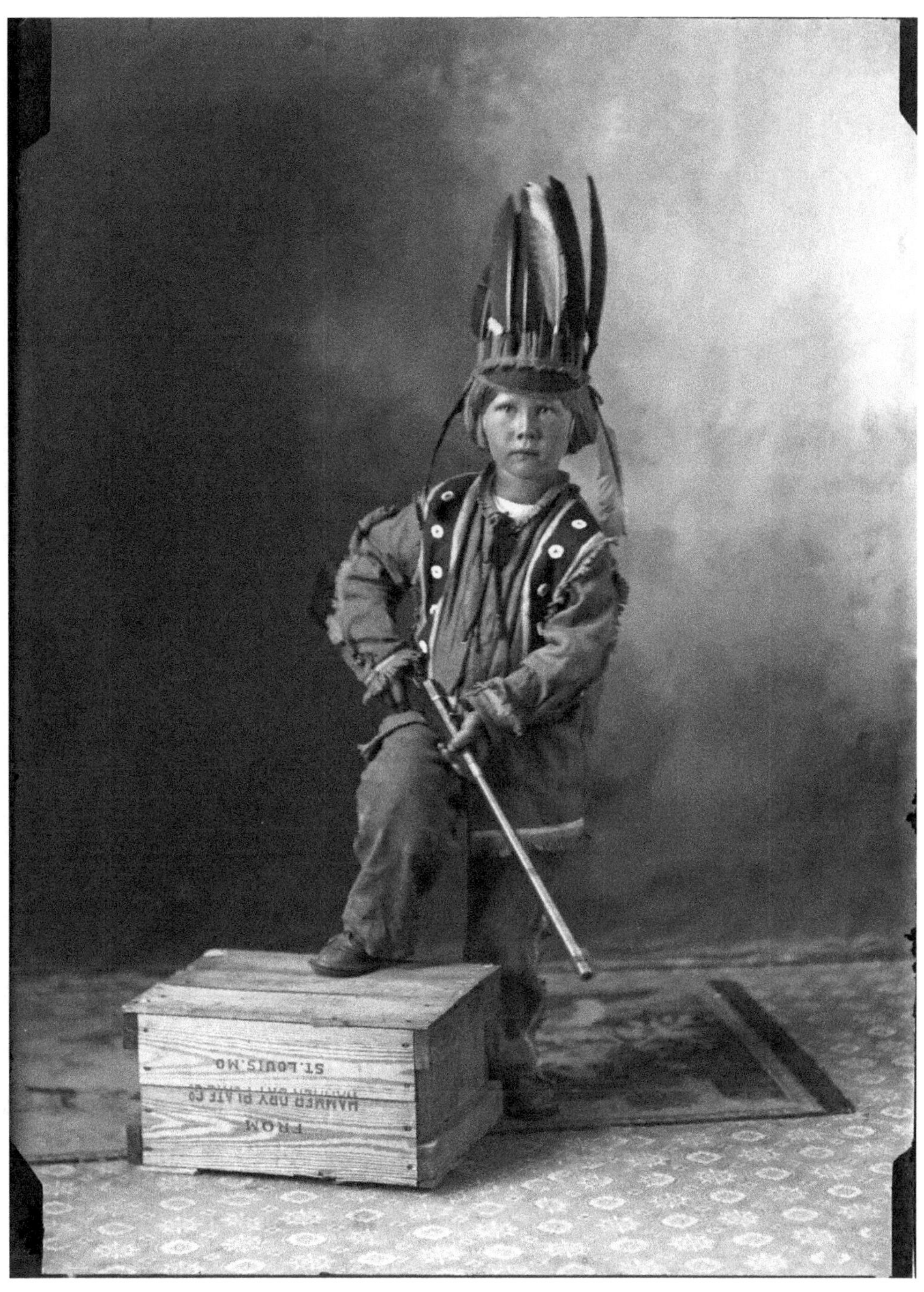
FROM
HAMMER DRY PLATE Co
ST. LOUIS. MO

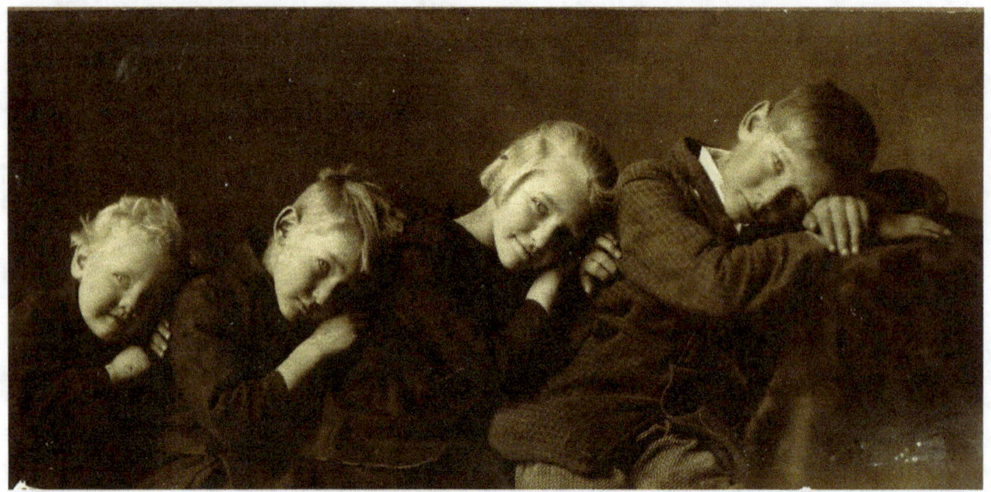

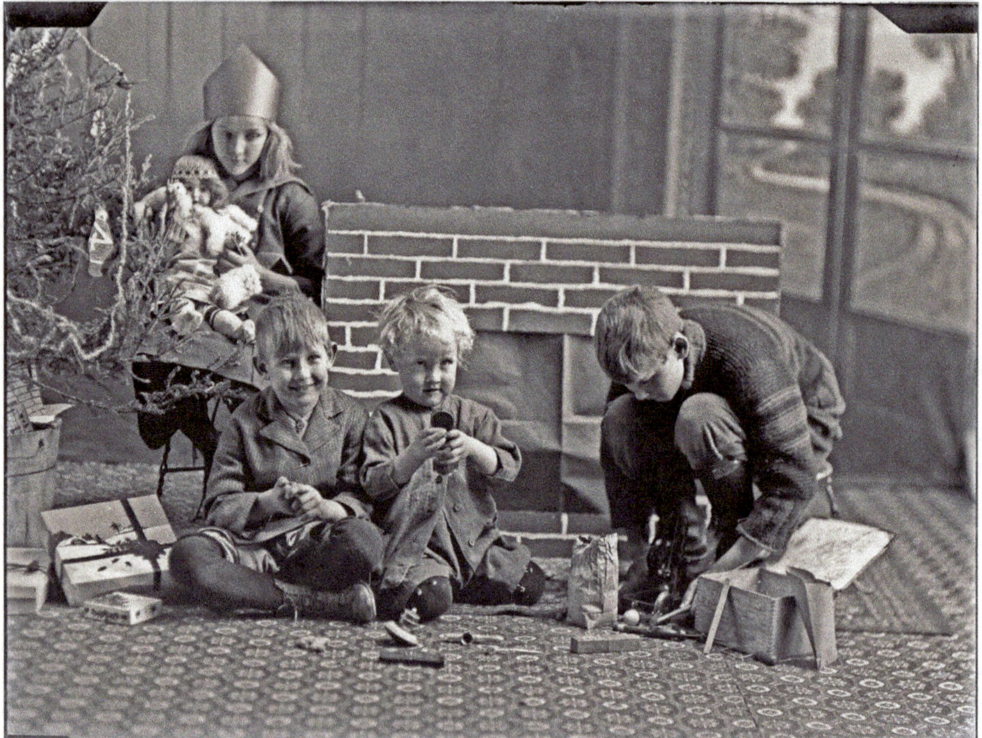

Top: Ebon, Bert, Alpha and Clarence. Ca. 1920.
Bottom: Christmas for the Flaten children: Alpha, Bert, Ebon and Clarence. Ca. 1921.
Photos: GC Flaten, IU Archives.

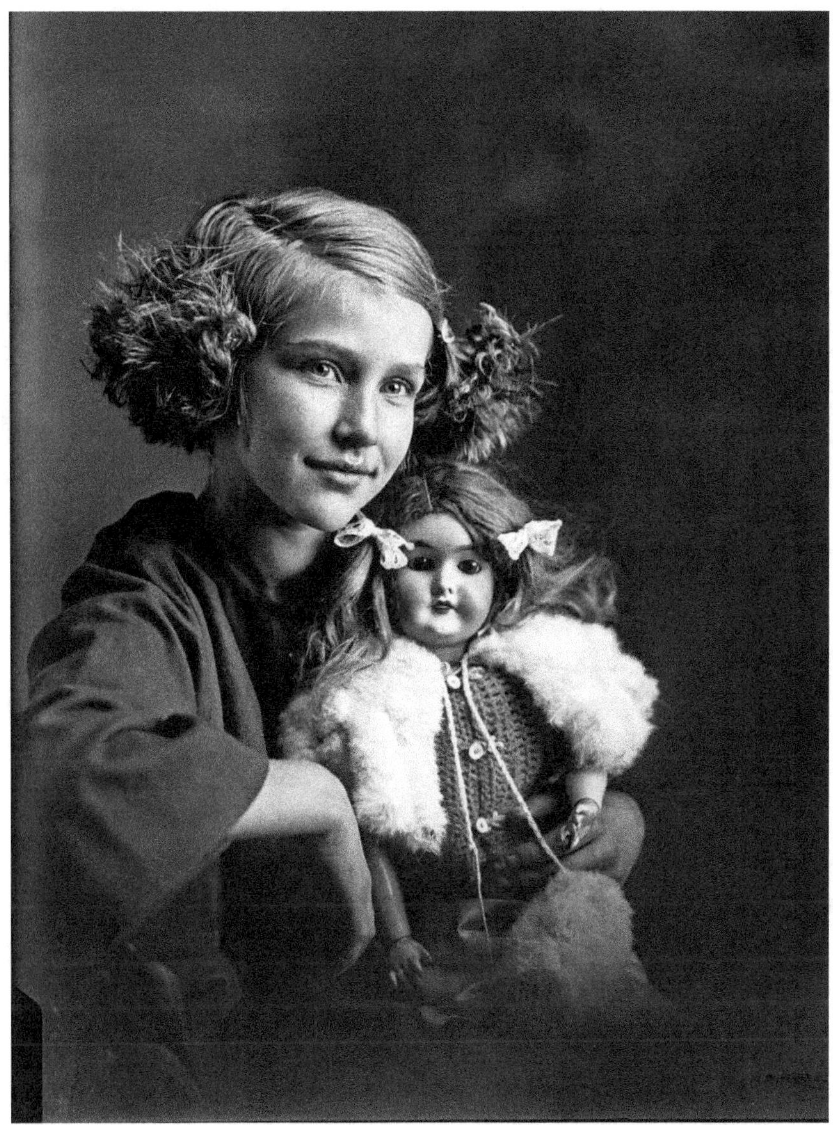

Alpha Flaten with one of her treasured dolls. Ca. 1922. Photo: GC Flaten, IU Archives.

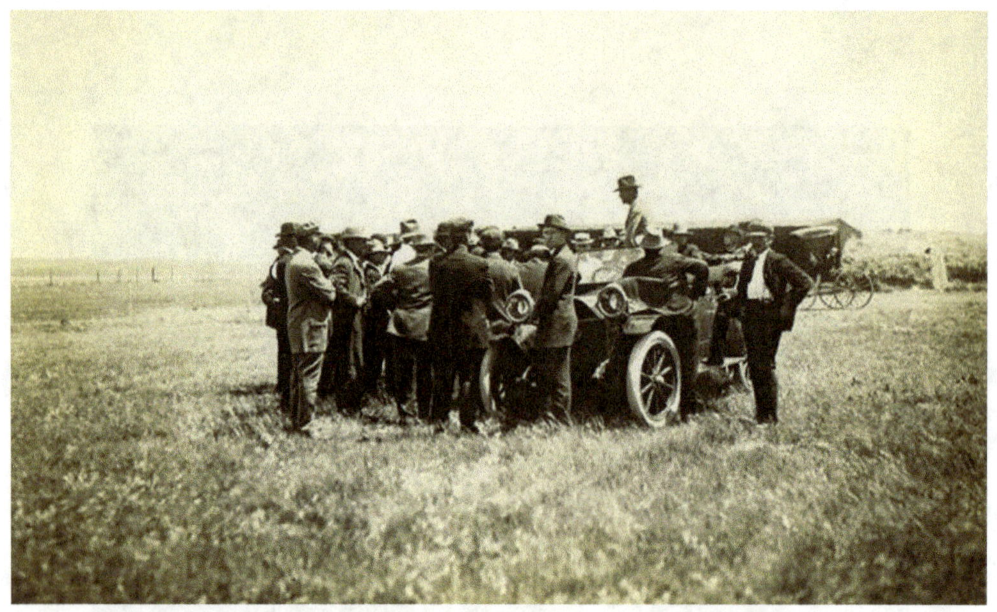

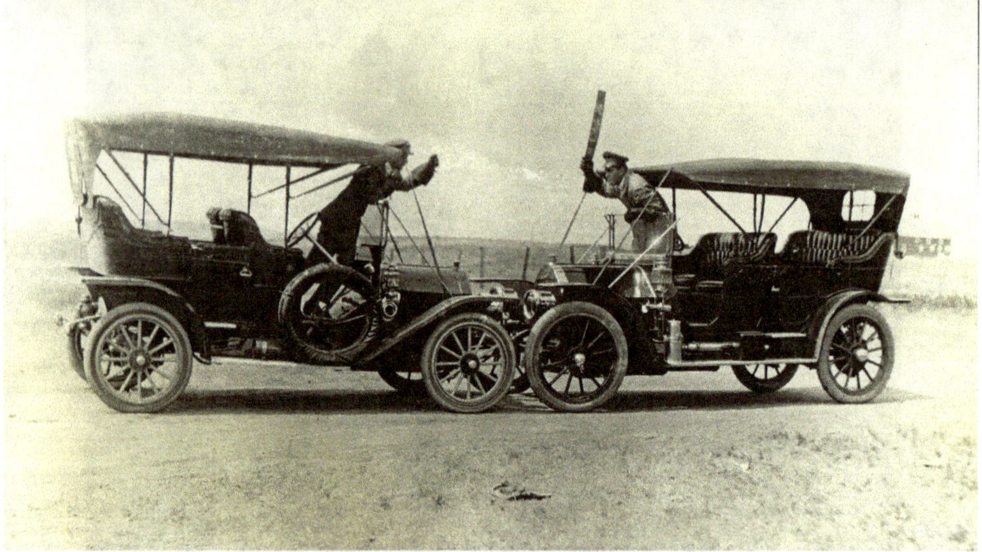

Top: B. Byron Bobb, AKA Alfalfa Bob, speaking to farmers about tariffs and crops.
Bottom: Prairie fender bender. Most likely a staged and comical accident for use in an ad or promotion.

Photos on this and facing page, GC Flaten, IU Archives.

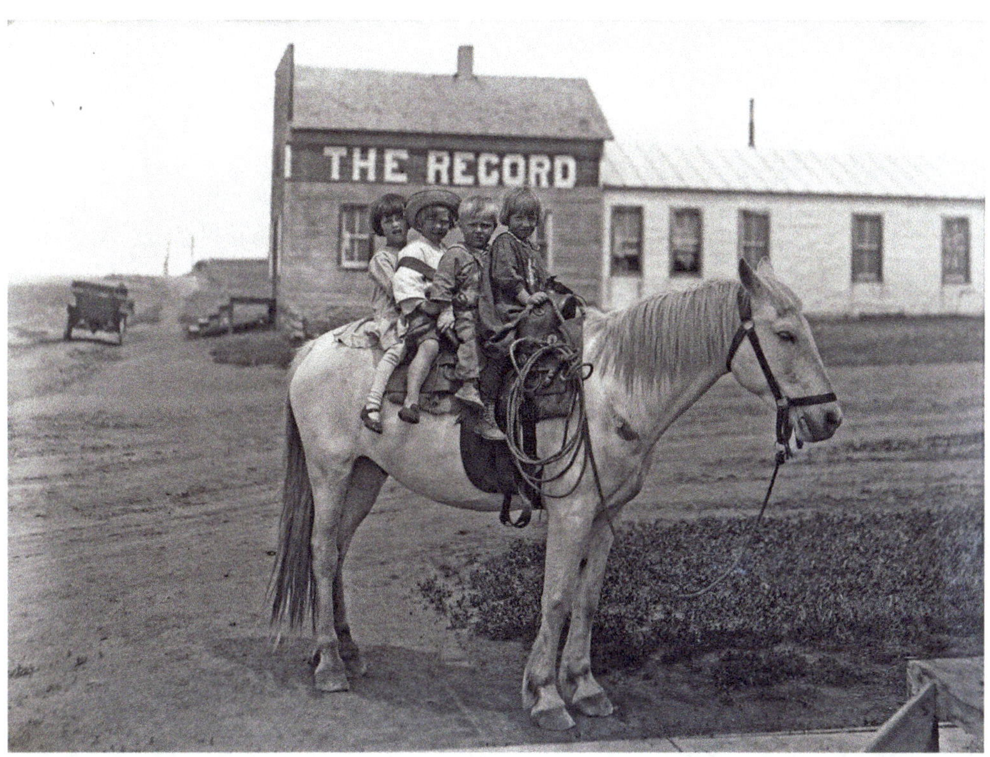

Top: Hettinger Childhood. Clarence (with hat) and friends on horseback. Ca. 1915. In background, Hettinger's town newspaper, The Record. Below: Children parade outside of the Hettinger Public School, opened in 1910.

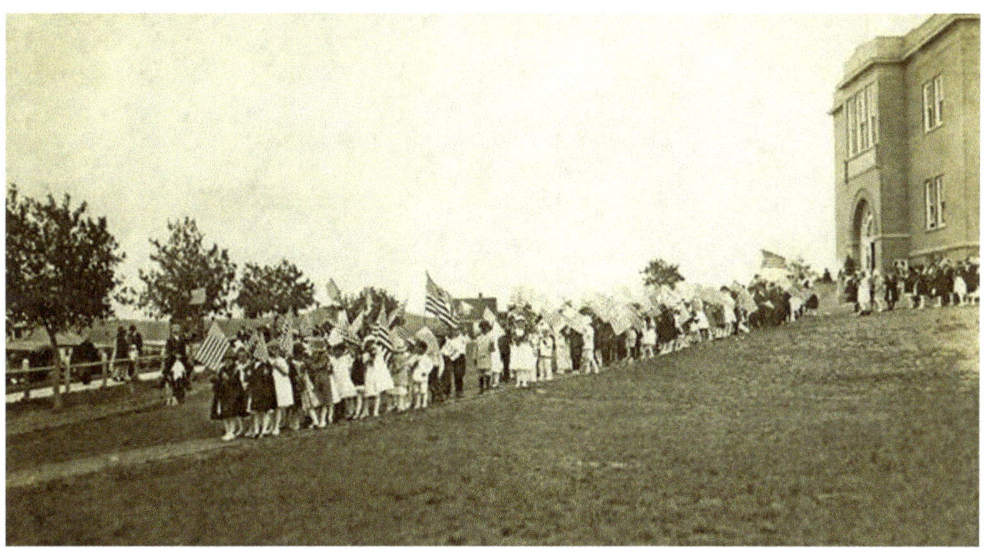

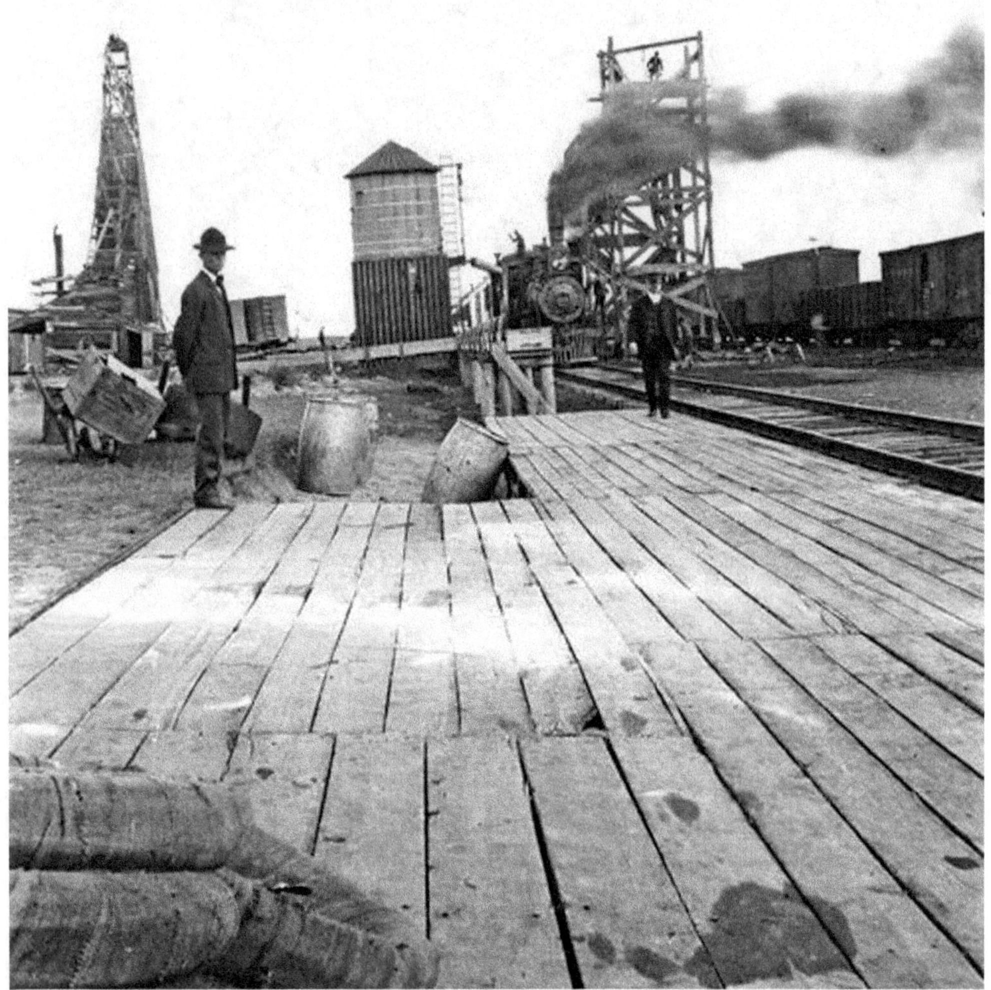

Hettinger train station. It was always hoped by the citizens that Hettinger would be designated a "Division Point" by the railroad. This would have meant Hettinger would become the most important stopping place between Chicago and Seattle. This hope never materialized. Photo: GC Flaten, IU Archives.

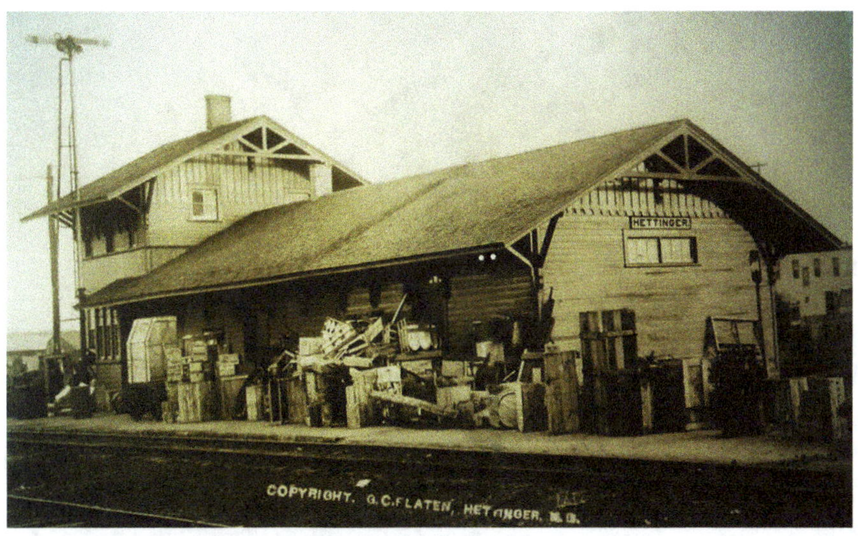

Above: Hettinger train station. Photo: GC Flaten, Dakota Buttes Museum.
Below: The Hettinger train station. Photo: GC Flaten, IU Archives.

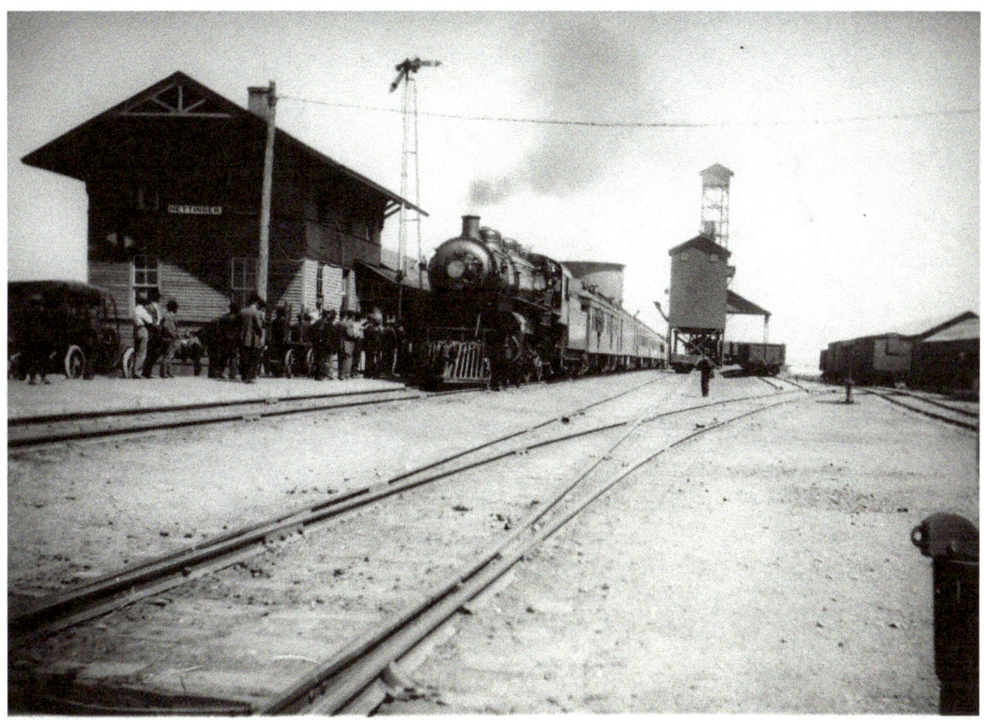

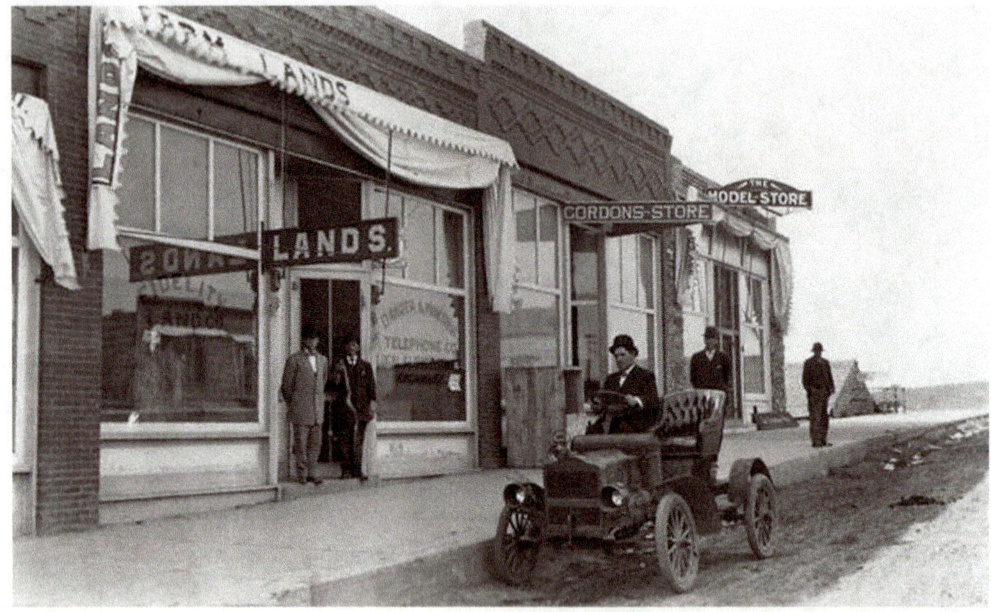
LANDS
LANDS.
CORDONS-STORE
THE
MODEL-STORE

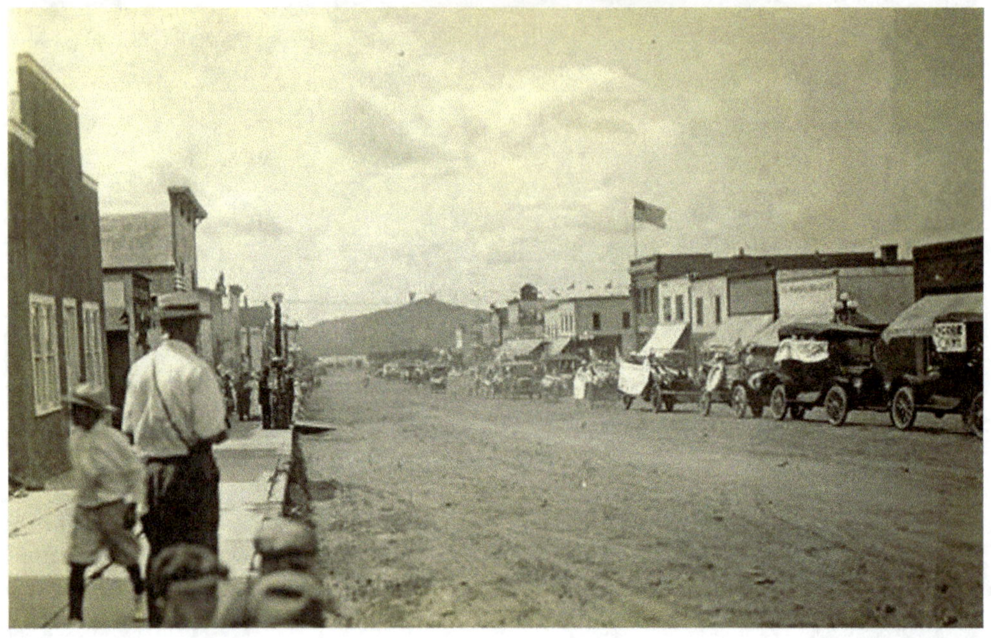

Opposite page: Top: The Model-T was a sign of progress. Ca. 1912.

Opposite page: Bottom: A parade that includes cars, possibly in Hettinger. Ca. 1912.

This page. The highway which formed the Yellowstone Trail was built by volunteers. Knowing it would bring traffic through their town, the local stretch of the Yellowstone Trail was built by the citizens of Adams County.

Right: Clarence poses next to a sandstone marker. 1914.

Below, the new highway section in Hettinger. May, 1914.

Photos by G.C. Flaten, IU Archives.

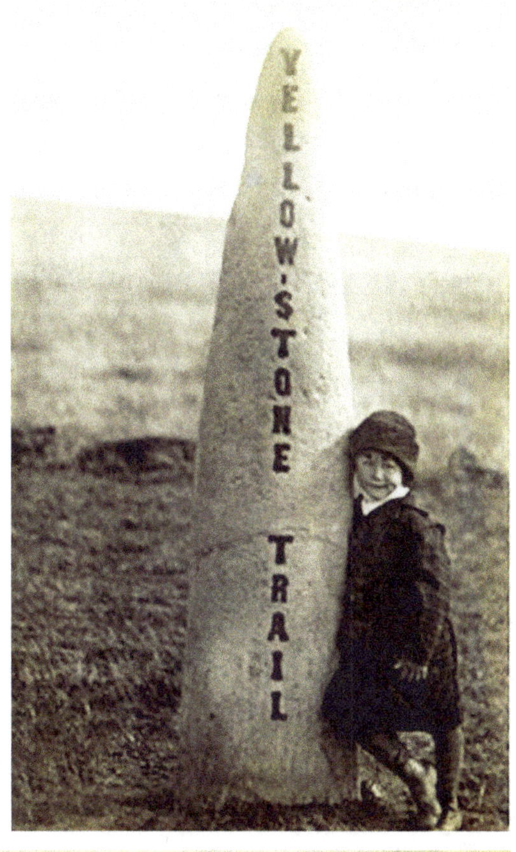

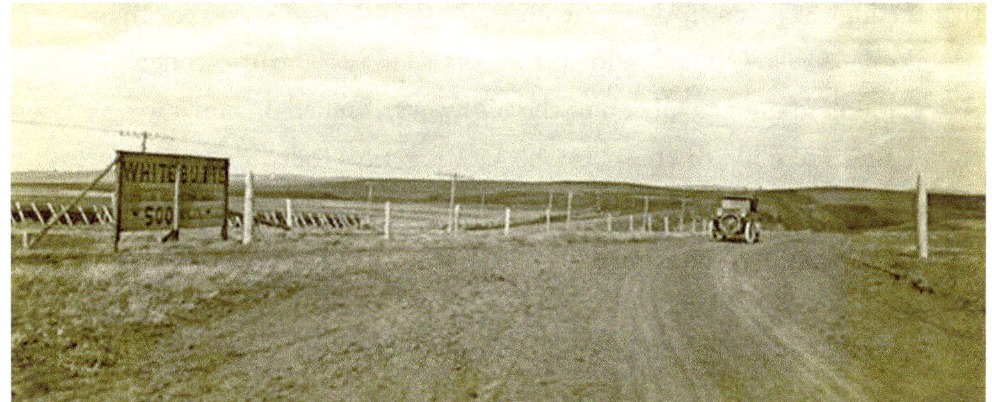

(Value $560) and then wisely sold her homesteaded land in Harding County for $1,000 according to her daughter Alpha. She was now quite well off. (Unfortunately, her brothers hung on to their claims and eventually lost them.) She must have been quite a saleswoman to have pulled off that sale, especially since Harding County was still in a drought.

1911. THE YEARS OF PROSPERITY

Life in the Golden Oak House was good indeed. Some elderly townfolk—as recent as 2007—still recall their parents' stories of happy childhood times spent visiting at the Golden Oak home. Back then, Ollie enjoyed homemaking, the house was always filled with visitors, and in quick succession, she had three more children: Alpha in 1912, Bert in 1915, and Ebon in 1918. Ollie sewed all of their clothes and nursed Alpha through polio, and later, Clarence through the influenza of 1919. The town's history of this time period was very exciting, filled with changes and general prosperity.

And big news arrived for Hettinger as it became a stop along the famed Yellowstone Trail. The Yellowstone Trail Association, responsible for building the first transcontinental automobile highway, had designated that the highway pass through the northern tier of Adams County, then pass through Yellowstone National Park on the way to Seattle. Since the Association did not actually build the highways, it relied on convincing town commissions to build their section. So Hettingerites rolled up their sleeves to build: May 22, 1914, was designated as Trail Day. Markers of natural sandstone with "YELLOWSTONE TRAIL" marked points along the highway through Hettinger.

Also, Hettinger had been granted $10,000 by the North Dakota legislature to operate the state Agricultural Experimental Station associated with the state agricultural college. It was located very near the Flaten's Golden

Oak home. The early work involved experiments to convert native prairie land to farmland. B. Byron Bobb, known far and wide as "Alfalfa Bob" (also "the alfalfa king of western North Dakota") was a local legend among farmers, and used to travel around informing farmers about the benefits of alfalfa and issues such as tariffs.

And even the daring Charles A. Lindbergh barnstormed into the Wolf Butte nearby picnic area. It was a thrilling era.

Of course, the news wasn't all positive. The much-rumored appointment of the Hettinger Railroad Depot as a "Division Point" had never materialized—the dream that the original settlers had their hopes and dreams set on, that one day Hettinger would be transformed from a mere stopping point to the most important railroad stop between Chicago and Seattle. But they kept hoping.

When his father died, G.C. traveled back to Minnesota for his father's funeral in October 1911 and filed paperwork so that the estate could be administered. After paying for the funeral and court costs, the final sum of $6,328.77 (worth $187,000 today) was to "share and share alike" among G.C., A.C., and Sena. However, it needed to go through probate and be published in the newspaper so that no one would contest it. Finally, in June 1913, the final decree for distribution of the funds was made.

Bessie improved upon and finally filed on her claim June 20, 1913. Since there were many rules to follow, she and the rest of the Flatens relied heavily on the advice of their close friend, attorney and land law expert, Paul Boehm.

The Golden Oak House, the 1915 Census tells us, was now filled with residents: G.C., Ollie, Clarence, Alpha, Bert, Paul W. Boehm, and Wesley C. Aunger. But where was Bessie? Living with another family member, perhaps. But Bessie and Paul spent plenty of time courting. Paul finally proposed to

Bessie, and they were married on January 14, 1916, with G.C. and Ollie as witnesses. There was undoubtedly a fine party at the Golden Oak House that night.

Paul also had an "off-farm" investment: he optimistically purchased land in Dickinson, land containing coal deposits with mining rights. (The land contained a very fine lignite grade of coal, which allowed for above-ground coal mining.) Soon, Paul and Bessie started their family.

WWI. THE NEW WORLD ORDER

And then the "Great War" began, for the United States, on April 6, 1917, and it destroyed the existing order and ended with shocking repercussions.

On September 12, 1918, G.C. had registered for the war, but the war ended only two months later on November 11, 1918, so he did not see service. The end of the war was actually the beginning of the longest, darkest period in history for the town of Hettinger and for all those who had worked so hard to build up their beautiful town from nothing.

True, previous to the war, farm crops were sparse during the 1910-12 drought. But there were outstanding years: 1900 to 1920 was called the "Gold Age of Agriculture," as the average gross income of farms more than doubled and the value of farms more than tripled. The dynamics of farming were changing at this time. There was demand for more land by farmers who were mechanizing their operations with steam engines. But many of the smaller farmers who had taken out loans to buy their neighbor's property were unable to meet their payments, and small farm mortgages were foreclosed.

All of the overproduction during the world war led to a sudden steep drop in demand after the war, which led to a drop in crop prices, which is turn led to a stagnant economy. More banks closed in 1921 than any other year, and farmers demanded relief from tariffs on foreign markets. This decline did not have a rebound.

During the Depression in the 1930s the drought grew worse. Some years nothing grew but Russian thistles. In 1934 many cattle and sheep were purchased by the government and shot. Many depositors lost their savings in the bank when banks simply went out of business; more farm mortgages were foreclosed. The only bright spot was that a shift to the mechanization and motors placed greater emphasis on better roads and bridges. But there was no call for photography. It was hard to promote desolation and despair. And who could afford a portrait? G.C.'s livelihood and dreams disappeared. The collapse of the economy caused widespread misery and shredded the fabric of family life.

Even the Boehms felt dark changes. In 1920, the Boehm household had settled together on 8th Street with a full house: Paul (41), Bessie (32), their two sons Daniel (3) and Benedict (2), Bessie's mother, Anna Evans (71), Bessie's sister Emma Guyer (30) and her husband John M. Guyer, Jr. (26), and Anna Bauer (48). Paul continued to practice law, trying cases from California to Wisconsin, and continued to be involved in city and county matters. But around this time, Bessie left the household to go live in California. Whether it was during the winter season, to escape the snow or for some other reason, it is not known. When Bessie left to go live in San Diego, California, she gave birth to two children there —Adelaide in '21 and Benjamin in '23.

As for the Flatens, the era of the so-called "Roaring 20s" was a despairing nosedive into poverty. It was anything but a time of prosperity and it shoved the Flatens into a very steep decline, the likes of which none of the children had ever known.

This economic collapse was so profound and unsettling that it's impact defined the lives of not only that generation, but also of both of my parents,

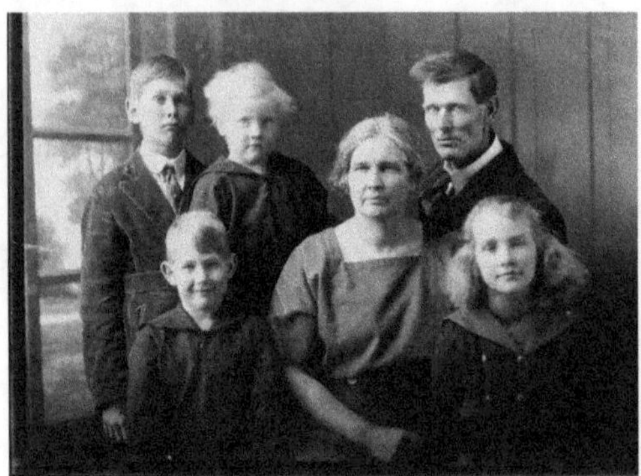

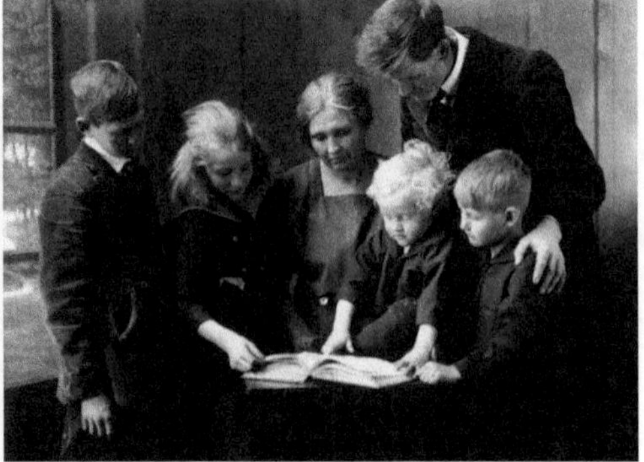

The Flatens moved from the House with the Golden Oak into the back room of the Flaten Photo Studio in 1922 in order to survive their uncertain economic circumstances. Even that proved to be a problem. They then moved to a farm and lived in the granary. Inset: an interior photo of the studio showing one daybed. Photos: GC Flaten, IU Archives.

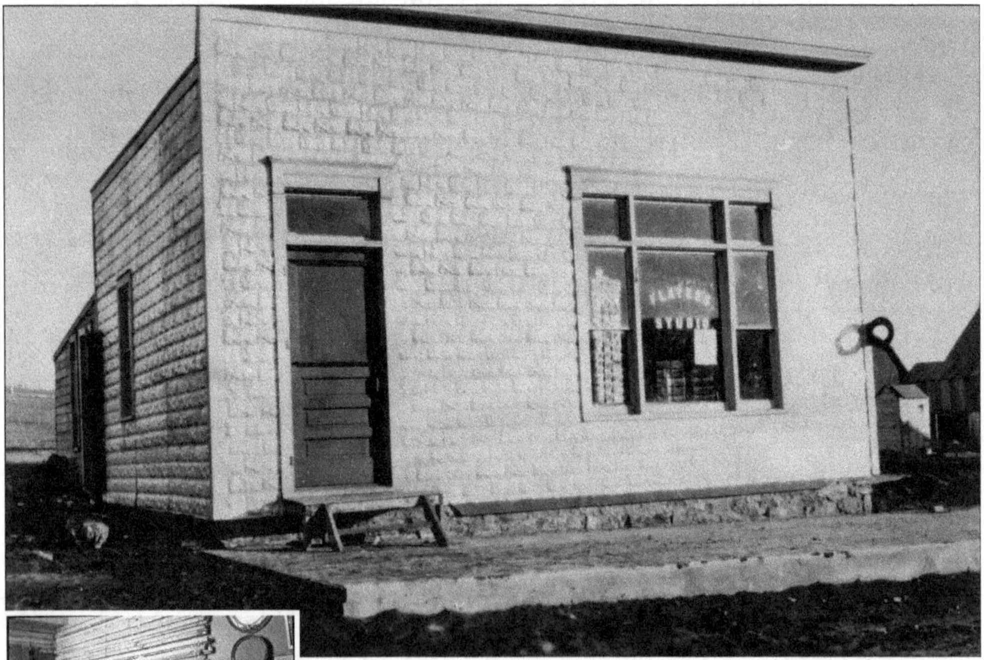

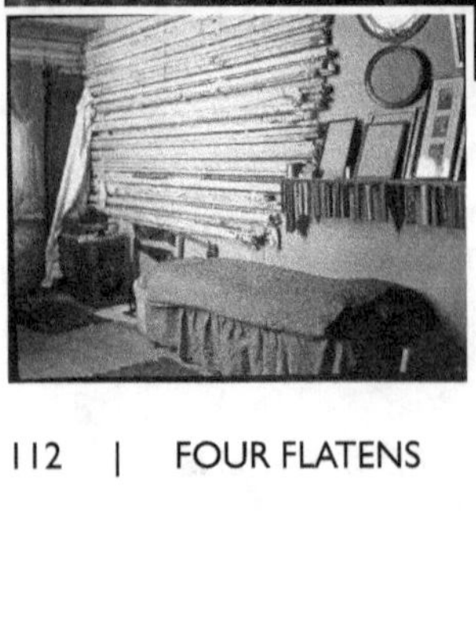

and consequently it passed down to me and my siblings. The lesson was this: make do with what you have.

1920-1923. THE FLATEN STUDIO YEARS

In 1920, forced to move from their beloved Golden Oak House, they now retreated to the back room of the Flaten Studio on Main Street. The children were young (Clarence, age 9; Alpha, age 7, Bertram, age 4, Ebon, age 1 ½) and Alpha remembers this as a time of great struggle. "The photography studio was one small bedroom for six people, no running water, bathroom (it was out back), a tiny kitchen and eating area, and a small space we called our living room. The rest of the building was used for his business." But the business could not survive the general economic collapse.

1923-1928. THE GRANARY YEARS

Sadly, the family finally sold the Golden Oak House in 1923 to R.A. Richardson, who operated the mill at the grain elevator. Since the makeshift life in the Flaten Studio was miserable, G.C. decided to move again, against Ollie's wishes, to a farm where they lived in the granary. It is hard to image a more impoverished situation. Alpha recalls: "Then in a few years my Dad wanted to move out on a farm and there was nothing but a little old granary which was unfinished on the inside so it must have been very cold. Against my mother's wishes this became our home for five years."

Could their living quarters have been any worse? The farm granary was a building that held grain. Typical granaries of the era were built on concrete piers, and raised off the ground which provided ventilation; they were made of wood in an elongated box style and had a gabled roof but no eaves. There was a center door and a hole in the gable for making deposits of grain into the compartments inside. A distinctive feature of a granary is lack of windows so that vermin do not enter. Often, they were double-walled for maximum protection from the elements. There was one large door on the side of the building where grain was loaded. This building was not fit for livestock.

Yet, the 1925 North Dakota State Census shows that G.C., Ollie, Clarence, Alpha, Bert, and Ebon were living in the granary along with Ollie's mother, Anna Evans, age 77.

During this time, according to Ollie's grandson Bill Flaten, Ollie left the family to be with her sister Bessie in California, leaving G.C. and the boys to fend for themselves with meager resources. "I remember when I was a kid, Ron [Bill's brother] noticed that Grandma did not like us boys. She was never mean to us; she just preferred to ignore us. So, I can understand Grandma going to visit her sister Bessie, to relax under the California sun with her daughter, leaving the boys to run wild on the streets of Hettinger, North Dakota."

Their last year in the granary in Hettinger, 1928, was quite unstable. Somehow, Clarence injured his leg which created a flesh wound to the upper third of his inner leg. Only two of the children continued to go to school for the 1927-28 year: Clarence starred on the High School Basketball Team in 1928, and both he and Alpha finished their year at Hettinger High School. But Bert's records show that he was repeating the 6th grade and was in attendance for only the 1st semester and Ebon's record appears as if he did not attend fourth grade at all.

By late 1926, desperate to improve the family circumstances, Ollie went to Sioux Falls, South Dakota to look for a rooming house she could live in while renting rooms and where the kids could go to school. While there, she talked to her brother John, who was single and farming his inherited acres. He asked her if she'd like to buy his farm. He knew that Han Bendik had asked his sons if, when they wanted to sell their land, they could try keeping it in the family. Ollie loved the idea of buying John's place and so she and G.C. decided they would do so, and they would all move to South Dakota where Ollie would be near her family. John Evans would live with them and her mother, Anna Evans, would, too.

So, the Flaten family left Hettinger. Of this journey south, there can be no better account than that of Ebon's son, Bill Flaten:

"When in 1927 the Flaten family left Hettinger, North Dakota for the John Evans farm by Dell Rapids, they loaded the furniture, camera, etc. on a railroad car but they had an old truck and a calf that could not be included. Grandpa, who could operate a camera, incubator, raise honey bees, was not going to drive that contraption. Grandma did not drive and your Clancy (Clarence) was already in Dell Rapids in High School. They decided to let the expendables drive it (Bert and Ebon.) So it was Bert, age 12, Ebon, age 9, on a 400-mile road trip. I can now only imagine Grandpa Flaten saying "Listen here, Bert, go East on U.S. Highway 12, cross the Missouri River, stay on U.S. Highway 12 when you go through the big city of Aberdeen, S.D. Continue East until you get to Milbank, S.D. Then turn right and go South on U.S. Highway 77, that will take you to Dell Rapids. Look up Clarence and he will show you how to get to the farm. And Ebon, you nine year old, do as you're told!"

A NEW LIFE IN SOUTH DAKOTA: THE JOHN EVANS FARM: SECTION 14

In 1928, near Dell Rapids, South Dakota, they settled on the John Evans' farm, which Ollie purchased "at a fair price" (she always emphasized) from John.

Ollie was pleased with her prospects; her young children were in school, and her mother Anna and brother John lived with them and helped out. She had less time to sew because she was busy with a new venture: raising turkeys. Her grandson Bill remembers her this way:

> "She raised the turkeys, dressed them, packed them in barrels with ice and shipped them to Fox Brothers in Chicago. She operated an incubator in the basement and had three brooder houses with chickens in them. In order to save money, Ollie slept in the brooder houses at night and kept them warm by stoking the stoves with wood and cobs instead of coal. She would also slip up to the house to check the incubators and turn the eggs." To her daughter Alpha, Ollie had great fortitude: "She was determined to pay the debt. She was a remarkable woman to accomplish what she did with so little to work with. By sheer will she pulled herself up again and she was a very good woman and happy. In the big house on the farm, she used to get up and be making breakfast & I'd hear her singing the song from the movie Oklahoma. She sang 'Oh What a Beautiful Morning, Oh What a Beautiful Day.' When any of the relatives came to South Dakota to visit they always came to our place. She didn't have much to offer them but made them feel at home and welcome whatever she had to offer."

Bill also recalls her feisty character. "Grandma was raising turkeys (not chickens) during the 1930s. She complained to her brother Ole Evans, next farm to the north, that his sons (Chet & Kenny) were stealing chickens, so Grandma switched to turkeys, challenging her nasty nephews to steal those birds. Ebon and Bert cursed those turkeys all their lives and Bert refused to eat any bird meat, especially turkeys. … But it took Grandpa to read the instruction manual [for the incubator], and he raised strawberries and produced honey from beekeeping."

But truth is, Ollie was practical: there was a big market for turkeys. The

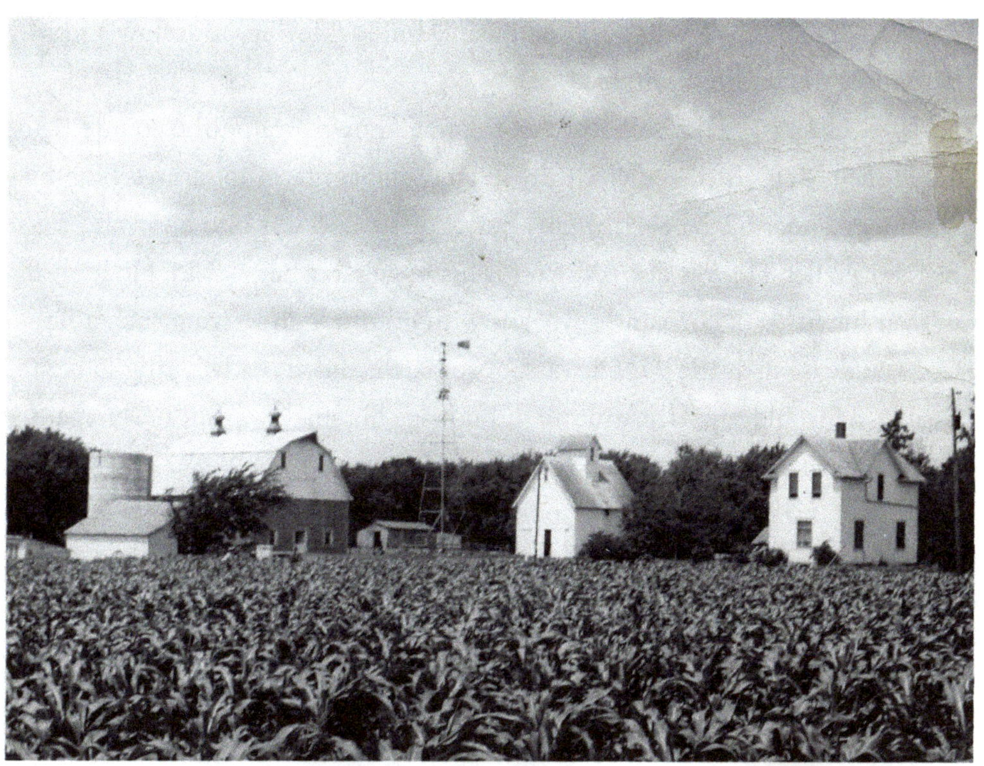

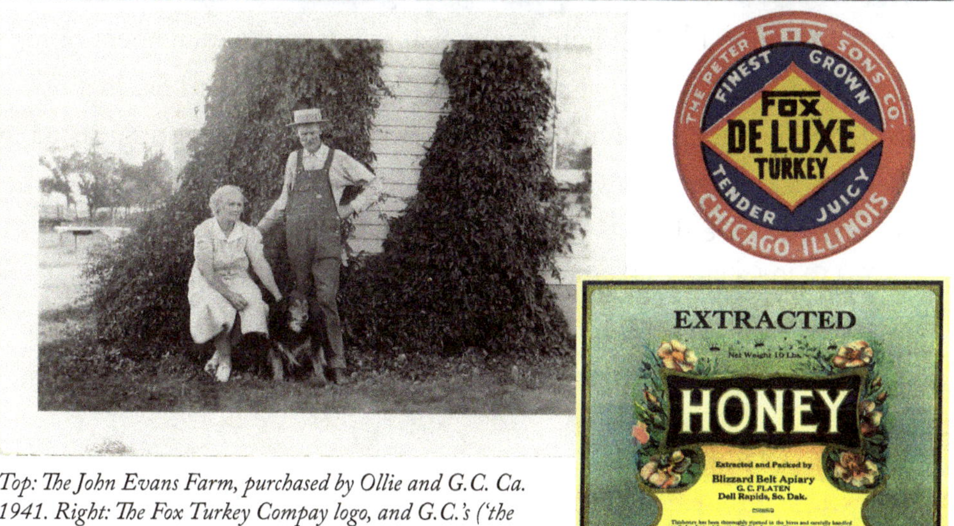

Top: The John Evans Farm, purchased by Ollie and G.C. Ca. 1941. Right: The Fox Turkey Compay logo, and G.C.'s ('the Honeyman') honey label, Blizzard Belt Apiary. Photos by Clarence Flaten, IU Archives. Logos: Collection of author.

Fox Brothers in Chicago had a good business model for her to follow and it was, simply put, more profitable.

G.C. employed his charm and became known around the county as "the Honey Man." Still genial, he drove around from farm to farm, selling his own honey under his label "Blizzard Belt Apiary" and was also known as a great storyteller. He was also known for his huge strawberry field. He looked out over his fields of corn and soybeans with gratitude for having such a fine farm. On days when the winter was not so harsh, and an early spring looked possible, he would say, "The ground did not see his shadow." But never again was he known as the photographer.

Very far from his starting point as teacher and photographer in Bricelyn and then as photographer in Hettinger, G.C. finally set his photography equipment aside in a dark shed not to see the light of day again. Later, Clarence was intrigued by these artifacts and was captivated by his father's stories of stereopticon shows. G.C. began his life on a farm, obtained an education and became a professional photographer. He returned to farm life for stability. But it is his photography that attests to the excitement of his years in North Dakota and that continue to resonate. They are a fascinating printed record for all time of history during a particularly interesting period in the West. I am sure he was aware of the unique opportunity he had to record the life of the early settlers.

By 1940 he and Ollie finally paid off their farm. On the census that year, he states he worked 60 hours per week, 52 weeks per year. Living in the house were Gunerius (G.C.), 66; Ollie, 65; Clarence, 29; Bertram, 25; Ebon, 23.

G.C. and Ollie finally retired from farming. When their son Ebon got married in 1947, G.C. built a small home close by in Sherman (near Dell Rapids), while Ebon continued to farm the property. G.C. died August 20,

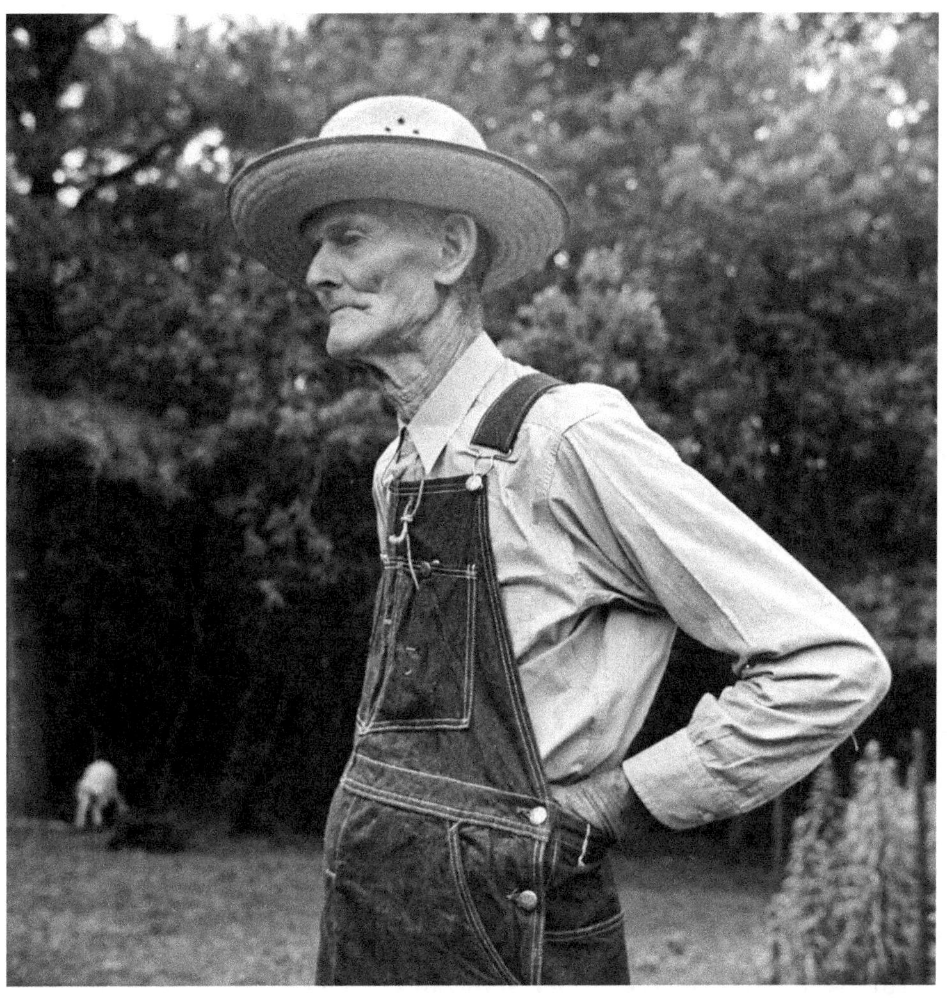

Gunerius Flaten, South Dakota. 1950. Photo by son Clarence Flaten, IU Archives.

1953, and Ollie went to live in a nursing home near where she had been born, in Hills, Minnesota. She had beautiful white hair, but she also had dementia at the end, forgetting names and people. Once when Clarence went to visit her with Mary, Ollie turned to Mary and said, "Mary, have you met my big boy Clarence yet?" She died later in 1971, and both she and G.C. were buried at the Norway Cemetery in Garretson, Minnehaha County, South Dakota.

Ollie held onto the land, the precious land. The parcel that Bendik Evans had not envisioned would go to one of the girls, went to his daughter Ollie. The Southeast Quarter (SE ½) of Section 14, Township 104 North, Range 48 West of the 5th P.M., Minnehaha County, South Dakota. Through endurance, the Flatens were still landowners.

In her will, after she died October 21, 1972, she followed the Norwegian time-honored custom. She willed her three sons the farm "share and share alike," and to her daughter Alpha, the equivalent in cash of $8,000. It was decided by all of them however, that Ebon, who wanted to purchase the farm, would buy it from them for the sum of $36,000. Thus, the land passed to Ollie's youngest son, Ebon. It was later inherited by Ebon's son, Bill Flaten, who, when his mother Florence went into a nursing home in 2004, sold the acreage to someone and the farmland to his cousin Roger Haak (Alpha's son) as a contract for deed. When Roger passed away from a heart attack in 2017, the land was sold to a large farmer in the area.

The following poems were written by G.C. Flaten when he lived in Sherman during his retirement years. Some may have been submitted for publication. In these poems, he reflects.

SOFT WHISPERS

I sit and dream, as the shades are falling,
Of one dear face I would like to see;
A voice from out of the past is calling
And whispers softly her name to me.

That parting day was both cold and cruel
It tore asunder my aching heart,
Why take from me that one precious jewel
That was to me a living part?

I sit and dream as the leaves are falling,
The thought of her charm wanders back to me.
That voice from out of the vast is calling
And whispers softly her name to me.

That love from out of the vast is calling
And whispers softly her name to me,
A pale white hand in the dim light scrawling
Her magic name on eternity.

THE COWGIRL'S RETREAT

From the crags the eagle screaming,
Wakes the coyote that is dreaming
In the sagebrush far below.
Haughty hawks are nimbly gliding,
Other birds in haste are hiding
Where the densest thistles grow.

Here, the cowgirl tanned and jolly
Laughs at old dame fashion's folly
As she skims across the plane.
She was freedom's queen appointed,
To a long and peaceful reign.

Little did she dream tomorrow
Would transform her joy to sorrow,
While her heart was young and gay.
But she took the thing for granted
When her haunts were plowed and planted,
All her tragic doom betrayed.

Now she looks and all around her
Everything she dread has found her,
Fields and fences mar her way.
Known trails she used to travel
Now are heaps of dust and gravel
And she turns her steed away.

LOVE NEST

We'll build our little love nest
Out beneath the stately pines,
We'll plant around the doorway
Friendly morning glory vines
From beneath the snow capped mountains
We'll gaze upon the sea
And forget all care and sorrow
In this kingdom of the free.

We'll build it in the dawning,
In the dreamy by and by,
When at last it is completed
It is time to ask us why.

We'll build our little love nest
In some sweet secluded spot,
Close beside the rushing river
We'll place our little cot.
We'll hang our swaying hammock
Where the dainty ivey twines
While we watch the sun set arrows
As they lodge among the pines.

We'll build our little love nest
Far out in the golden west,
Where the air is pure and balmy
And the storms do not molest,
We'll nest among the roses
Where the peach and apple blush,
While we listen to the music
Of the robin and the thrush.

THE MILKY WAY

Cosmic highway our fathers found,
Hemmed by eternity all around,
Winds through the endless blue,
Marked by the beacons of gleaming spars,
Paved with the dust of crumbled stars,
Until it fades from view.

Nebulous masses along its course,
Spurred by the phantom of hectic force
Muster, move, and obey.
Wandering comets from murky space
Scramble past in a frantic race
Light and adorn the way.

Pathway unmatched by mortal man
Not even the greatest mind can scan
The depth of its mystery.
Glittering chariots swiftly spin
Filling the space with their rhythmic din,
Into oblivion flee.

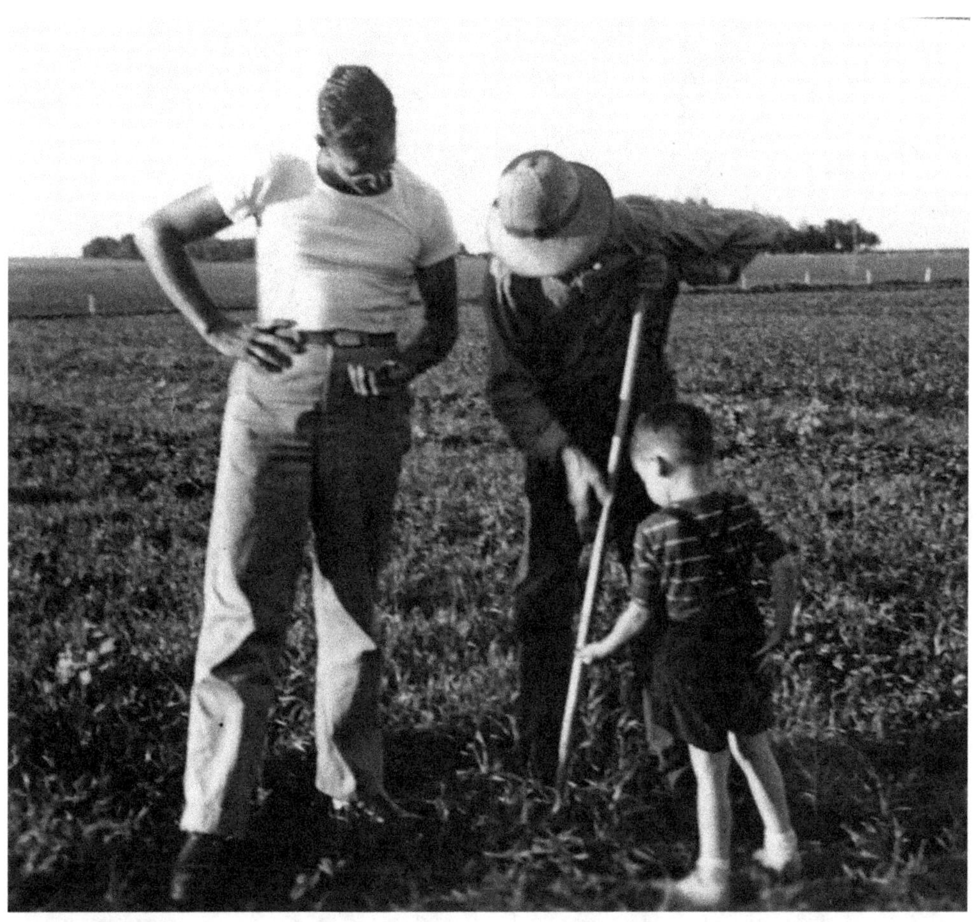

Three of the four Flatens: Clarence looks on as his father Gunerius shows his grandson Christopher how to use a hoe. South Dakota. Ca. 1946. Photo: CM Flaten, IU Archives.

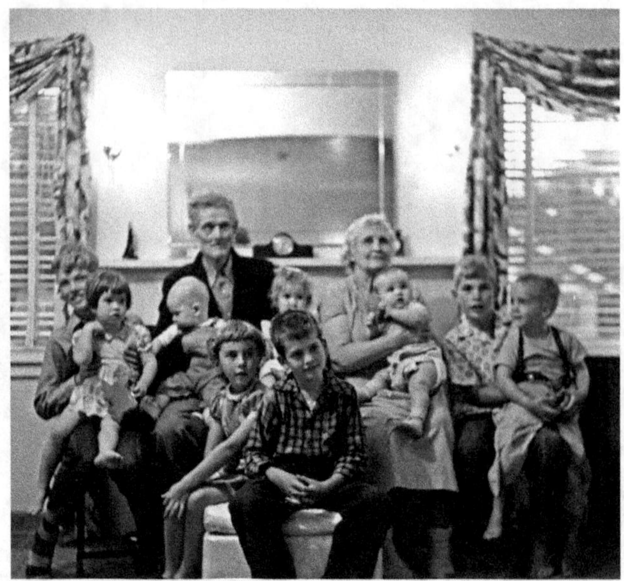

1950. In the front room of Ollie and Gunerius's farmhouse in South Dakota. (Front Row, L to R) Joyce Haak and Kit. (Back Row, L to R) probably David Haak , Peggy, Grandfather Gunerius with two unknown infants, Grandmother Ollie with Brian, probably Jerome Haak and Larry.

1950. The Family Reunion in Garretson SD. Front row, L to R: Brian on Grandma Ollie Flaten's lap, Jerome Haak, Diane with her mom, Alpha, Gunerius Flaten with baby Ronnie Flaten (or Roger Haak?) and Joyce Haak on his lap, Larry Flaten, David Haak and Kit. Back row: Peg standing with Mary Flaten and Florence Flaten.

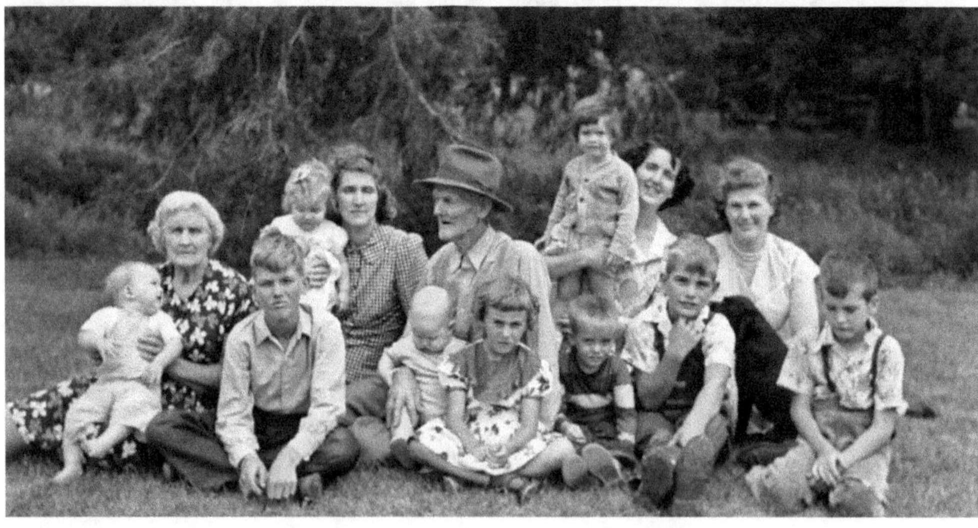

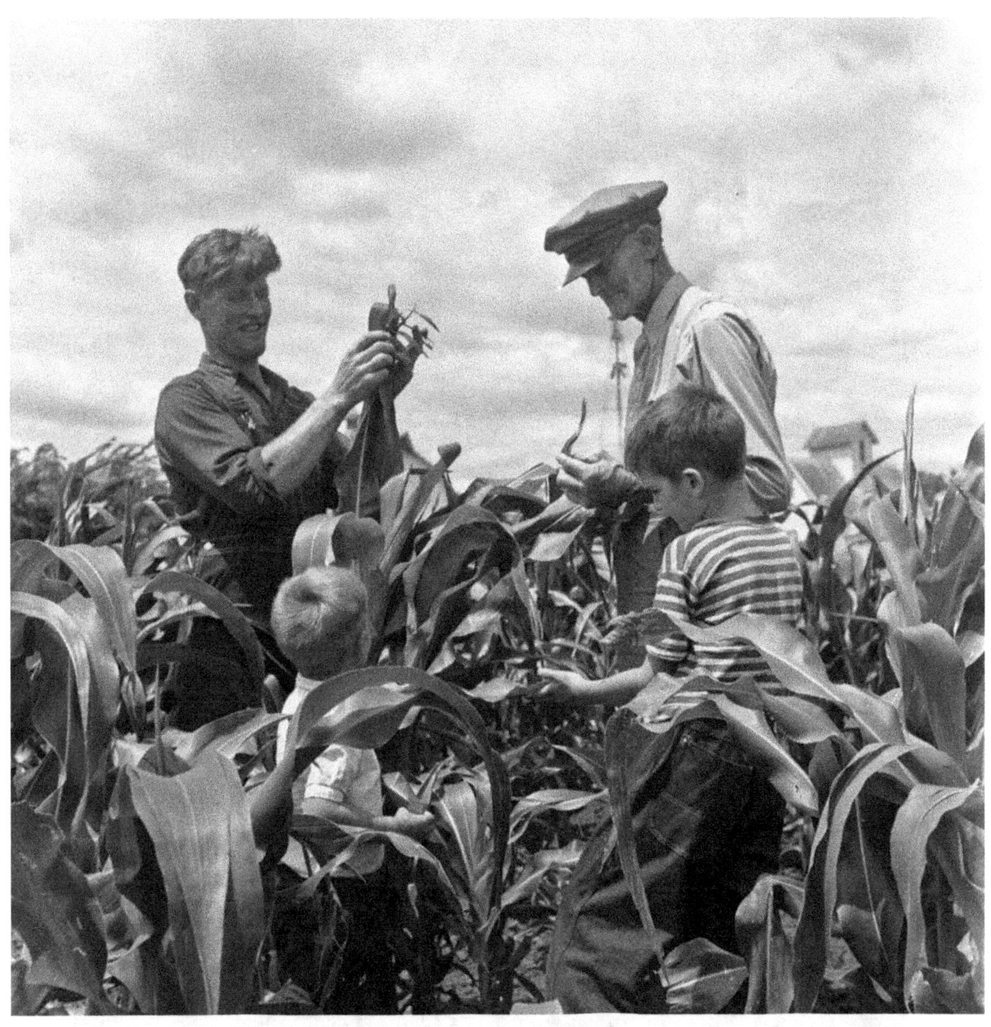

Gunerius (standing right) with his grandsons Larry Flaten (front left) and Christopher "Kit" (front right). Standing left is Ebon Flaten. Photo by Clarence Flaten in his father's corn field in South Dakota.

Photos on this and facing page: Clarence Flaten, IU Archives.

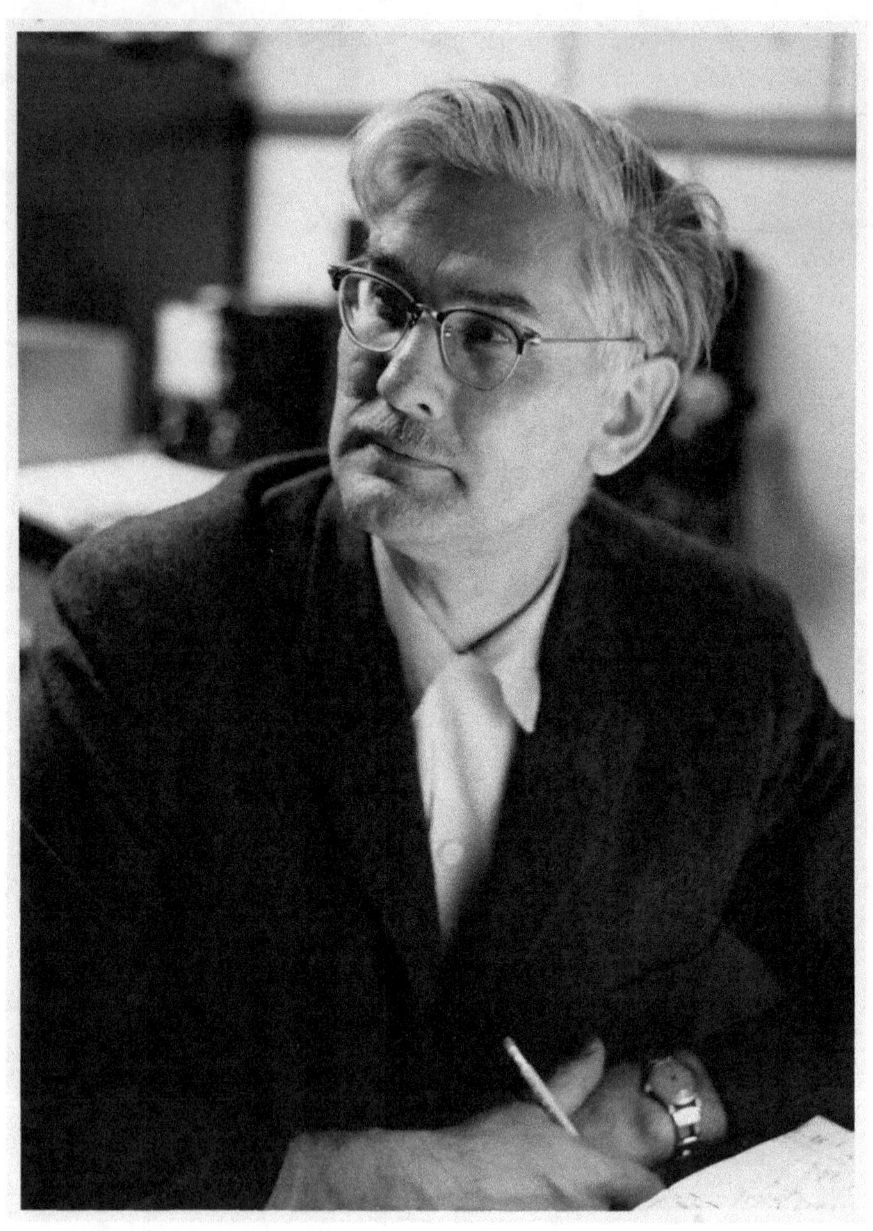

Clarence Malven Flaten, IU Archives

CHAPTER THREE

CLARENCE MALVEN FLATEN 1910-1974

MY FATHER CLARENCE MALVEN FLATEN RARELY SPOKE OF his childhood or any other aspect of his life. I am sure it was because he was too busy and, after all, I was only but a child, unable to ask the right questions. The farm in South Dakota came to mind when I tried to picture his own childhood, but now I realize that the town of Hettinger, North Dakota was where he grew up. He was not born on a farm but rather lived in town, in the Golden Oak House, later moving to a two-room photo studio, and then to a granary on a farm when he was thirteen. Yes, he did spend time on a farm from 13 to 18 while going to school in Hettinger and Dell Rapids, and he spent six years on the family farm in South Dakota after he graduated from high school, so the narrative we learned (that while riding tractors, he always was reading a book) makes some sense. But like his father Gunerius, he was mostly attracted to books. He wasn't really a farmer at heart.

After the family left Hettinger, he had made the transition to his new high school in South Dakota very well; when he graduated as a senior from Dell Rapids High School in May 1929, he earned a cup at commencement for "Best All Around Student," since he had maintained the highest grade among senior boys. He even starred as the leading man in the school's play—this despite the fact that he had been living in a granary for the previous five years, very unsupervised. It spoke very well of the training he had received in the Hettinger Public School system, but it also showed incredible individual resolve and self-discipline. He also pursued interests, one being music.

On his own, he ordered a violin from the Sears & Roebuck catalog, but he had to sneak to the barn to play it since (according to family lore) his grandmother Anna Evans believed the violin was the instrument of the devil. Alpha said that he was self-taught on various instruments. He always placed music very high on a list of values for himself and, later, his children. Where did his love of music originate? I would love to know.

So, Clarence read while plowing with the tractor. Although his Norwegian heritage pointed him in the direction of farming (in the 1900 census, 54% of Norwegian immigrants' children were farmers), Clarence inherited Ollie's determination, as well as G.C.'s interest in higher eduation. As he looked past the alfalfa and wheat fields to a very different life, he remembered a mentor in Hettinger, his uncle, Paul Boehm.

For ever since his Uncle Paul had graduated from the University of Michigan (UM) in 1905 with a degree in law, he highly recommended UM to Clarence, and he probably wrote a letter of recommendation for Clarence. So, in 1934, at age 24 (which was older than most college students), Clarence applied, and was accepted "with reservations" to the University of Michigan to study Forestry. This was a moment of luck that forever changed the course of his life. It is safe to state that he was elated. Very soon thereafter, he hopped a train and left for Michigan with his family's blessing.

ANN ARBOR, MICHIGAN

He arrived at the University of Michigan in the Fall of 1934, enrolled in the Student Union and dedicated himself to his studies. There he was truly a fish in water. After his first year, he didn't return to the farm but instead stayed in Michigan and was employed by the University in their Forestry School, doing mapping and surveying, timber cruising and teaching dendrology. (I had to look it up: it's the scientific study of trees.)

Joining him in 1936 were his Uncle Paul and Aunt Bessie Boehm, who moved to Ann Arbor, where Paul began to practice law. Soon two of their children, Adelaide and Dan, moved there to attend the university. And when they gathered together for parties, Clarence brought out his beautiful new Gibson guitar and perhaps his devilishly tuneful violin.

In 1938, Clarence graduated with a BSF, and applied for graduate school. Meanwhile, he went to work for the Ford Motor Company in Dearborn, MI and while working at Ford, he took a night class in photography, a skill he found much more interesting than working on the assembly line. He shared this interest with others as a member of the Photographic Guild of Detroit. After completing graduate school in 1939, he continued with a course in photography at UM, and in 1940 was hired by the Michigan State Conservation Dept. Institute of Fisheries under Dr. C.J.D. Brown ("Brownie") to do drafting, map work, aerial photographs, and motion picture work, and to devise new camera equipment for their scientific surveys. He later remarked, "Photography is at once a language, craft, and an art. It has something for almost every inquiring mind."

While working at the University of Michigan in the dorm cafeteria at Mosher Hall, earning his way through college, Clancy met a wonderful, vivacious Irish gal from New York, Mary Frances Browne, who was also waiting tables while getting her teaching degree from the University. Both "Clank" and "Frannie Mae," as they were known to their college chums, were living on a shoestring and their romantic courtship stories reflected such.

"We didn't have enough money to go to the movies, so Clancy and I would go to the theater and stand outside and smell the popcorn!" laughed Mary years later. Once, when they were able to afford a dinner at a restaurant, Mary suggested to Clancy that she would like to take a spoon for a "souvenir," but Clancy told her, "If you really want the spoon, I will buy it for you." This

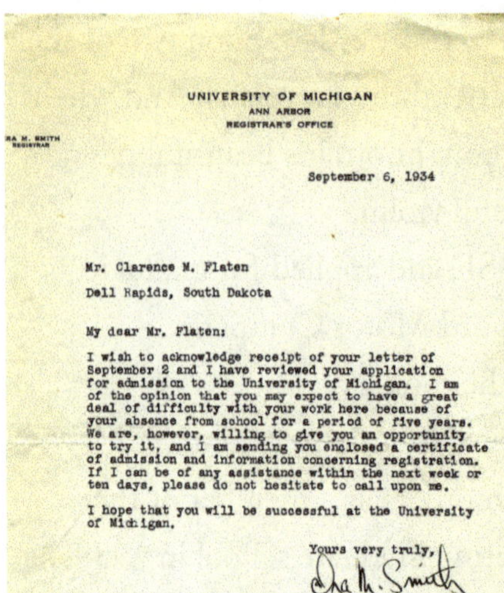

UNIVERSITY OF MICHIGAN
ANN ARBOR
REGISTRAR'S OFFICE

RA M. SMITH
REGISTRAR

September 6, 1934

Mr. Clarence M. Flaten

Dell Rapids, South Dakota

My dear Mr. Flaten:

I wish to acknowledge receipt of your letter of September 2 and I have reviewed your application for admission to the University of Michigan. I am of the opinion that you may expect to have a great deal of difficulty with your work here because of your absence from school for a period of five years. We are, however, willing to give you an opportunity to try it, and I am sending you enclosed a certificate of admission and information concerning registration. If I can be of any assistance within the next week or ten days, please do not hesitate to call upon me.

I hope that you will be successful at the University of Michigan.

Yours very truly,

Ira M. Smith

IMS:I. Registrar

Left: Clarence's acceptance letter to the University of Michigan (Class '38). Below: seen at right, with the School of Forestry UM 1938, and the Institute for Fisheries Research, Mich Dept. Conservation Ca. 1940. Photos: IU Archives.

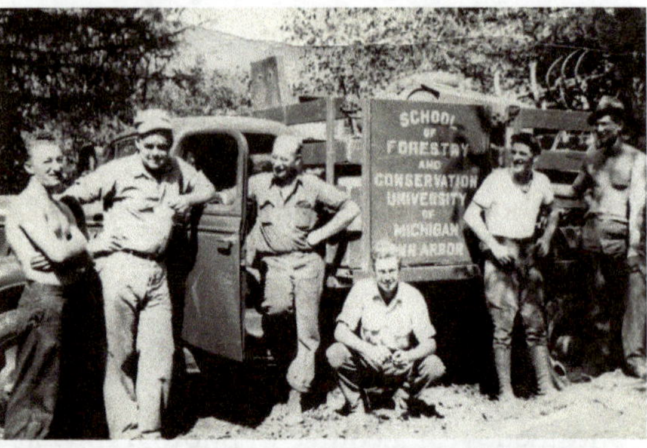

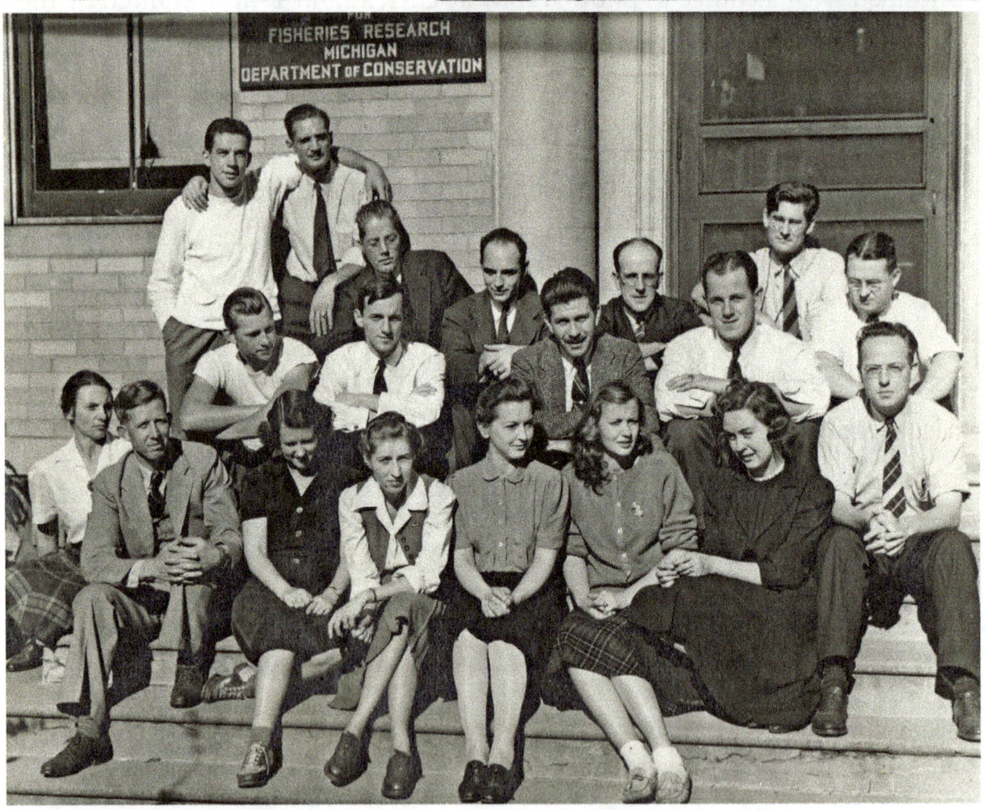

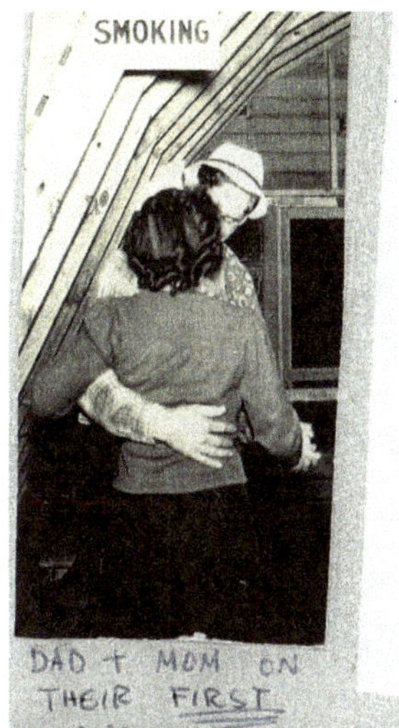

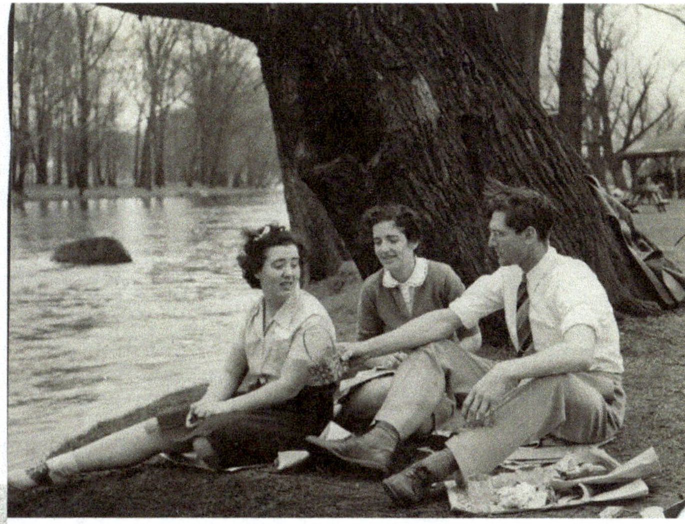

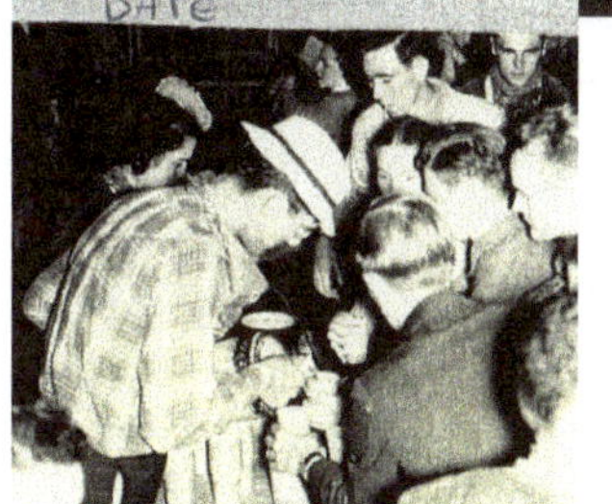

Clarence and Mary's first date was at a party given by the forestry school, where she helped him serve refreshments. Left: from their first date. Photos: collection of Margaret Daisley.
Above, Mary's sister Winifred Browne joined Clarence and Mary for a picnic. Photo: CM Flaten, collection of the author.
Below: Clarence and Mary on a date, perhaps overlooking Niagara Falls when Mary worked in Buffalo in 1939. Photos: CM Flaten, IU Archives.

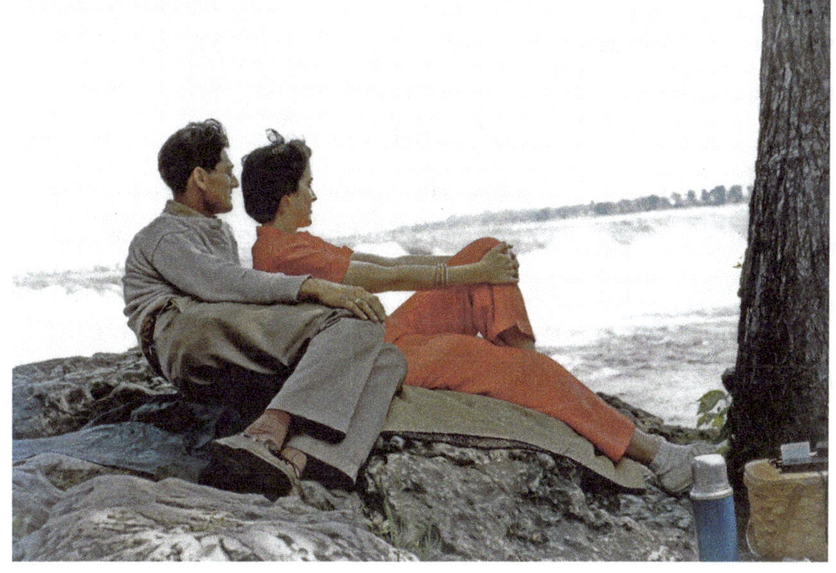

is the moment Mary made her mind up: his sterling honesty was where she would put her lifelong trust.

Another repeated family story about their courtship, this one also illustrating Clancy's gallantry, as captured by their daughter, Peg, who recalled: "The Night Mom's Underwear Fell Off While on a Date With Dad." She wrote it down in a letter she sent to her mother:

"You were walking home from a dance and as you were walking along, the elastic broke on your underwear and it fell off, it just kind of slid down around your ankles and of course you were very embarrassed. But Clancy Flaten didn't say one word. He just quickly scooped them up and put 'em in his pocket to help you avoid any embarrassment. And of course, your House Sisters, your Dorm Sisters, never let you forget it! I believe the story was that Christmas they got you a gift, and it was some very fancy underwear."

The repeated family stories summed up our family values: honesty, thrift, and gallantry. These stories were a bedrock definition of who we saw ourselves to be, the type of people we were, our moral genetic code. They made us very proud and we admired our parents.

Mary graduated in June of 1939 and accepted a teaching position in the Fall at Amherst Central High School in Buffalo, New York. It was understood that this degree was practical, to help her family out, but Mary was also very happy to be out on her own, even though her heart remained with Clancy back in Ann Arbor. That winter, she invited him home to meet her parents at Christmas, and there, they announced their intention to marry, and took a stroll along Jones Beach, very much in love. It was a backdrop for the beginning of an exciting adventure together. Love would conquer all. But there was a big problem for Mary's parents: Clarence was raised a Lutheran, and the Brownes were strong Irish Catholics.

Marrying outside of the faith was against their religion, her father insisted, to which Mary said, "Well, what kind of a Catholic are you?" referring to Luke's years habit of tipping the police on the block in New York, part of the regular method for thanking cops for keeping his small grocery store safe. But to Mary, it represented an irregular "payoff" and now she dramatically threw this imagined hypocrisy back in his face, as was her style toward the overly dramatic. But she was hurt. To her, Clarence's demonstrated honesty and proven character spoke much louder by example than her father's professed Catholicism. Though Mary always took her faith very seriously, she was sure her "mixed marriage" was a very blessed match.

They were married July 15, 1941, in their beloved Ann Arbor. Clarence Malven Flaten of Dell Rapids, South Dakota and Mary Frances Browne of Queens, New York wed inside the rectory of St. Mary's Catholic chapel on campus. The priest who married them, Father Allen Babcock, had informed them that since Clarence was a Lutheran and not a Catholic, church doctrine barred him entry into the church sanctuary for their ceremony.

Did this difference in religion matter to Clarence's parents? Clarence's mother had come from a very strict, conservative Lutheran background and G.C. may have been slightly inclined that way. They did not come to the wedding, but it was most probably for financial reasons, so standing in for family was Clancy's cousin Dan Boehm as Best Man, and Mary's sister Winifred as Maid of Honor. Mary's parents were present as well, and did in the end put differences aside. The Brownes were proud of their first-generation Irish American daughters, both of whom attended UM.

Very much in love, Clancy and Mary made a home at 3010 Geddes Avenue in Ann Arbor. Peg recounts how lovestruck they both were, in her letter to her mother:

> "...when you and Dad were first married, one of the places that you rented, only later did you realize there was no sink in the kitchen. And

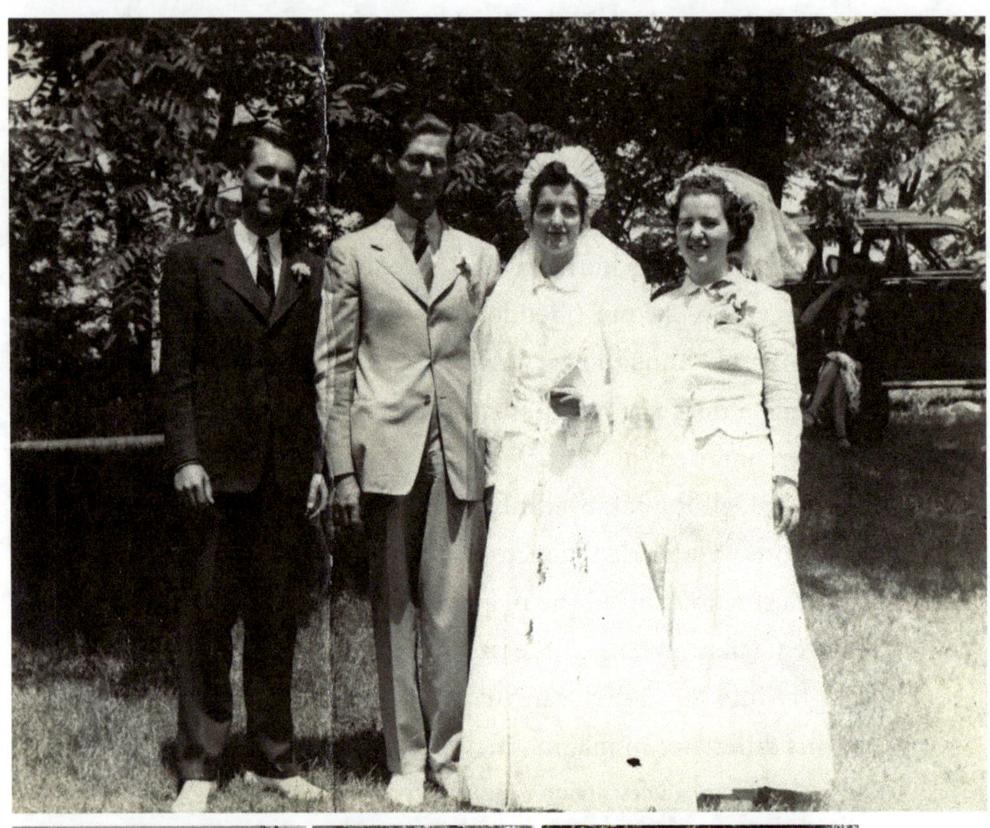

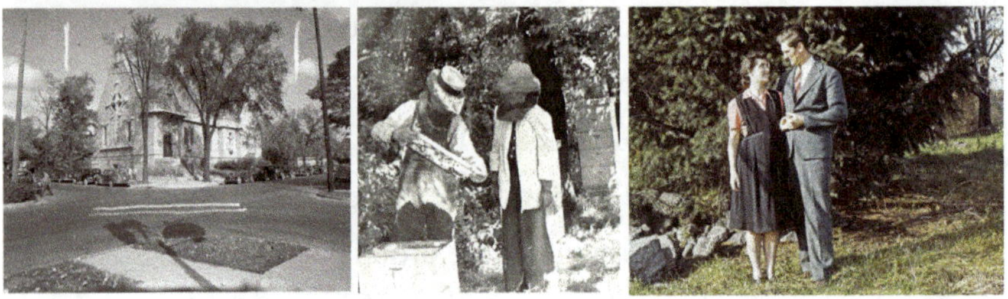

Wedding Day, July 15, 1941. Clarence's cousin, Dan Boehm, was his best man. Mary's best lady was her sister, Winifred Browne. They were married in the rectory of St.Mary's Catholic chapel at the University (bottom left from online source). For their honeymoon, they traveled to South Dakota where Mary met Ollie and Gunerius (center), G.C. shows his beehives to Mary. Right, Mary, pregnant, and Clarence, shortly before he reported for military service. 1942. Photos: CM Flaten, IU Archives.

you wound up having to do dishes in the bathtub. And the reason that you didn't notice was that there was such a beautiful view and light in the kitchen and you and Dad were just taken with the view from inside looking out. And who thinks about doing the dishes? Who WANTS to think about doing the dishes? What the heck.... Do 'em in the bathtub!"

For their honeymoon, he drove her home to South Dakota to introduce her to Ollie and G.C. and the beehives and all. She loved the visit. But Ann Arbor was their new home as it still was an important place for extended family. Adelaide, who had moved to Ann Arbor to attend the university married Dan Suits in 1942. Dan Boehm married Mary Jean Sanford there in 1948 while attending the university. They all remained in Ann Arbor. Life was idyllic.

WORLD WAR II

The bliss of married life was soon gone. Five months after they were married, on December 7, 1941, Pearl Harbor was decimated by the Japanese and the United States entered World War II. Clarence was inducted by the Selective Service into the U.S. Army on October 15, 1942. He reported to Fort Custer, and then to Sheppard Field, Texas for basic training. Since he was already a professional photographer with the Michigan Conservation Department, the Army recognized this and sent him for additional training at Lowry Field, Colorado, allowing him to hone his skills for military assignments. However, he had to leave Mary, who was pregnant.

While he was away training, Mary gave birth the day after Christmas to their first son **Christopher ("Kit") James Flaten**. But she could not manage on her own, so she and Kit moved to Queens, New York, in June 1943, to an apartment next door to her parents so that her mother Margaret could look after Kit while Mary worked for a radio station selling ads.

Meanwhile, after two years of basic training (Alabama, Colorado, Texas), Clancy went on to Officer's Candidate School (OCS) in Miami, Florida. In May 1944, as Captain, he entered active service and was assigned as a photographer to Chabua and Barrachport, India, in the U.S. Army Air Corp's 1333rd Division. This Division was assigned to the North Burma Campaign, part of the larger China-Burma Theater.

CLANCY'S ASSIGNMENT: THE NORTH BURMA CAMPAIGN

During WWII, the U.S. allied themselves with Chinese Nationals against the invading forces of the Japanese. North Burma was particularly important because of a supply route which the Japanese used through the Himalaya Mountains. It became essential to disrupt that supply road.

In June 1944 the combat strength of the U.S. Tenth Air Force was reconstituted as a tactical air force of two fighter groups and one troop carrier group (plus administrative and service elements) to support the North Burma Campaign. The Eastern Air Command (EAC) had 5 subordinate air commands: the Strategic Air Force (Anglo-American); the Third Tactical Air Force (mostly RAF and 12th Bombardmt) and 459th Fighter Squad; **the Photographic Reconnaissance Group (Anglo-American)**; the Tenth Air Force; and the 293 Wing RAF, charged with defense of the Calcutta region.

The main mission for the EAC, which included Cpt. Flaten's 1333rd Division, was to disrupt the entire strategic supply and transportation routes which ran through the Himalaya Mountains, especially along the major "Stilwell Road." Keeping this key supply route open for the Chinese Nationals (who fought alongside the British and American forces) was essential in halting the ongoing Japanese invasion of China. Because there were no accurate maps of much of the area, the 1333rd Air Corps flew photo-

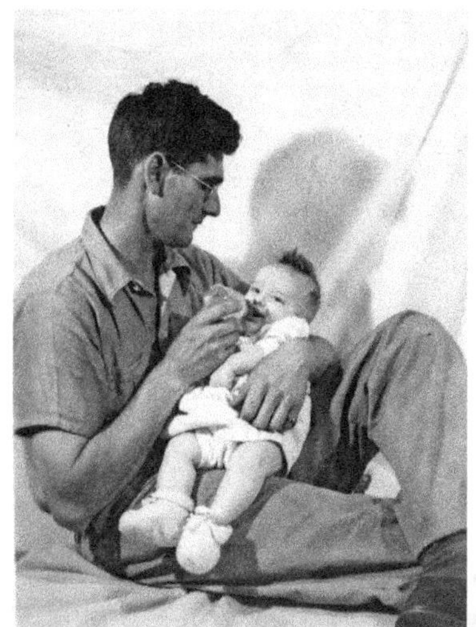

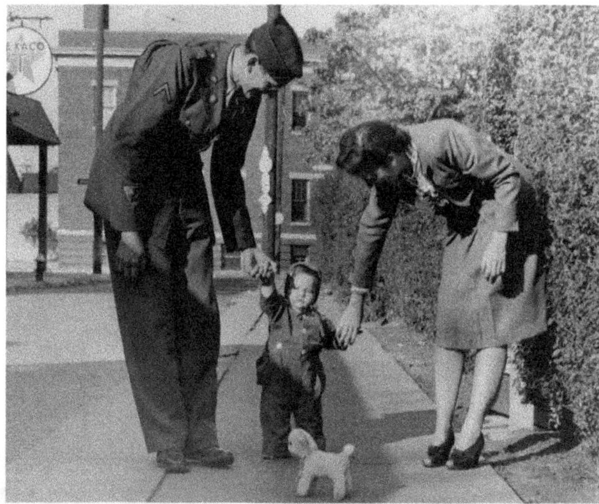

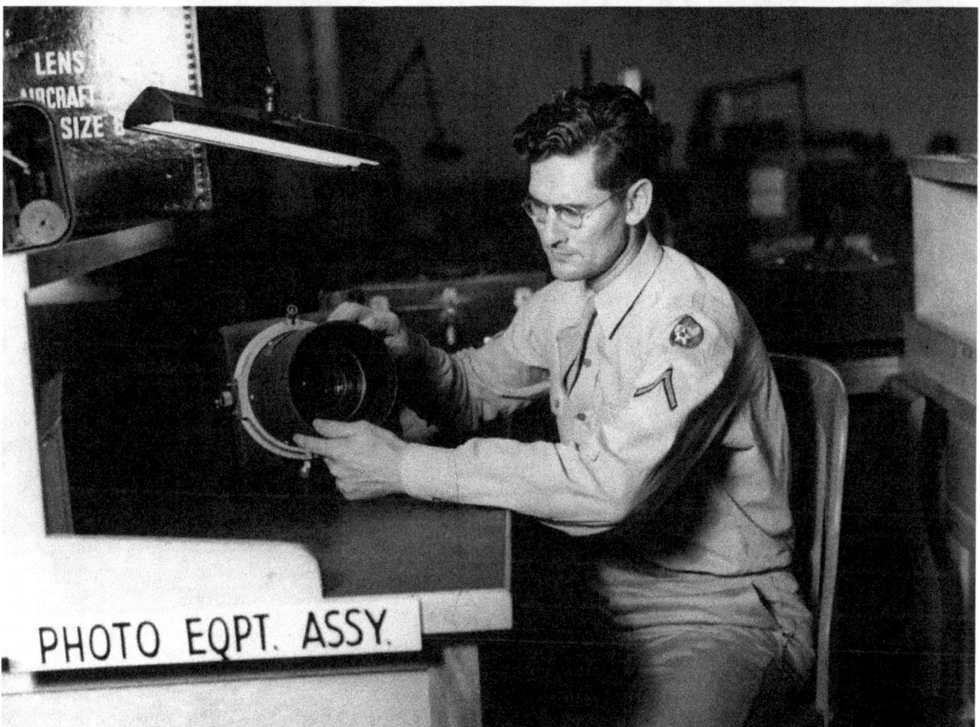

Top left: Clarence took leave from Sheppard Field TX to return to Ann Arbor to meet Kit for the first time, May 1943. Top right: Clarence on second furlough with Kit and Mary in Queens, NY Oct 1943. Below: PV2 Clarence M. Flaten inspects Army K24 camera lense. Top photos by CM Flaten, IU Archives.

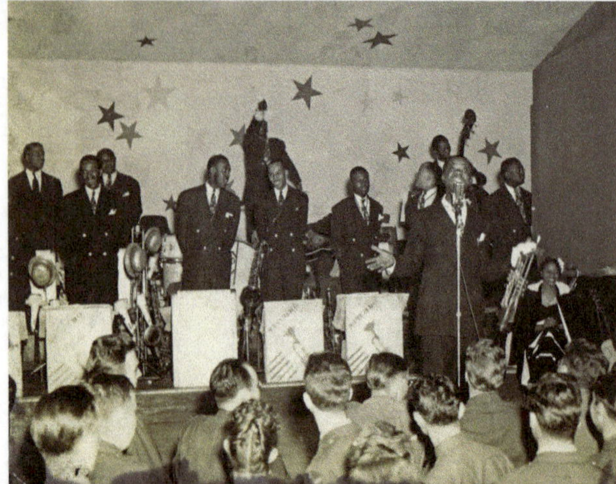

Left: A young Louis Armstrong and his band "Sachmo" perform at Brookley AFB, Alabama. December 1943.

Below: the mess hall. Don't Fatten These Swine: garbage for Hitler, Hirohito or Mussolini.

Below: Errol Flynn speaks at "Bond Drive" Brookley AFB.

Deer hunting party near Mobile AL.

This and facing page, Photos CM Flaten, (except for portraits) IU Archives.

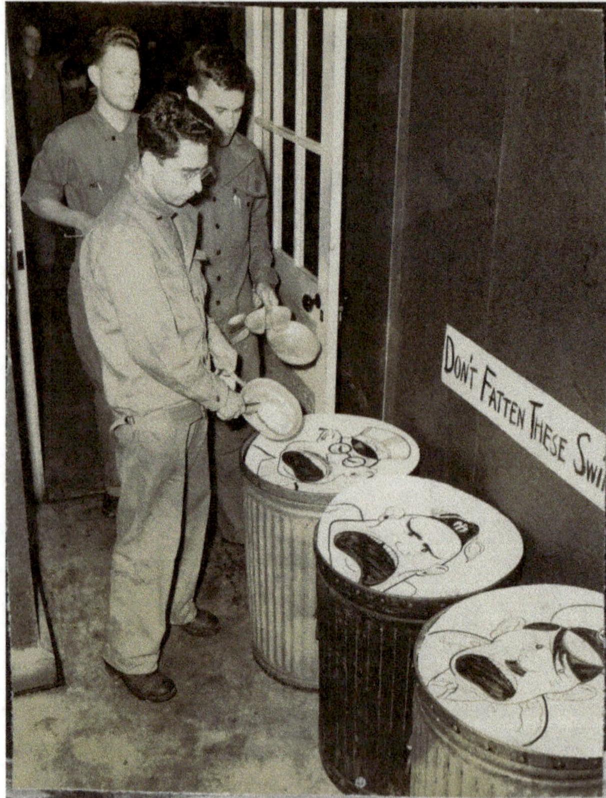

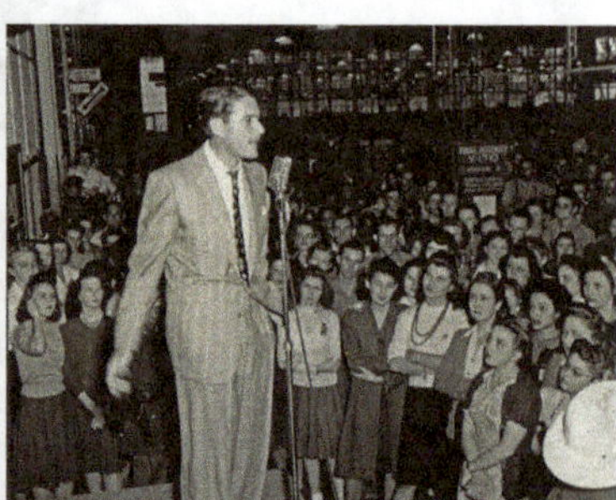

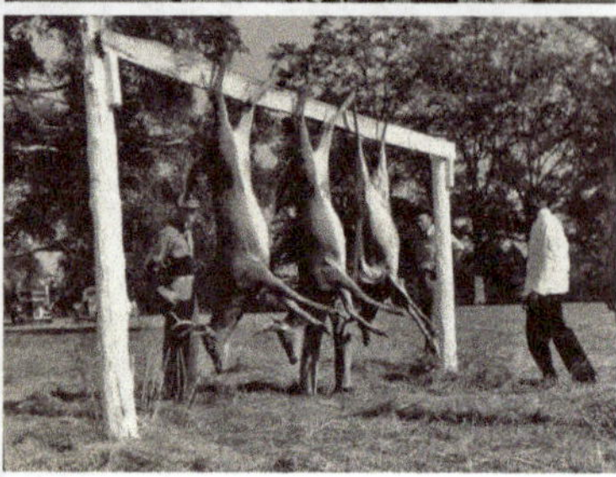

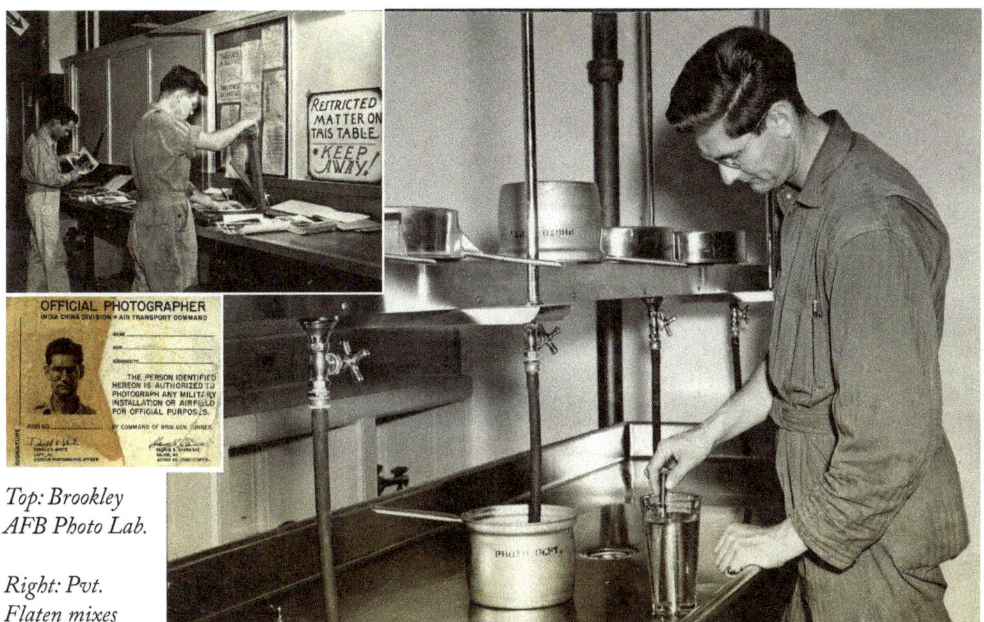

Top: Brookley AFB Photo Lab.

Right: Pvt. Flaten mixes chemicals, Lowry Photo School.

Right: Flaten with cameras.

Below: Sioberg, one of Flaten's photography instructors, US Army Air Corp - Flying Cadet. Brookley AFB.

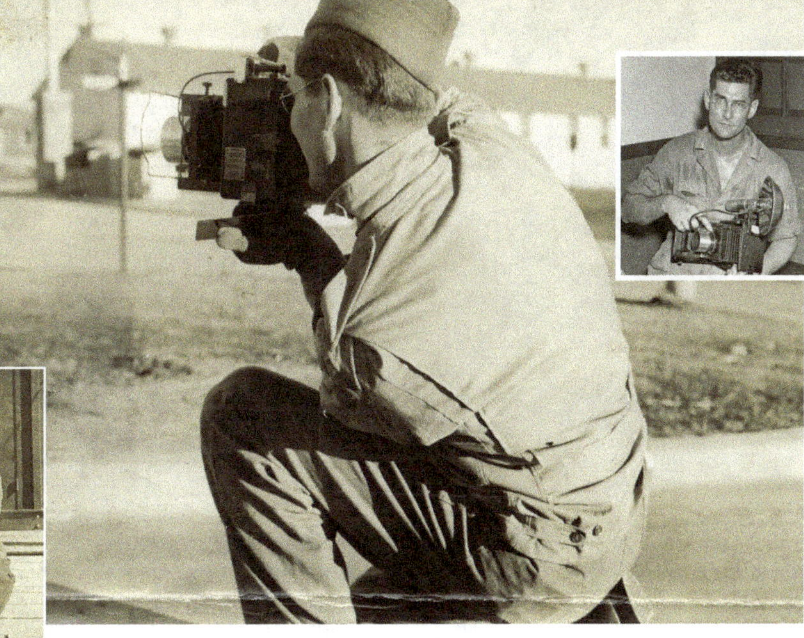

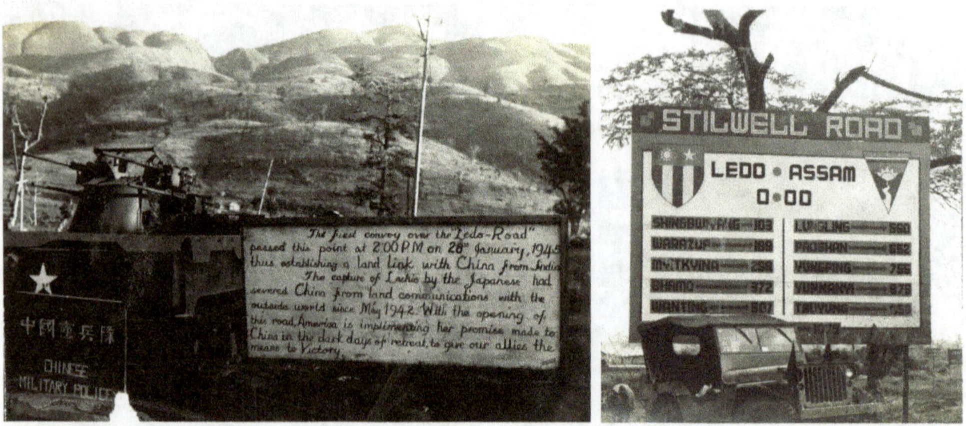

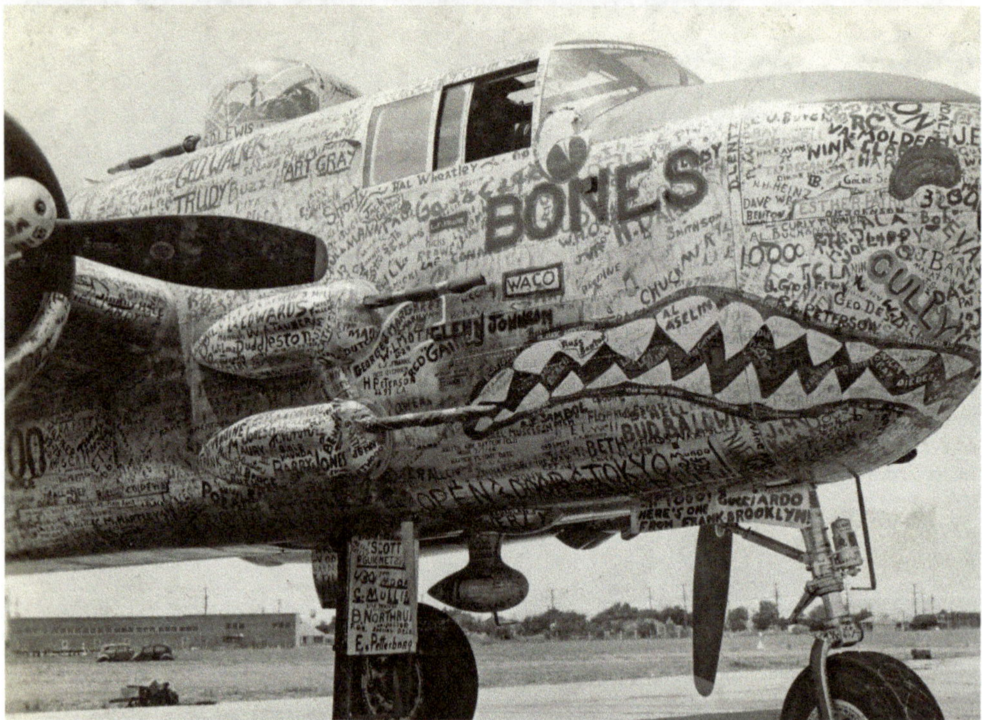

Top: A sign posted at the Ledo Road in the China Burma Theater, a road which was critical for transport. "The first convoy over the 'Ledo-Road' passed this point at 2:00P.M. on 28th January, 1945 thus establishing a land link with China from India. The capture of Lashio by the Japanese had severed China from land communications with the outside world since May 1942. With the opening of this road, America is implimenting her promise made to China in the dark days of retreat, to give our allies the means to Victory." Hand printed sign reads, in full: (Chinese characters), then in English: "CHINESE MILITARY POLICE". Right: The Stilwell Road: sign with distance markers.
Below: "Bones" WWII B-25 Bomber. Photos by CM Flaten, IU Archives.

Right: Mount Everest in the distance photographed from a B-25 Bomber.

Right: "The Hump Club: A Happy Haven," a club named after the Himalaya Mountain range, "The Hump." Those who flew over the mountain called it "flying the hump."

Below: aircraft flying the hump.

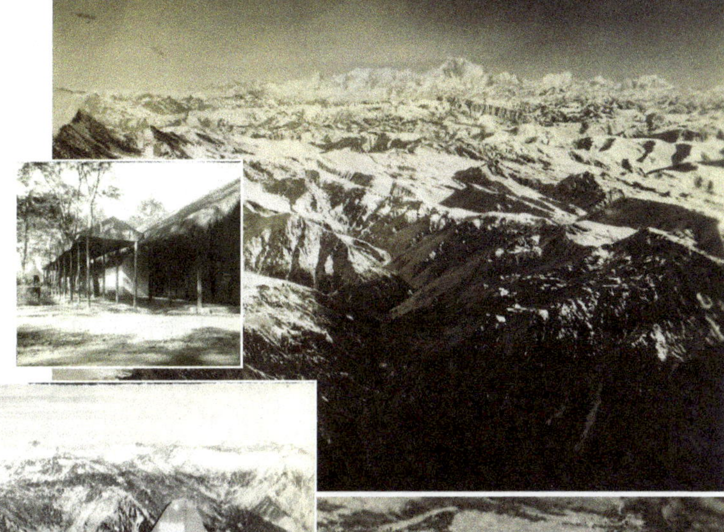

Above: Military Transport C-47 WWII Aircraft in flight.

Chabua WWII Airfield from 6,000 ft.

Photos by CM Flaten, IU Archioves.

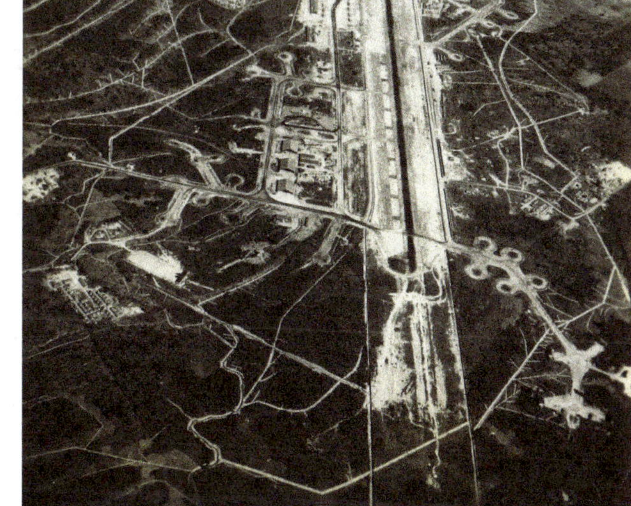

reconnaissance missions to produce aerial mosaics. Flaten's assignment was to take low-level verticals, reconnaissance strips, obliques, and pinpoint shots used by both air and ground personnel for target designation. These aerial photos were most valuable to map the trail that needed to be bombed in order to disrupt the supply routes.

This assignment was extremely dangerous. As Wing Photo Officer, he flew in transport planes over the Himalaya Mountains, some of the tallest mountain peaks in the world which include Mount Everest, the highest mountain in the world. Flying over these high mountains was also known as "flying the Hump." The planes in which they flew were so experimental that many of them crashed in the Himalayas because their aluminum fuselages were unable to withstand the pressure of the upper altitude. There were so many crashes that the long string of wrecks was called "The Aluminum Trail."

Overhead, Allied fighters swarmed over the dirt trails all day long, bombing and strafing the Japanese. Japanese supplies could only be moved at night, a task made extremely complicated when the monsoon rains began. During that time, the Japanese were starved out and paralyzed.

Fighter sorties supported the infantry. Between March and July 1944, 221 Group flew 9,000 sorties. Their colleagues of 224 Group flew about 5,,000. During siege operations in North Burma, Northern Sector Air Force averaged 33 fighter sorties a day. This figure is low considering these were flown during monsoon weather so that good flying days saw many times the 33 figure flown. The RAF expended 25,000 rounds of 40-mm ammunition in ground support during the first 6 months of 1944. In the same period the fighters dropped 9,327 tons of bombs. Although the fighting was aggressive, the tactics were debated. The problem was known as "The Stilwell Problem" referring to the General's failed strategy. As this problem continued to be fought, his tour of duty ended on April 16, 1945.

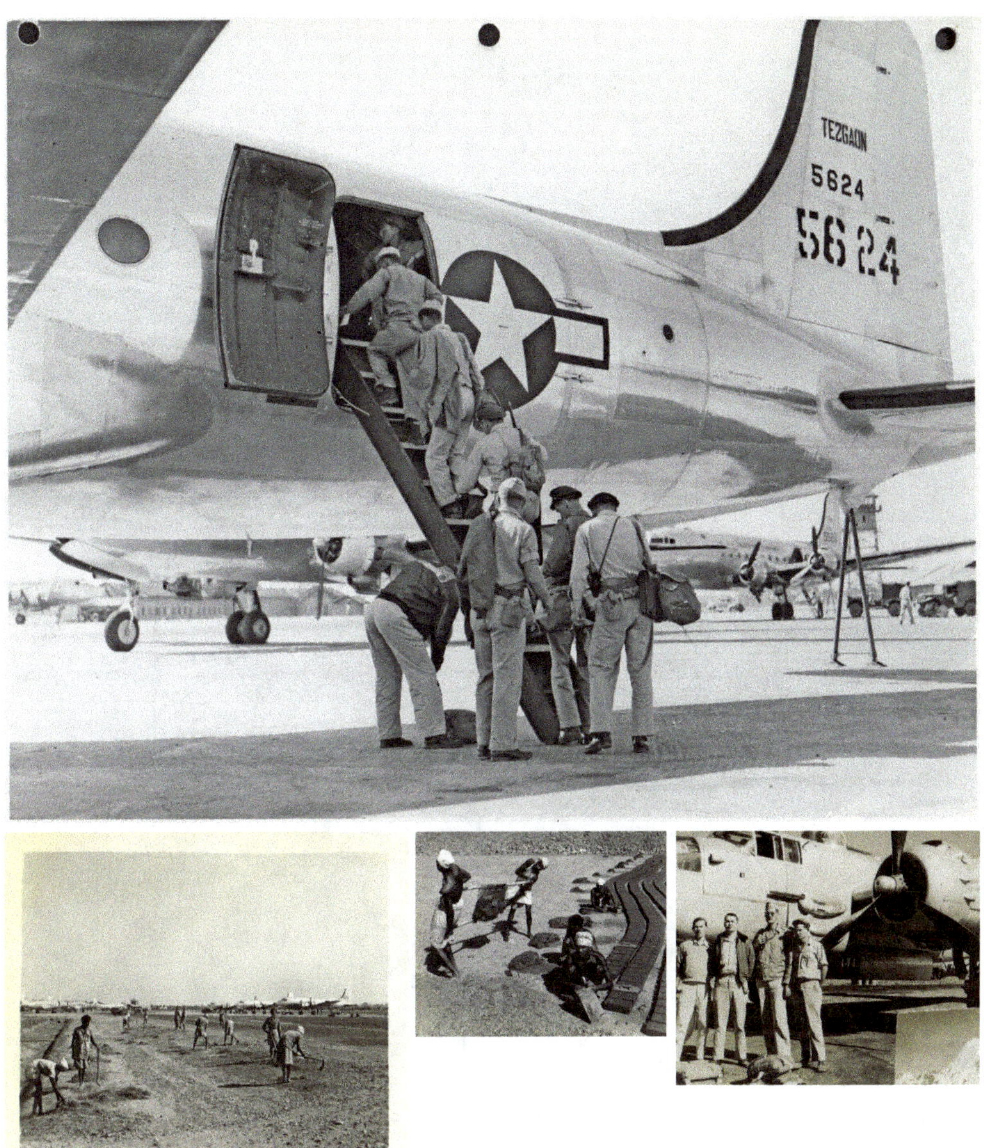

Top: The aluminum fueselages were prone to buckle under the heavy pressure at the high altitude of the Himalaya Mountains. Soldiers board a U.S. Air Transport Command Planes in India.

Below: Men contructing an airfield. Brick mason, bricklayers and workers. Right: Flaten and aerial flight crew.

Photos: (except bottom right) CM Flaten, IU Archives.

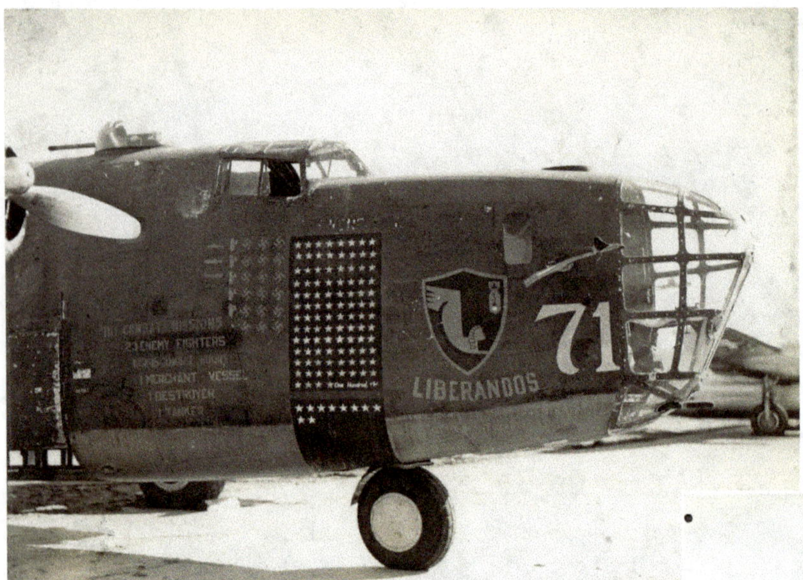

Left: The "Blue Streak" WWII B-24D Bomber.

Middle: WWII Aircraft on runway: B-24 Liberator bomber and a spotter or trainer on runway.

Below: A-24 Banshee SBD dive bomber piloted by Capt. David. 1944.

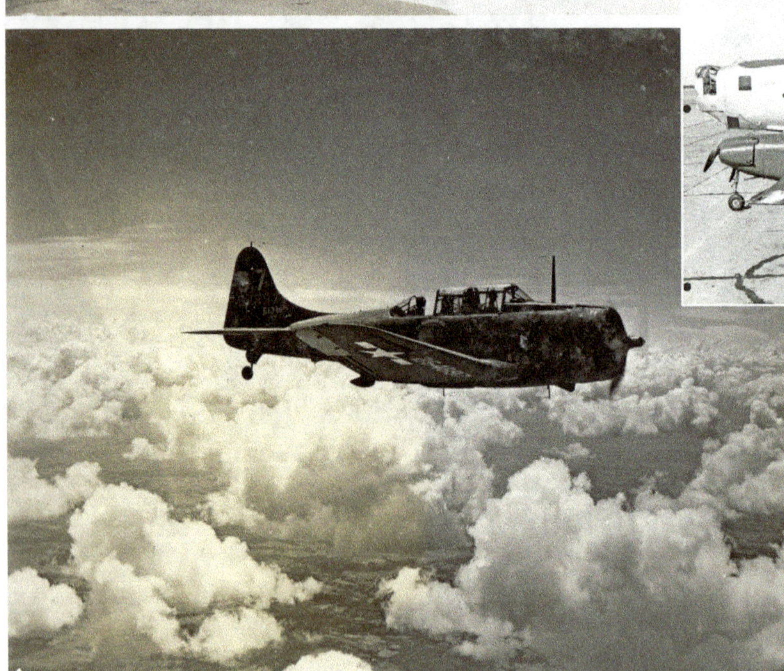

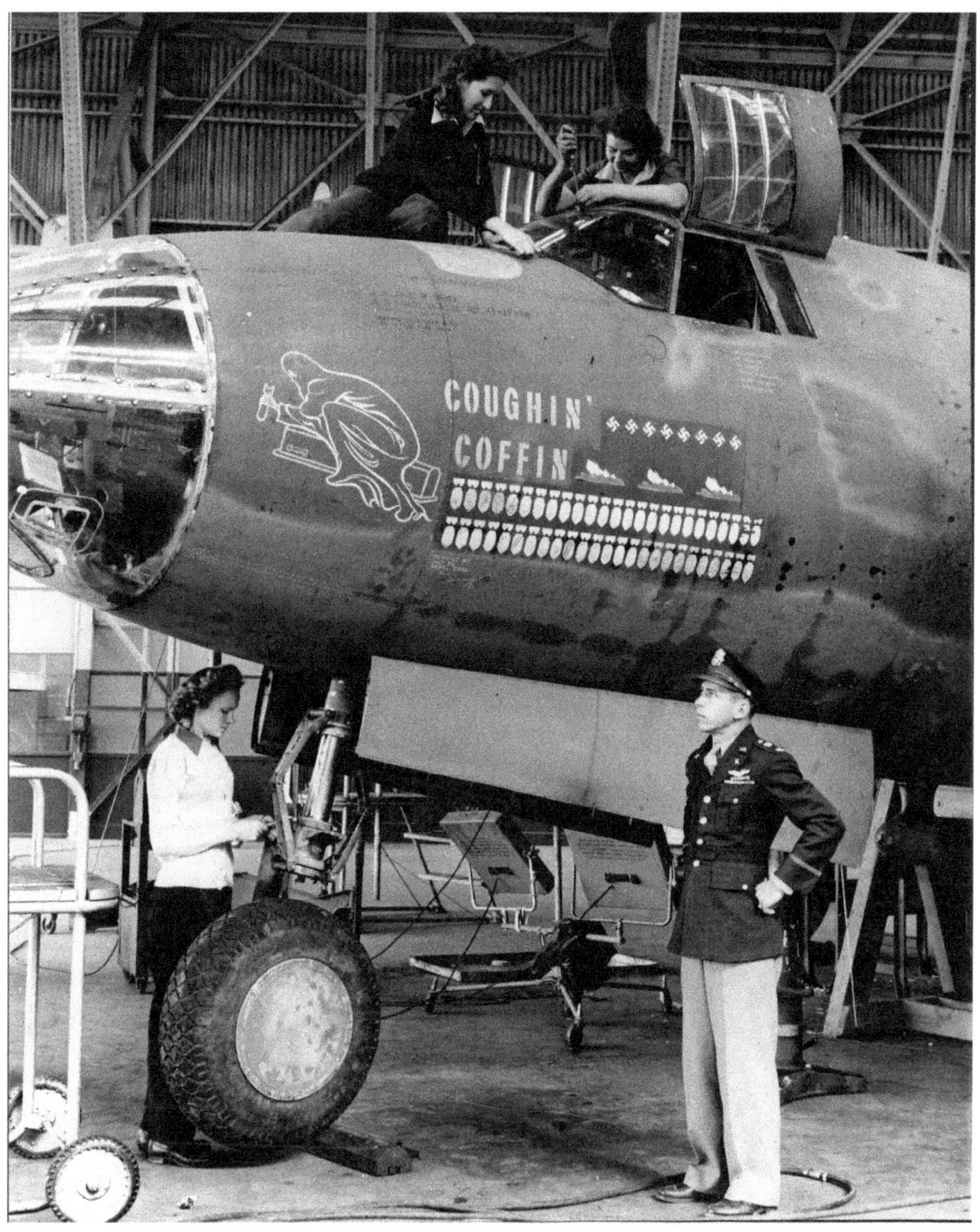

Many types of aircraft were required in order to overcome the difficult challenges of altitude, terrain and extraction. Above: Maj. Prichard, Air Service Command with B-26 "Coughin' Coffin" veteran bomber on tour. Nov 1943. Photos by CM Flaten, IU Archives.

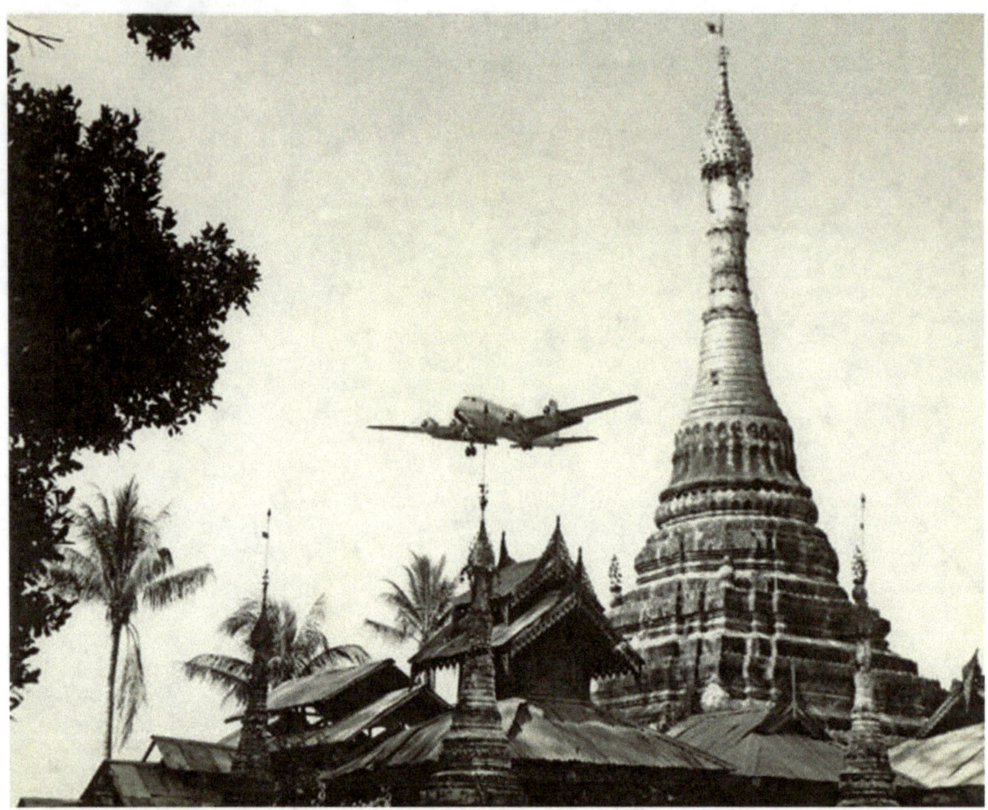

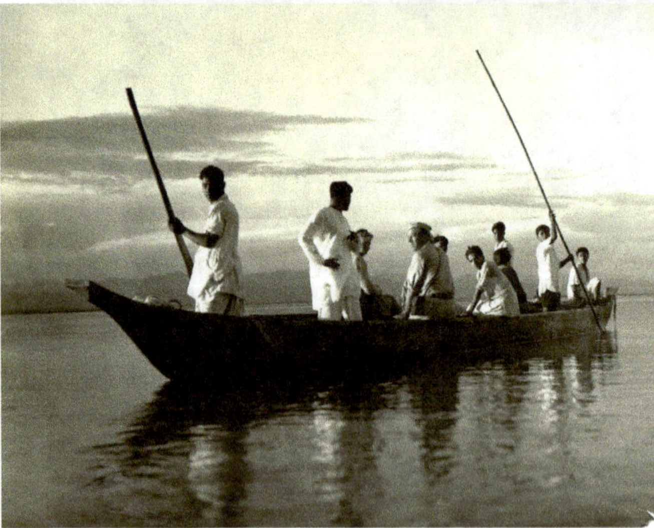

Flaten photographed the geography and people of Burma and India. These photographs represent a small selection of his portraits of the land and people. He visited a tea plantation, a fair, villages, markets, temples, a cremation site, a project built using elephants, larger cities and smaller towns.

Top: Burmese pagoda at Mylchina with airplane overhead.

Bottom: Men in river boat with long poles transporting soldier and woman.

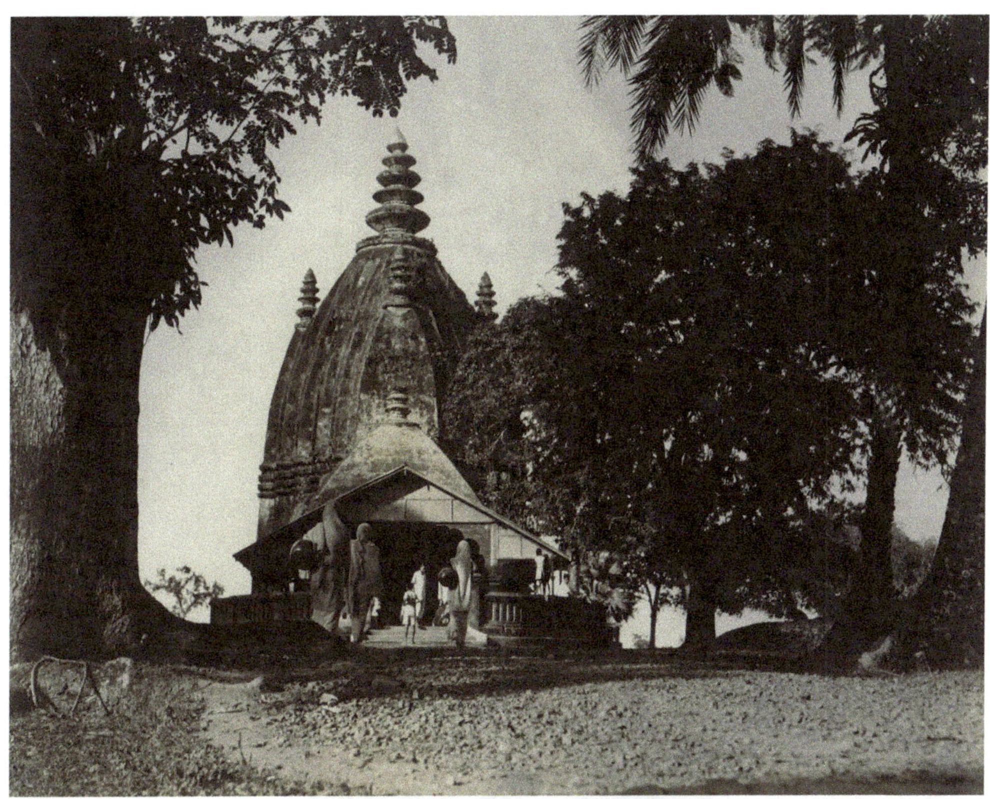

Above: Women with veils entering a temple.

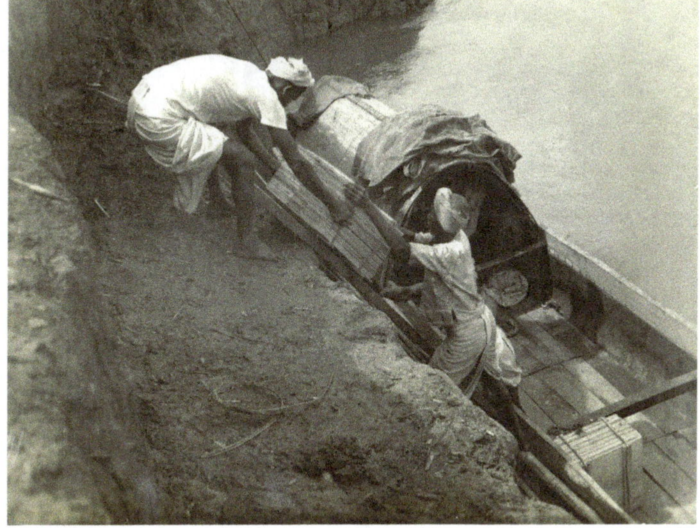

Right: Men with turbans and dhoti on river boat loading building material.

This and facing page: Photos by CM Flaten, IU Archives.

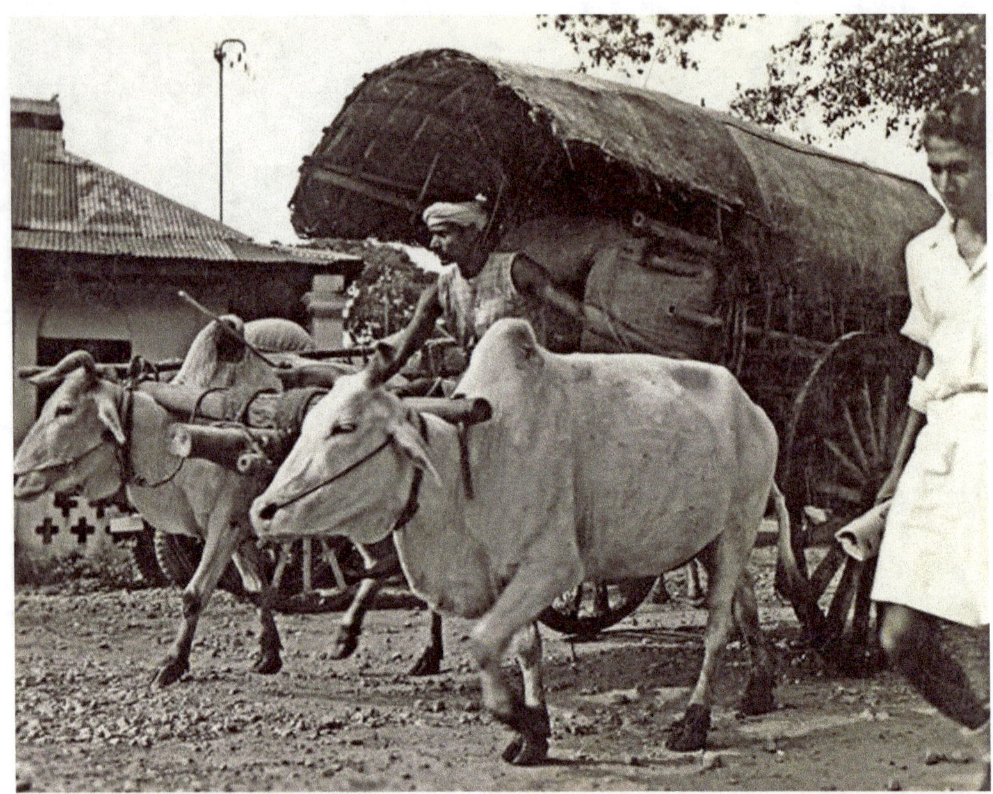

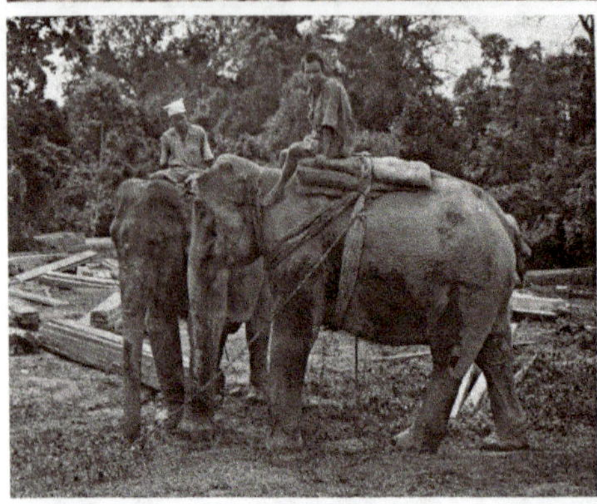

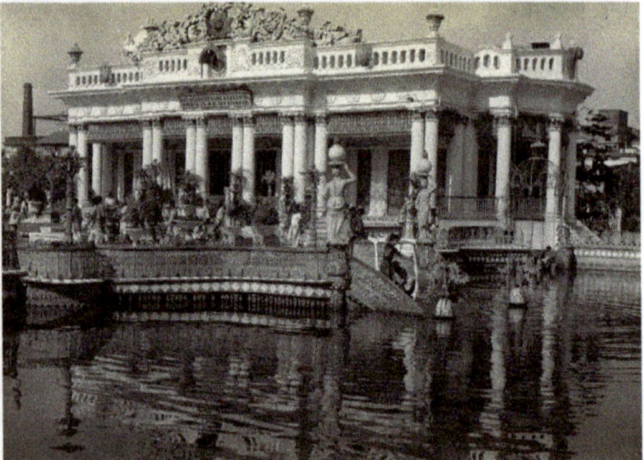

Above: Indian man driving cart with two yoked water buffaloes.
Left: Indian Elephants used in construction project, Sadiya India.
Right: Rai Buddree Dass Bahadoor house, Jain Temple, in Calcutta, West Bengal, India.
Photos: CM Flaten, IU Archives

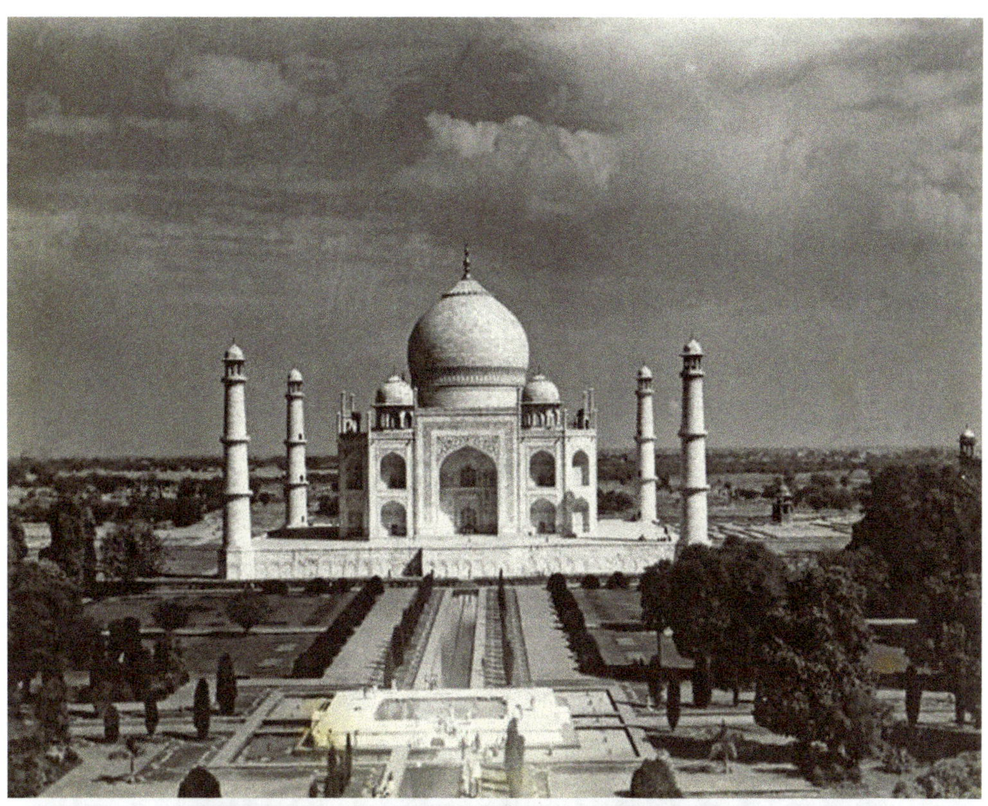

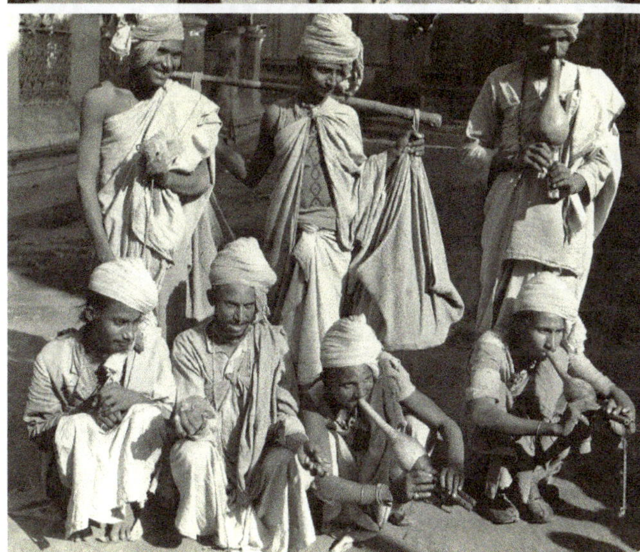

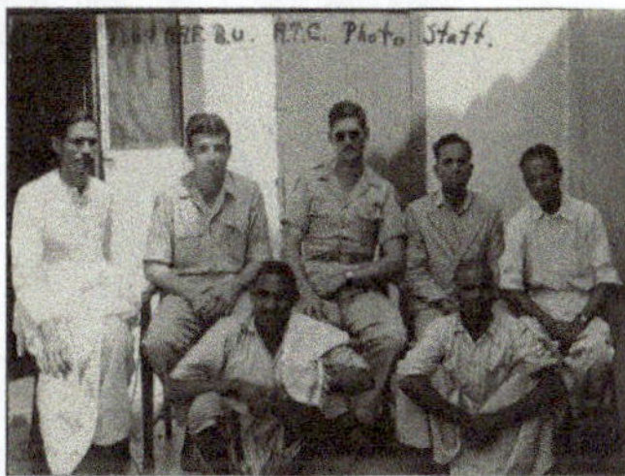

Top: The Taj Mahal.

Left: Village street musicians in turbans playing gourd pipes.

Right: Capt.Flaten and officers. Photographer unknown.

Photos: CM Flaten, IU Archives

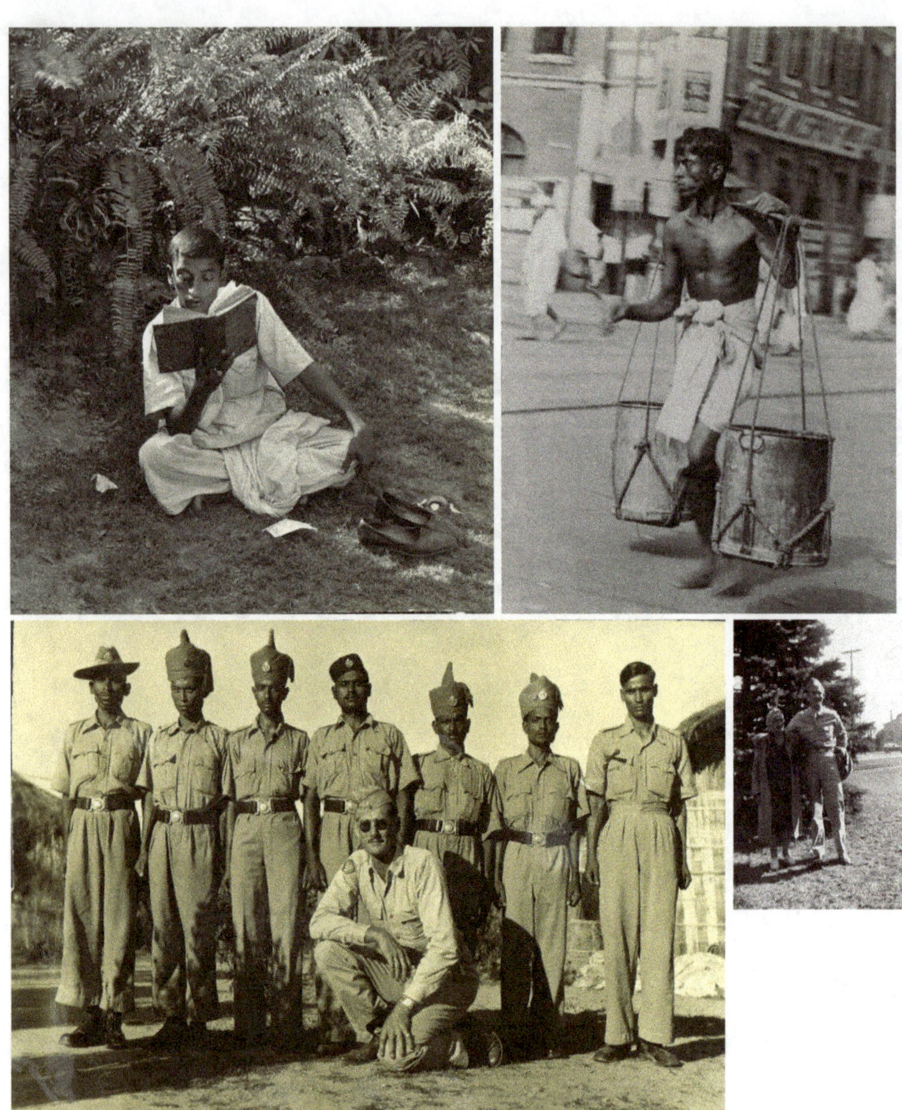

Top: young man on the grass reading a book.
Right: man carrying two large pails with a neck yoke.
Bottom: Flaten and officers.
Bottom right: Bert Flaten with mother Ollie Flaten. Bert fought on Normandy Beach and freed Nazi prisoners at Ebenzee.

Photos: Photographer unknown for Bert's photo. Other Photos: CM Flaten, IU Archives.

Four months later, after Clarence finished his assignment, Hiroshima and Nagasaki were bombed on August 6 and 9, and a surrender was called on September 2, 1945 (V-J Day). I do not know what date Clarence flew back to the states. Did he stay to continue his photography? His brother Bert returned to Sioux Falls, South Dakota to the farm. Bert had served his country by landing on the beaches of Normandy, and afterwards, he helped free the prisoners of the Nazi concentration camp at Ebenzee, Austria.

A year later, Clancy officially separated from active service in June 1946, Fort Dix, New Jersey with the rank of Captain, Air Corp, U.S. Army and returned with Mary and Kit to Ann Arbor and to his work with the Michigan State Conservation Department.

He and Mary added another son, Lawrence (because it sounded like "Clarence") in February 1947. At the same time, Clarence was offered a new position at Indiana University in Bloomington, Indiana as Chief Photographer of the Audio-Visual Center, so they headed south to Indiana. They were not the only ones to leave Ann Arbor.

Also leaving beloved Ann Arbor was Paul Boehm, who moved back to Hettinger; he ran for Judge of the 6th District Court in Hettinger in June 1942. Three years later, this man of great influence, Clarence's uncle, passed away on May 20, 1945, only twelve days after VE Day in Europe, and he was laid to rest near Hettinger with his wife Betsey and their son Ben. Paul chose for a final inscription on his granite tomb the last stanza from a poem called "Where" by Heinrich Heine, the famous German writer and poet. (Heine's tomb in Paris has this same stanza.)

> *Immerhin mich wird umgeben gotteshimmel dort wie hier und wie todtenlampen schweben nachts die sterne uber mir. Heine.* After all, God surrounds me there as here. And the stars that hover over me in heaven shall be lamps above my bier.

CLARENCE AND MARY IN BLOOMINGTON, INDIANA

In 1947, Clancy and Mary arrived in Bloomington to exciting new prospects. He had just been accepted at Indiana University as Chief Photographer of the Audio-Visual Center, and she, though having a teaching degree, chose to stay home with Kit and Larry. She very proudly emphasized that this was an intentional choice and that mothering was as important a profession as any other. "I feel like I belong here!" she would say of her feelings about her new home, Bloomington.

They were newcomers to a town built by industry and limestone, quarried and constructed by the old settlers: the Wheelers, Slusses, Thrashers, Hunters, Stogsdills, Carmichaels (native son, Hoagy), Woolerys, Waldrons, Hunters and McDonalds, and so on, whose elaborately chiseled and tilted headstones now quietly commemorate a dust-covered past in Rose Hill Cemetery on the west side of town. The new generation of Bloomingtonians were young people like themselves: ex-GIs, a triumphant generation, now focusing the same energy that won World War II on education and modernization and improvements. Their modern visions would be enshrined in new architecture built with the local Indiana Oolitic limestone and the skill of expert local stone carvers, the very same material used to build the Pentagon and the Empire State Building.

The town was growing. Swelled ranks were part of a Midwest demographic trend but also a large national trend. The nation's official center of population in 1910 was squarely in Monroe County and by 1940 it had moved only slightly westward. In Bloomington, telephone service expanded to over 6,500 phones. New schools, bus lines, police, parks, churches and a manufacturing plant were built. Rogers opened a block manufacturing plant and the Weddle Brothers construction business was established. More parking meters were a sure sign of increased automobiles and commerce. And although the old Showers Furniture Company continued with earnings reports, their revenue was declining; the developing technologies of television and radio being manufactured at the new RCA and Sarkes Tarzian plants were the guarantees of progress.

The university was expanding integration efforts. The first black basketball player started on the I.U. basketball team. The Gables restaurant, the city swimming pools and scout troops were open to all. The university was becoming more cosmopolitan and drew celebrities from across America. Local Hoosier war hero Ernie Pyle was honored. And celebrities like Frank Lloyd Wright, Vladimir Horowitz, Paul Robeson, Jimmy Dorsey, and Count Basie came to perform and lecture.

Now that Clancy and Mary were in a transforming world at peace, Clancy focused his attention on the next mission: professor, educator, scientist, microbiological photographer at a state university. "It's the best place to be in the world," he declared as we spent time together in his office one afternoon on campus. He cherished the mission of education and the university, and its administrators, in turn, encouraged his ideas, dedication, and innovations. Like Mary, he truly felt as if he belonged.

They rented a bungalow on South Washington Street, and added a daughter and son, Peg and Brian, and then little Liz, to the family. But they needed more space, so they loaded the family into their Studebaker and drove southwest of town toward Bedford, where they found an old farmhouse on Airport Road. On July 27, 1951, they purchased it from William R. and Lilly E. Hughes. Perhaps William and Lilly had heard rumors that the Fair Board would soon relocate to the adjacent property and had decided to sell, but for now it was wonderfully isolated.

They moved into the old clapboard, one-story white farmhouse with wrap-around porch, somewhat similar to Clancy's family farm home in Dell

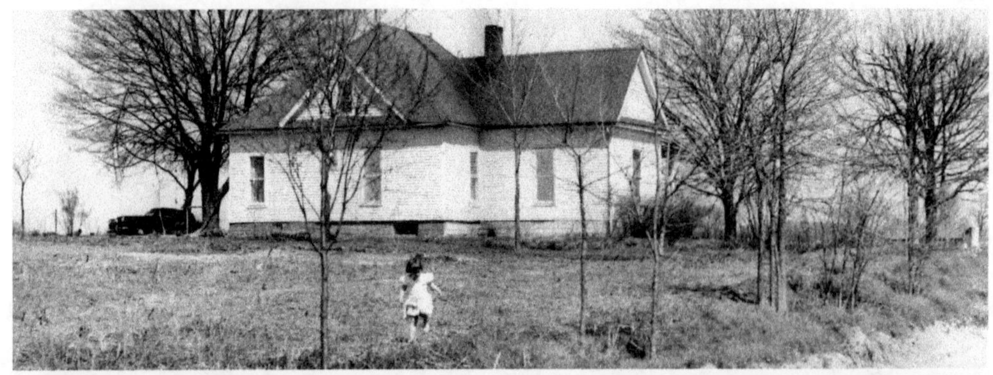

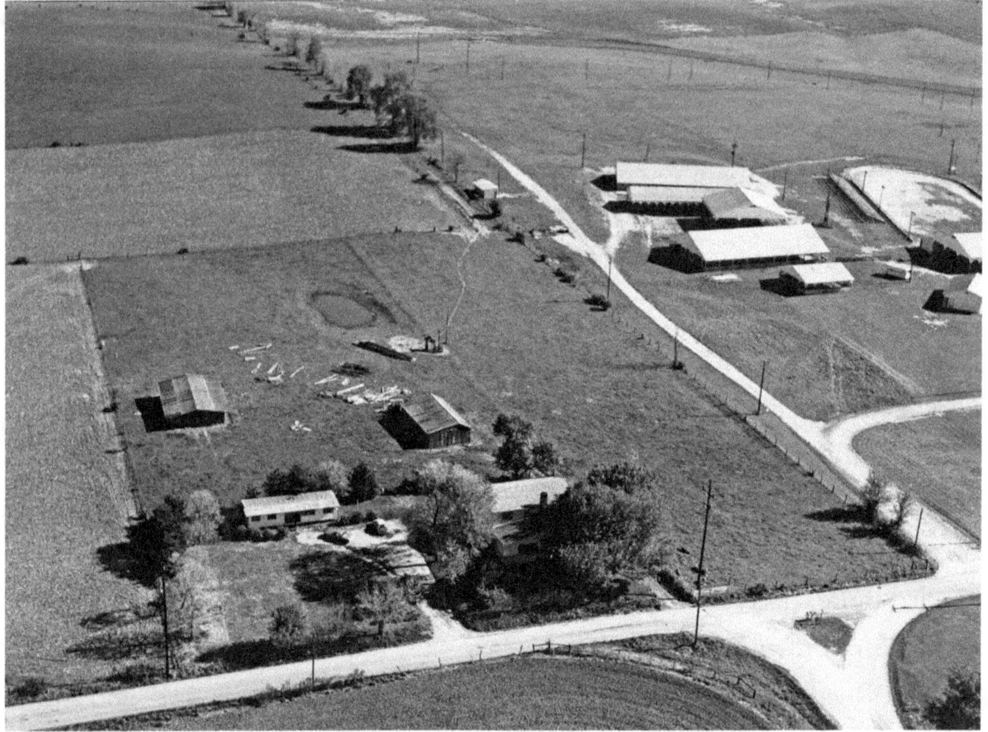

Top: Peg plays in the yard of their new home, an old farmhouse on Airport Road. Photo: CM Flaten, IU Archives. 1951.

Bottom: An aerial view of the farmhouse, with barns in the back, and the Monroe County Fairgrounds buildings to the right. Unknown aerial photographer. (Was it perhaps taken by Capt. Flaten?)

Photos: CM Flaten, IU Archives.

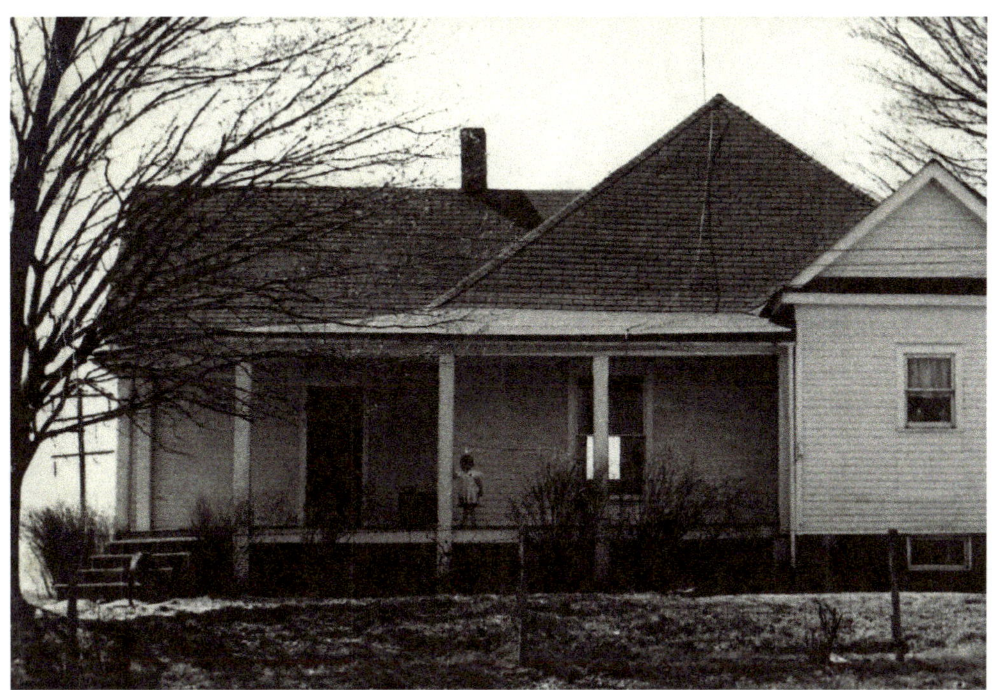

Top: the original farmhouse.
Right: Wayne McConnell plowing with a Case tractor near chicken coop. 1951.
Below: McConnells cows grazed in the fields which surrounded the farmhouse.

Photos: CM Flaten, IU Archives.

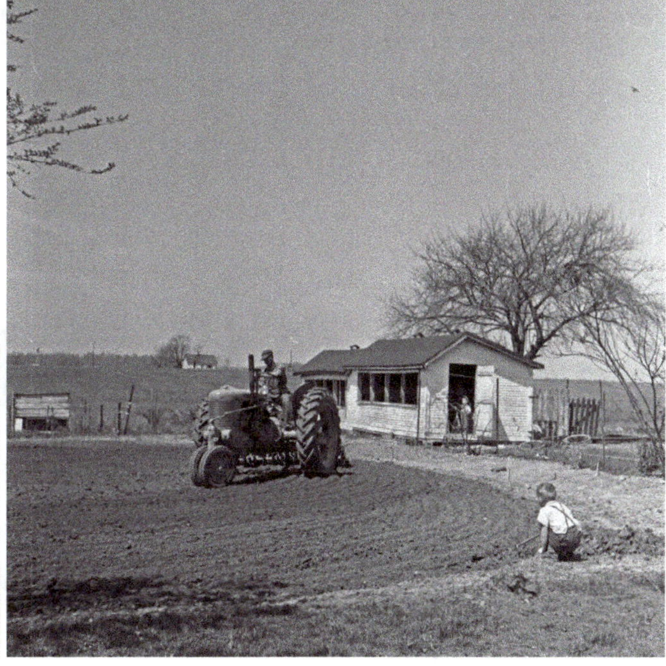

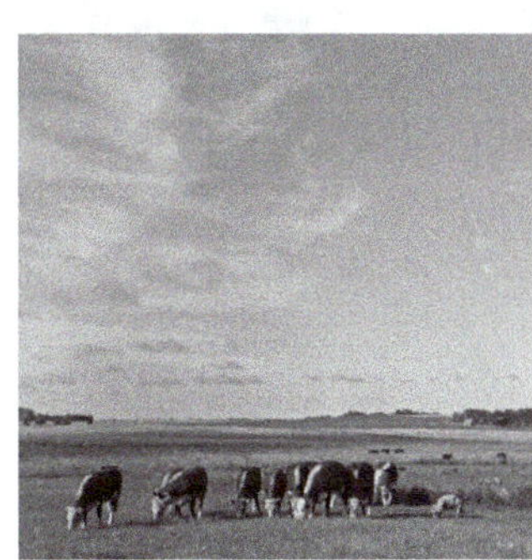

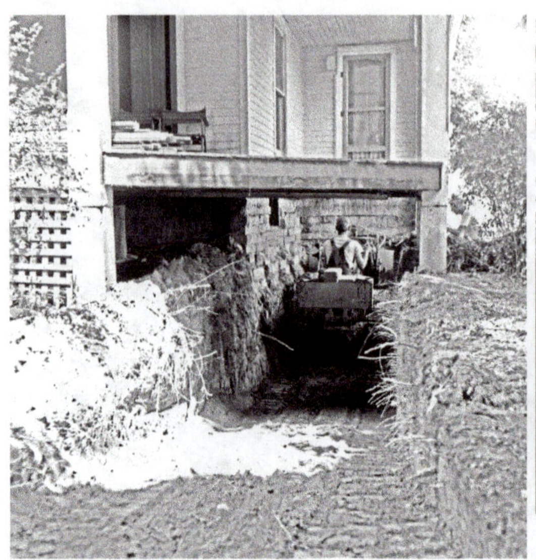

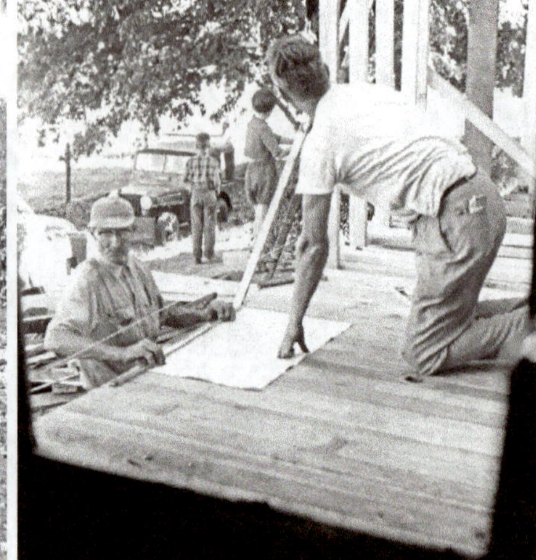

Above: the home under reconstruction. A basement coal bin was dug, the furnace was upgraded with a stoker and blower, and a second story was added. Ca. 1955. Top right: Clancy and Mr. Criswell work on the construction of a front addition. Ca. 1964. Right: Clancy at work, Marianne in foreground. Ca. 1955. Below: The old chicken coop, still standing. Ca. 1960. (collection of the author.) Below: the home gains an upper story. Children are off to school: Peg, Larry, Brian and Kit heading to St. Charles School. Ca. 1955.

Photos: CM Flaten, IU Archives

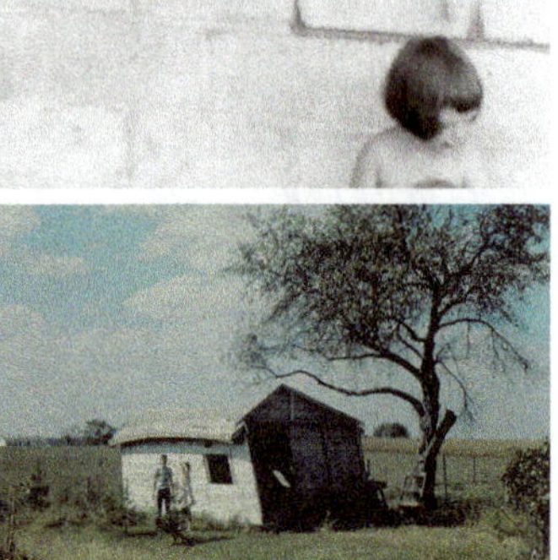

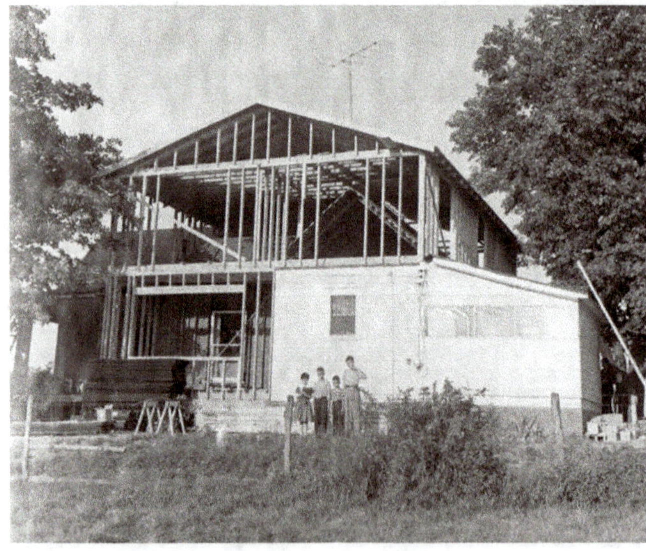

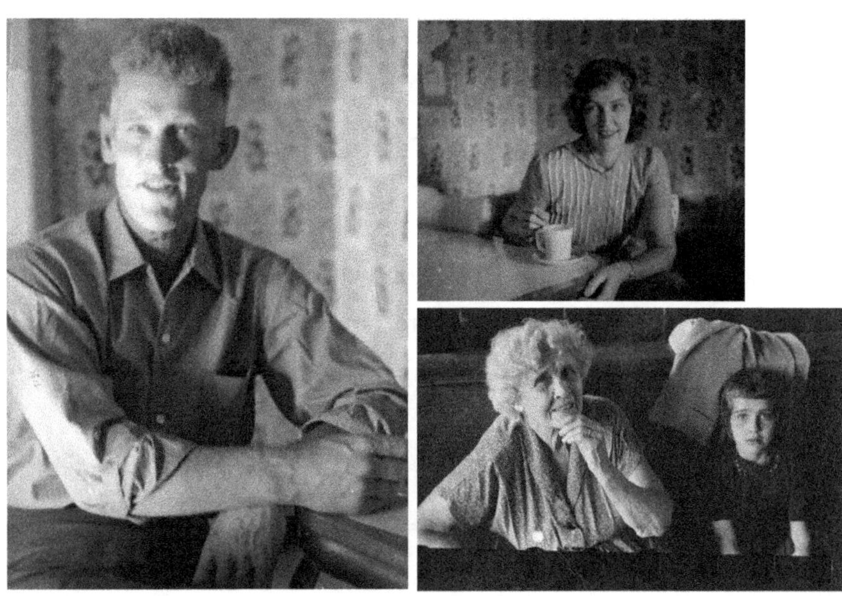

Family were welcomed visitors on Airport Road. Above, Clancy's brother Ebon Flaten and sister Alpha Haak, and his mother Ollie Flaten with Liz Flaten. Ca. 1959.
Below: Luke Browne with his grandchildren: left to right, Kit holding Sugar, Brian, Georgia, Peg, Marianne, Larry and Liz. 1954. Photos: CM Flaten, IU Archives.

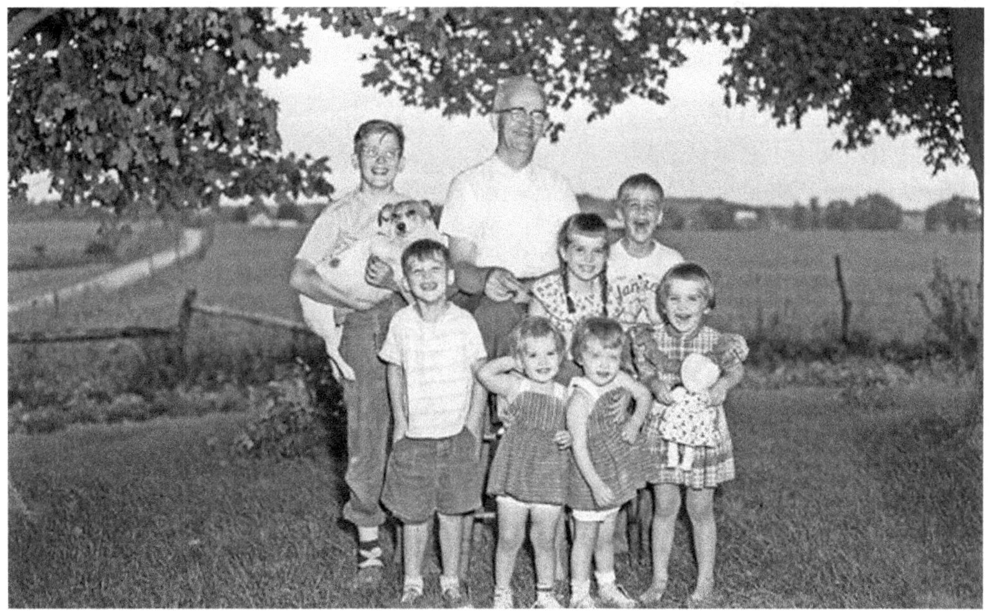

Rapids, sited on three-fourths of an acre of land next to cornfields and pasture. It was here that I came into the world. They moved in with five children in tow by this time: Kit, Larry, Peggy, Brian ("the big kids"), and little Liz, only a month old, cradled in a bureau drawer. In short order they added three final "little kids," my twin Marianne, myself, and Tom. This magnificent old farmhouse became our forever home, certainly a place I resurrect in my dreams, always a stop on my pilgrimage back to Hoosier pastures, a landscape which built my essence and reticence from its karst and clay soil and its iron-tasting well water.

Now there were eight kids, two adults, and later, Mary's father Luke Browne would move in. As a Catholic, Mary chose wonderfully long saint's names.

THE BIG KIDS
1942. Christopher James (Kit)
1947. Lawrence Martin (Larry)
1948. Margaret Anne (Peggy)
1949. Brian Lee Michael

THE LITTLE KIDS
1951. Elizabeth Kelly (Liz)
1952. Georgia Neal and Marianne Evans (the twins)
1956. Thomas Anthony (Tom)

CLANCY AS FATHER

I never met G.C. nor my great-grandfather Christopher Aslesen. But I certainly knew my father, who was a giant in my eyes. He was 6 feet 3 ½ inches tall, loving, and rather stern with steel grey/blue eyes and a thin and scratchy "pencil" mustache. Daddy's demeanor was Nordic, stoic, gentle, serious, silent, and intense. References to his heritage were unspoken but I later recognized them in small ways. For example, in our house, the combined playroom and dining room was lined with a wainscoting of horizontal pine wood, a particular favorite of his, who, having no decorating opinions other than this single one, insisted that Mom never paint over it. Perhaps it reminded him of the days in the Golden Oak house? This feature is very Scandinavian in any event. He loved woodworking and trees. He had a degree in Forestry and Fishing. And he also loved the violin. And most of all, learning. These things I could see. Of his family history I knew little.

AIRPORT ROAD: HOMEWORK

It was 1955, and we were setting down roots. The first year in the old farmhouse there were no bathrooms, just an outhouse, and the water in the kitchen was from a pump. There was also a pump well in the backyard. Major updates were needed. The biggest challenge was to make the house bigger. Clancy rolled up his sleeves and bent over the wheel of the radial saw to make another cut. Mr. Criswell, a local carpenter, was pounding in nails and putting up the framing to the second story on our farmhouse. A bulldozer was digging a new basement for a coal furnace. All of this industry came of necessity.

Clancy at the same time entered the I.U. Graduate School (it would take four years to earn his Ph.D. in Botany) while carrying a full-time teaching load. There was little time for individual attention, so we kids played around the yard together, and we always looked out for each other. One of his scientific projects during this time was the production of a slow motion film that captured the development of the cardiovascular system of a chicken embryo. Often, he would have to drive to the lab to check on the chicken incubators—a slightly ironic echo of what his mother Ollie had done at her farmhouse.

While he built and worked and studied, we kids were running around in bare feet, mindful of the nails. Family possessions were laid on the grass. A stray dog chewed on a spear that Clancy had brought back with him from India and the dog died. Infant Liz played in the wooden playpen while Peg and Brian played cowboys and "Spin and Marty." Kit and Larry threw the basketball up to the homemade wooden hoop, then ran over to explore the old chicken coop on the property. "Let's build a chemistry lab!" we decided and ran to collect a box of old glass test tubes which Dad had brought home from the lab.

Clancy remodeled the home with four upstairs bedrooms and a bathroom upstairs and downstairs, each with only a bathtub, never a shower. And since the water heater would only heat so much water, we had to share the same bath water. Once a week, each of us would take a bath, dry off and dress, and then let the next person in turn take a bath in the same water. Yes, it was soapy and scummy by the time I got my turn, and not very hot, but before I got in, I skimmed the surface and added a few cups of hot water from the tap. It was an early lesson in thrift. Today I never take a shower for granted and I certainly have no love of soaking in a tub.

After reconstruction, Clancy also maintained the house, which was heated by a huge old iron coal furnace in the basement. He would rise before anyone else and stoke the furnace in order to get the house to start to warm up. First, he would clean out the clinkers. These were the burned remains of the coal which he then carried out in a coal pail to the driveway and dumped there for traction. I must say those clinkers, dull jet black and as hellishly jagged as a coral reef, were extremely painful to run across when we ran barefoot around the yard. One summer, my sister "Lucky Liz" was the star of the summer when she won an entire dump truck of fresh gravel at the County Fair. I'm not sure where the clinkers went after that, but he continued to stoke the furnace for the rest of his life.

All the while he maintained everything else, too. We joked that "Dad never sat down to watch TV," which was absolutely true. Sometimes when we kids were watching something on TV, he would come into the room on his way to a project, and stop and stand briefly before continuing on to his original task, and we would tease him. "Come on, Dad. Sit down." We did not appreciate his constant responsibilities. There was one exception.

The only program to cause him to stop and stand (but never sit) and watch more than a minute was "Hogan's Heroes," a comic treatment of WWII POW camps. It must have been a twist to see a situation comedy develop from a life-and-death hell-hole war which had only ended a decade earlier. But he thought it was quite funny, especially the doofus character of the German sergeant. But, since there was always something to fix, he was soon on his way. Mom joked that when we first learned the name for a "hammer," we called it the "damhammer" because Clancy was always exclaiming, "Where's the damned hammer?!!", annoyed that we had not returned it to his grey Craftsman toolbox. He never rested. Once I asked him what he thought death was like and he replied, "It's a time of great rest." Certainly, for a man who worked strenuously his whole life, this would be an attractive reward.

The actual airport on Airport Road, up the road about one-half mile, was Kisters Field, a small airport named after a local soldier Lt. Gerry Kisters, who had received the Congressional Medal of Honor from President Roosevelt in 1944 for wartime heroism. The short tarmac was for small private planes and local Lake Central Airline flights. It was very modest. Sometimes we would all jump in the Studebaker and take a short one-minute ride there just to watch planes come in and to watch hobbyists fly their model airplanes. The buzzing sound was most pleasant and could be heard all the way home.

For Clancy, this might have reminded him of the Army Air Corps, flying over Burma, scouting through India. Back then, WWII never seemed that far away. We had a trunk of Dad's war stuff that we kids would sift through. We used his canteen, backpack and camp gear when we took pasture hikes. Some Sundays, Army jeeps from the nearby Crane Army base would come rolling down Airport Road, twenty or so at a time, on their way to bivouac at the Airport or elsewhere. We would stand by the side of the road and wave enthusiastically to them, just as if we were being liberated at the end of the War in Paris, and they would toot back! We would run into the house to call all participants to the roadside. The war has ended! The war has ended!

And at all times of year our large farmhouse was lit up at night; turning lights out when we left the room was impossible because the rooms were always filled. Sometimes strangers would stop by our house, knock on the door and ask if we were the "Airport Hotel," much to the amusement of my mother, and this became a story she would repeat again and again with the punchline, "Is this the Airport Hotel?"

In general, though, traffic on Airport Road was not heavy. It was slow enough for tractors, which were a common sight on the road, and we soon learned the body language to signal a friendly acknowledgment from vehicle to vehicle. If you drove past, you were to raise your index finger slightly, or if you were driving, raise it off the steering wheel as a salute. Any deviation marked you as an outsider. Car traffic was different back then. This was back in the days of "The Sunday Drive," a special family outing in the family car, although it was sometimes used derogatorily ("Sunday driver!!"), meaning the person just poked along. Each Sunday we easily noticed the Duff family (like us, St. Charles parishioners with eight kids) when they were out for their weekly "Sunday Drive" in their remarkably novel VW beetle bus. We would wave to them from our place in the yard and they would toot back. It was always something we looked forward to. What an adventurous life we led.

A DEGREE IN FORESTRY

We all remember fondly our best climbing trees, the maples. And thanks to Dad, there was also a beautiful elm tree which greeted us from the side of the drive as our car's tires hit the crunchy gravel. Nearby, he and Mary planted a beautiful anniversary tree, a white birch, along the driveway. In addition, he planted a boundary row of Norway pines along the perimeter of our property line, and they were lovely and practical as windbreakers.

We also had a row of American hornbeam trees, old heritage trees lining the property along Airport Road. One summer all the hornbeams had an infestation of bagworms. Clancy's solution to the infestation was to spray gasoline into each nest, and then light all of the nests on fire. It was thrilling to see all six hornbeams with many worm nests on fire all on a summer's eve. The worm nests were dropping out of the trees, burning, and it was something which was both amazing and repulsive, as the sizzling nests dropped to the ground, hundreds of worms wriggling to their deaths. This action saved the trees and they stood there decades later.

While he did not return to his farming roots, we did have a large vegetable garden some years. The boys mowed the lawn. But Clancy did not work out in the yard. He paid Mr. McConnell to turn the earth over by tractor for our vegetable patch.

Ours was not a well-groomed yard—the boys usually ran a quick mower over the "grass" making it all look at least uniform in color. Sometimes when Dad drove us through town on the way to mass at St. Charles, he would brake at a particular ranch house on a suburban corner lot and we would sit and laugh as we watched the same fellow mow meticulous stripes across his lawn week after week. It looked ridiculously obsessive to us and we enjoyed the show. I really loved how our father found humor in the simple things. We even named the house, calling it, "the house with the pretty lawn."

And although Clancy and the boys turned up a small garden in the early years, groceries were purchased at Jim's IGA up the road, a throw-back to the days of the pickle barrel and wooden floorboards. Being at the intersection of Airport Road and Highway 45 (the Old Bloomfield Road), we frequently waited in the car while Mom ran into Jim's for groceries. "I'll be right back! You kids wait in the car!" Waiting in the car proved interesting as we could comment on local personalities who happened to pull up.

Sometimes we spied Corrie Alcorn, the County "Ag" Agent—who we always referred to as "Corny Acorn"— jawboning with the farmers, and we would burst into gales of laughter saying that name, hiding behind the seat in case he saw us. Corrie, being a government agent was purportedly viewed with both respect and suspicion. His knowledge of solutions to field pests and fertilizers were helpful, yet wasn't he allied with a government scheme of farmer welfare? It was too much for us to sort out. Also of fascination while waiting for Mom to finish her grocery shopping, was the lethal tire pump, where someone once overfilled their tires, the tire exploded, and the man died. Once Mom came out of the store, there was always the invariable and predictable long wait in the crowded and hot car while she emptied the entire contents of her purse, piece by piece, in agitated frustration, onto the hood of the car, searching for her car keys, holding us hostage. I don't think she ever figured out a good system.

Clancy had a formal side. Even though it required a great amount of effort for Mary to launder and iron them, he insisted on a cloth tablecloth and napkins at each meal, and we always came to the table and stood behind our chairs until everyone was there, then said grace (Bless us, Oh Lord, and these thy gifts …), and only then did we sit down to dinner. We were called to the dinner table, sometimes by the old brass bell, sometimes with a call "Dinner's On!" We always sat together for two meals: breakfast and dinner.

When we had finished, we had to ask to be excused from the table. ("May I be excused, please?") We were made to first finish what was on our plates, with the admonishment, "Remember the starving kids in Korea." We had no idea why they would want our food, but it was important to finish what was on the plate in the name of obedience or to be sent to bed without any supper. And rules were always enforced in our home. It must have been Clancy's military training.

Sometimes Dad used meals as an opportunity to talk about science. He would have various quizzes at the dinner table, such as asking us to put a finger near a candle flame to determine what part was the hottest, or the paper quiz using the scientific "inquiry method"—asking us to posit why various scenarios might take place after looking at illustrations. In this way, he encouraged inquiry. We never, not once, talked politics. As I grew up (and even to this day), I am unsure which party Clancy and Mary voted for.

Once our meals were over, and since we did not have garbage pickup, Clancy would either burn the garbage in a big barrel, or he would bury it in the yard back near the fence line, or sometimes he would haul it to the dump.

CLARENCE'S LOVE OF MUSIC

Clancy's love of music and his insistence on lessons meant that he provided a common family language, an orchestra, a discipline, and a deep well of lasting and happy memories. He valued the permanence of music and said that it was a treasure that no one could ever take away.

"Did you come from a musical family?" was the first question people often asked us. Well, there was no long lineage of professionals, although Mary's side boasted two somewhat-famous performers. (Have you ever heard of The Masked Tenor? Eddie Rabbitt? Wikipedia has.) Mary always remembered her relatives' Irish dances in their basements complete with live

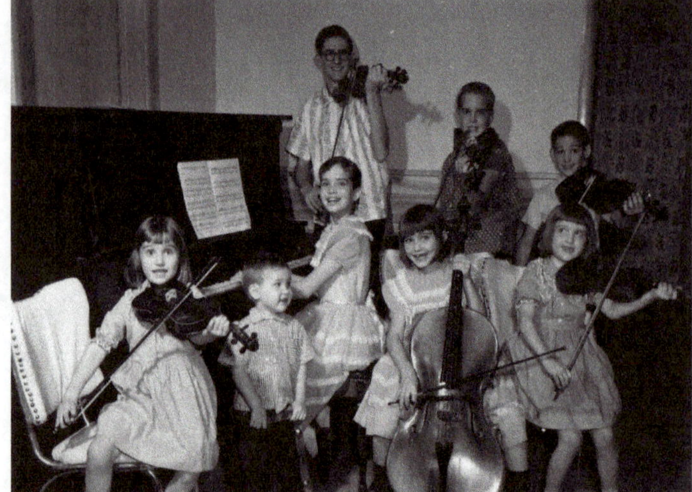

Left: the family's 1958 Christmas card pose. L to R, Georgia, Tom, Peg, Kit, Liz, Larry, Marianne, Brian.

Left: Kit playing a piano, Ca. 1955, and Marianne playing her Steinway grand at home. 1969.

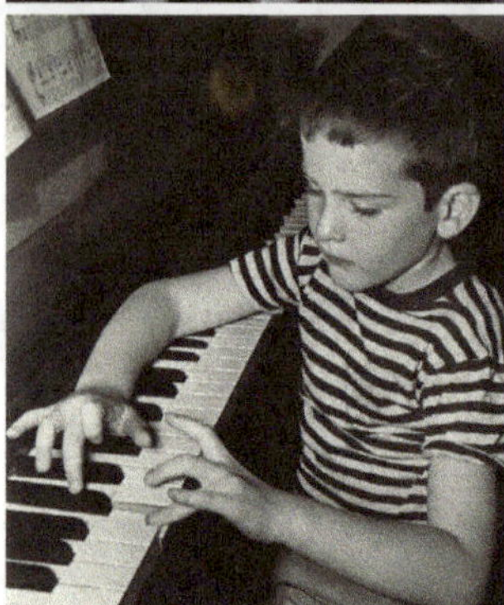

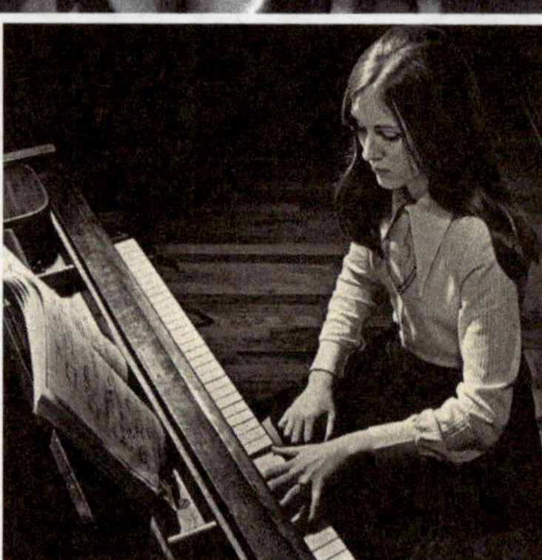

Below: The St. Charles Borromeo Orchestra led by Sr. Regina Marie McIntyre. 1961.

Photos by CM Flaten, IU Archives.

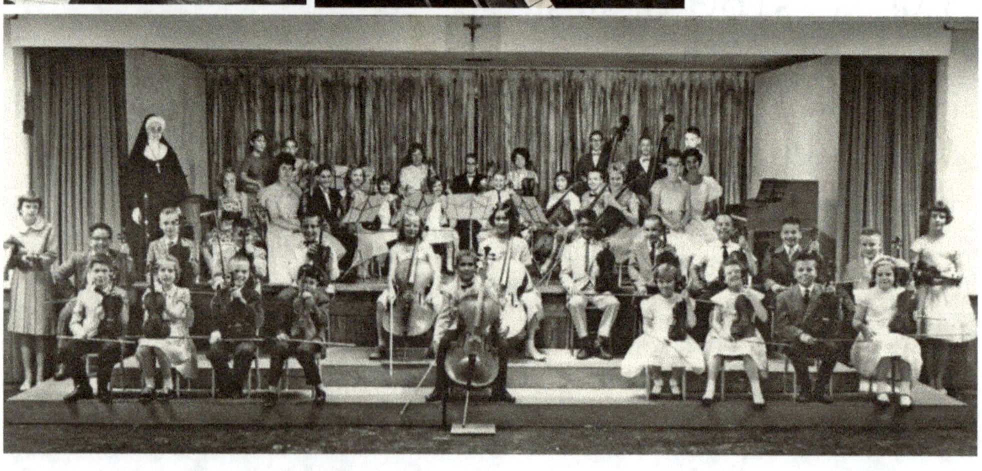

music. And she herself loved to sing and play the piano, especially at home parties. Mary's singing style was dramatic and she had a great talent for songwriting, especially lyrics. Although she had received some early piano lessons and grew up with a father who adored opera music, she played music by ear and could easily access the basic chords and modulate to any song on the keyboard. Her parents had parties in their Irish home and everyone played musical instruments, including her uncles.

Clancy played a beautiful Gibson guitar. His style of playing was low-key, soft and strumming, of unrecognizable songs, to which only he seemed to know the words "lo-lo-lo-lo …" but in those rare and relaxed moments for him, he who was exceedingly busy with work and responsibilities, it conjured a balmy shore, where Hoagy Carmichael's Stardust Melody held sway.

Once we entered first grade, all of us kids had to pick a stringed instrument to learn and were required to take piano lessons, encouraged to play, and hounded to practice. Early lessons at St. Charles School on piano, violin, viola, cello, and bass under the patient guidance of Sister Regina Marie meant we had our very own orchestra, and Clancy was our first conductor. Our first performance as a family orchestra was out in the country on the porch of a farmhouse on Curry Pike, back when it was all farmland. Clancy and Mary organized the family to play before an audience of farmers and their families, and it went well enough that we then performed at a meeting of the Farm Bureau Coop on stage at the County Fair Community Building. This was more to our liking, because we were paid with all of the ice cream sandwiches we could eat (which were more than the planners had counted on, I can tell you that). Mom never missed an opportunity for us to perform, she being quite a Stage Mother, and we even played in our living room for farmer Wayne McConnell and his sons, although they left after the piece with polite thanks, but noted it was something they had not heard before. We played yearly school recitals with memorable banana split parties at the house after the performances.

Clancy was very happy to have an after-dinner performance for guests, but he did have to coax us. After dinner, he would push back his chair and announce in a jovial tone, "I'm Old King Cole calling for my Fiddlers Three." This royal call meant that he expected us to pull out instruments and entertain. Very aware of the privileges we were receiving with our music lessons, yet terrified of being put on the spot to perform, we would plead, "Oh Dad! Do we have to?" After a bit of hemming and hawing and pleading, we would navigate our way through a tune with all its flaws, which always made King Cole merry and proud.

Clancy not only encouraged music, it was an absolute priority. There is a phrase Mary repeated to emphasize how important music was, on the scale of expenditures in the meager family budget. "Your father often said that the music lessons will be the *LAST* to go!" Sure enough, we did without dining out, movies, candy, birthday parties, fancy gifts and new clothes, and anything remotely considered an extra. We may very well have gone without food before Mary and Clancy canceled music lessons. My love of black humor had me inwardly chuckling at this declaration while I practiced my violin, as I envisioned my own cartoon sketch, where a quartet of bare skeletons are playing—the music, indeed, being the last to go.

When the violins needed a crack repaired or the finish revarnished, Clancy turned to his considerable woodworking skills. He took apart the violins at the kitchen counter and refashioned them to make them brighter and playable. He sometimes visited the university's luthier, Ole Dahl, and besides sharing an interest in the craft, also enjoyed the shared heritage of Scandinavia, Ole having been born in Denmark. Ole shared information about repair, and since Clancy had been a fine woodworker during college, having created a beautiful drop-leaf table, a jewelry box, and a cutting board and more for Mary, he had the patience it required to study, fit, glue, sand, and finish pieces. It suited his temperament.

There was, however, one damaged instrument which even he could not patch up.

One evening, when Mary and Clancy were out to a PTA meeting, we were left on our own. Larry was preparing his own meal: a Swanson chicken pot pie. I was in the other room, playing the Gibson. I got up and walked into the kitchen with the Gibson in my hand, just in time to see Larry take the pot pie out of the oven, and as he pulled the cookie tray toward himself, the small Swanson aluminum pie tin slid off of the tray, toward him, and landed right into his lap! Since the pie was scalding hot, the expression on his face registered horror, then shock. My immediate reaction was to laugh at his expression, since it was so dramatic. He jumped up, much angered, and chased me around the kitchen, whereupon I slipped, fell, and the guitar hit the floor with popping twang! The neck of the Gibson snapped. Clancy tried, at various times, to glue the neck and repair the damage, but the guitar was never the same. Although it was my fault, he never reprimanded me for it. He had a lot of patience.

A few of the children used their musical training to advance to a profession. Some of us continued studies with the faculty at the Indiana University School of Music, a place of unparalleled training. Marianne completed her professional degree, a B.A. Perhaps Clancy never sat down to watch TV, but very much later, after he and Mary had added the new Music Room, Clancy would sit in his comfortable chair after dinner and listen to many hours of Marianne practicing Schuman, Chopin, Scarlatti and others. He bought her the sheet music to his favorites: Hoagy Carmichael's Stardust, I Found a Million Dollar Baby, and other wonderful jazz pieces, all of which created the most restful respite for him from his responsibilities, schedules and teaching duties. Later, Liz, too, became a professional musician and received an M.A. in cello performance from Butler University in Indianapolis, Indiana. And I myself studied violin but realized I did not have the temperament to dedicate myself to musical discipline.

To further the family's interests and education, Mary and Clancy took advantage of the wonderful performances at the I.U. Auditorium, wanting their brood to be exposed to the very best in musical performances, especially the wealth of talent on the I.U. School of Music faculty. When my siblings and I were quite young, we went to hear the Berkshire Quartet perform many times. The music was completely new and fascinating, but we also had a laugh as we noted an audience member loudly snoring. And Larry, true to form, made a joke of the name of the quartet, calling them the "Berserk-shire Quartet," doing an imitation of someone wildly fiddling, which always made us laugh.

CARS AND TRANSPORTATION

Clancy liked new cars. But living in the country, it was because he depended on them to get to work.

At I.U., with prospects looking up and a growing family of four kids, Clancy walked into Harry Stephens & Co. in July 1950 and bought the car of the future, a bullet-nose 1950 9G Regal Deluxe 2-door Studebaker. This classic, built in South Bend, Indiana, came with a 1- and 4K-mile inspection and conditioning promise, along with a Lubrication Coupon Book for 12 chassis lubrications. The smooth aerodynamics of this car body meant it was quite challenging for us kids to crawl all over the body, but at least the bumper helped us to get a leg up. Mom constantly warned us to stop playing on the car. "Get off the car!" she yelled in exasperation, as we hung about the yard outside looking for entertainment.

According to the sales slip, the Studebaker was "Comanche Red" in color when Clancy bought it, but for whatever reason, he was later compelled (rust? an accident?) to spray paint the body a baby blue, one which made our family stand out of the crowd, this blue bomb on wheels with massive chrome handles and bumpers, round headlights, and large hood ornament. This car enveloped our family of nine as we sat "spooney" (Mom's word for sitting very close together) on its bouncy and upholstered front and back bench seats. The exterior car handles had a modern, space age touch. The windows rolled up and down with fat beautiful handles; the door opened with a pull of a solid chrome arm. And the armrests on the door were luxuriously padded. And it smelled so warm and cushy. Everyone piled into this car, all eight kids, with no seats belts. My favorite spot was right on Mom's lap, where I regularly rode, feeling very safe, peering out ahead through the large windshield. Dad always drove, as Mary only learned to drive much later, when her son Kit was old enough to teach her how.

But the old Studebaker's engine would not always turn over, mostly in winter. Clancy would push it down to the bottom of the driveway, out into the road. We would all pile in and wait for a car to come along to give our car a push so that the alternator would start. Yes, this was quite common.

Eventually Clancy got pretty tired of this and considered an upgrade. All of his future car purchases would always coincide with family vacations.

In preparation for an upcoming family trip out East to New York in the summer of 1959 to be part of the cast of an I.U.-produced educational film, "Long Journey West," and to see Niagara Falls, the Brownes, and Plymouth Rock, Clancy considered a new Ford. He had worked on the Ford assembly line and felt familiar with the product. Car loyalty was really big back then. That might be why, in 1959, he walked into the showroom of the

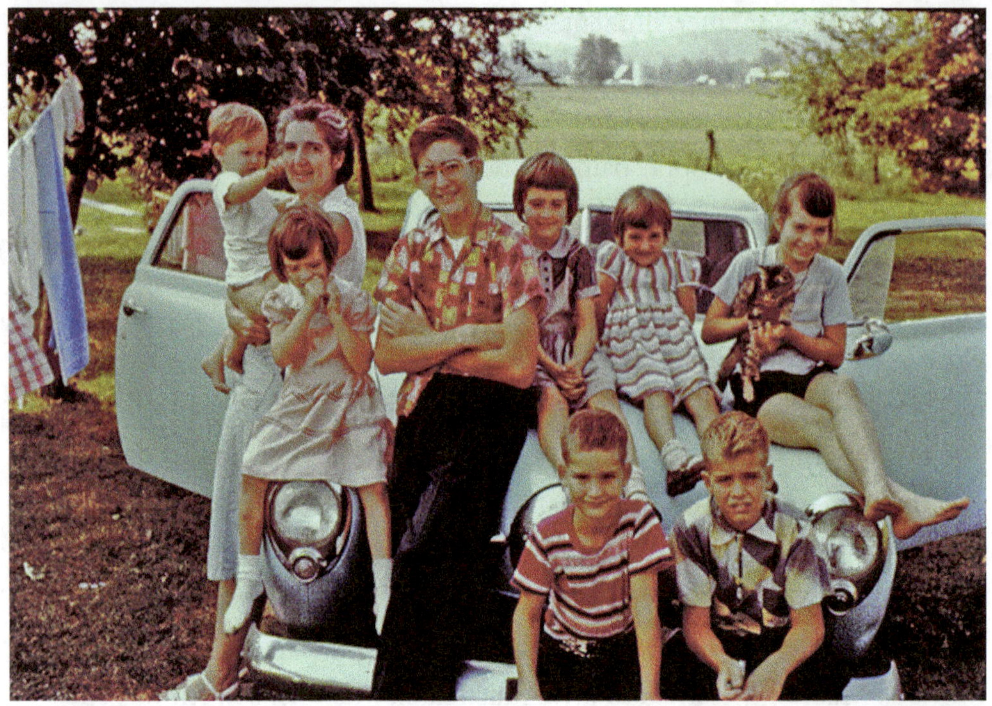

The family Studebaker. 1957. Photo: CM Flaten. Collection of author.
Right and below: 1959. The family prepares for a trip East in their new Ford Country Squire station wagon. The seats laid flat in the back and we all traveled without seatbelts. Standing in front of the car: Brian, Larry, Liz, Georgia, Peg, Marianne, Mary, Tom and Kit.
Photos: CM Flaten, IU Archives.

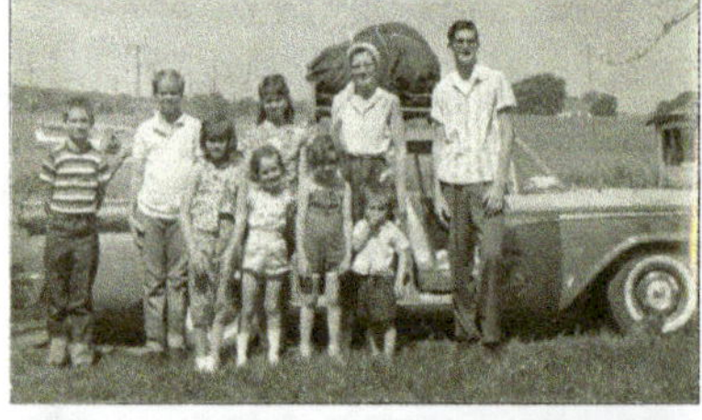

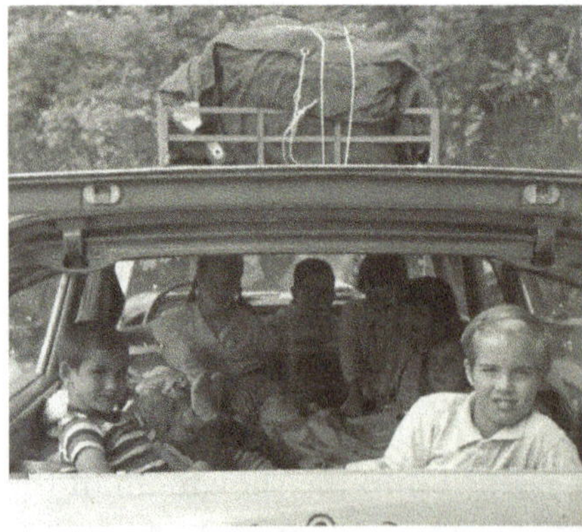

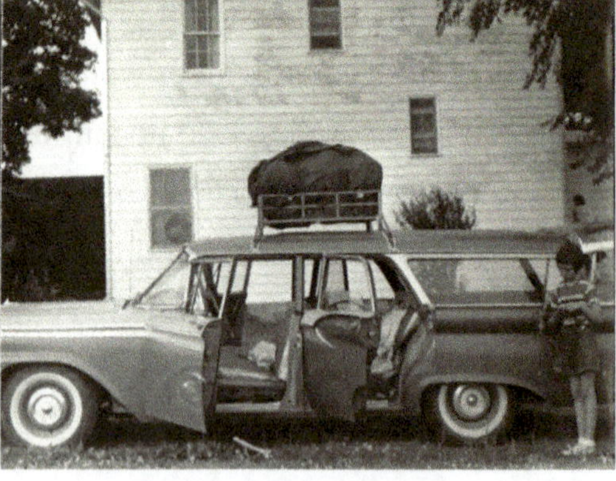

Graham Ford Motor Cars and bought a two-tone green, four-door Ford Country Squire station wagon. This modern Country Sedan featured a drop-down tailgate, a lift-up back window, and a luggage rack on top, perfect for loading all those sleeping bags and covering them with a tarp. I'll never forget the new car smell and the sound of the brand new radio as I twirled the dial in search of station reception. It wavered brrrrrreeerrreeeerreeerr as the invisible broadcasting waves beamed into space searching to lock onto a broadcaster's voice, sounding like an alien spaceship. And talk about new car smell! It was divine!

One winter morning, six of us piled into this station wagon to go to St. Charles School, and after having put the chains on the tires, Clancy cautiously plowed through the dangerously snowy Airport Road, and up on to the barely plowed two-lane highway leading into town. We made it past Melton Orchards and Leonard Springs Road, and past Grandview Elementary school, when straight ahead, Clancy saw a car sliding towards us, spinning out of control, and headed straight for our front end. He did something then, which we never heard him do, before or since, he cursed— *"Hell's Bells!!!!"*— and turned the wheel to the right in order to avoid impact. However, it was not in time, and though it did lessen the damage, we all felt the WHOMP of steel-on-steel impact, and it sent us sliding into the ditch and beyond into a barbed wire fence in the nearby field.

We all sat there for quite a while as the car cooled and Clancy took stock of the situation. Sometime later, we kids were given a ride back home by our old bus driver, Orville Combs, who was returning after having delivered kids to school. Meanwhile, Clancy stayed to arrange the tow. When we got back home, Mom did the only thing she could think of to make it all better: she made a special batch of hot cocoa and served it to us in small green ceramic teacups which were saved for special occasions. Later on, when Clancy came home, he complained not about the accident, but rather about the farmer, whose fence he had slid into, and who was now threatening to file an insurance claim against Clancy for repair of the loss of his old rusty, pathetic barbed wire fence.

Our next new car was bought around 1964 for a family trip out west to Boulder, Colorado in summer of 1965. Clancy switched loyalties and walked into OK Chevrolet, south of Bloomington High School on old Highway 37. The mint-new car, a long beige four-door Chevy Bel Air station wagon, boasted a mounted luggage rack and rear-facing back seat with an electric window. It also promised air conditioning via a tiny A/C single unit mounted under the front dashboard, a formula for a happy and cool trip for the passengers in the front seat during a very hot ride. But about halfway across Kansas, the small A/C quickly became overtaxed and frosted up, and we found ourselves in a Phillips 66 on the side of the road with an area cooled only by picnic tables and tall trees. Eventually we made it to Boulder.

Tom also remembers the car. "Larry might recall using the light tone brown Chevy wagon to haul garbage to the dump one hot summer day. The packed 55-gallon garbage container would not fit so we left the rear gate in the down position and held the hot, stinky garbage container steady—until Larry crossed the RR tracks on Curry Road causing it to jostle and spill forward into the rear seat foot well. It was a stinky, sticky, smelly mess. It took months (if ever) to eradicate the stench from the car."

After Clancy left work at I.U. for the day, he would frequently pick us up at the Monroe County Library, a central meeting point. One day, perhaps after the garbage accident, when Clancy came to pick us up after school, we went out to the car, which to our surprise had been left idling on the curb with key in ignition. I told him I was surprised he would do that, as anyone could steal our car! He said he only hoped someone would! This droll statement coming from my father was most amusing to me, especially since I rarely heard him make jokes, especially wry ones about stealing.

Perhaps due to the unfortunate condition of the Chevy wagon, Clancy then bought a sedan, a white four-door Impala. At the same time, there was another car in our driveway in the late 60s. Brian bought himself a GTO and fell in love with that car. He had purchased it in 1966 at age 16, but Brian and Mom returned to OK Chevrolet where Brian, having decided to join the Navy, enlisting December 13, 1967, sold his GTO and generously helped to make a down payment on another new family car, a reliable white Chevy Nova.

Again, a vacation became the impetus for a new car in 1970-1973. Clancy purchased a used Buick LeSabre four-door sedan, which was used on a later family trip to Colorado in 1973. He may have purchased this at the Fairgrounds at an OK Chevrolet sale, perhaps on a stroll over there on a summer's eve as he stretched his legs after dinner. It's possible.

INDIANA'S FATHER OF THE YEAR

Earlier, back in June 1960, the Indiana Retail Men's Wear Merchants held a "Father of the Year" contest, and unbeknownst to Mary, all her children sent in nominations. But it was Kit, attending school at St. Meinrad at the time, who sent in the winning poem describing his father:

A father must be many things
Besides a man who merely brings
A child onto the earth.
His job's not over then and there
For there is many another care
Which follows his kid's birth.
He's a patient corrector
And a courageous protector
This is what's meant by "a father"
In time of danger
He's a diaper changer
Which is often quite a bother.
To walk kids at night
Till the sun's early light
Peeks over the far horizon
Is the father's worst chore

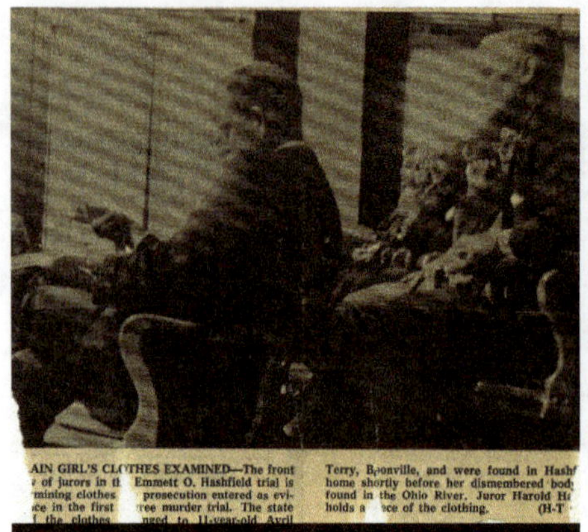

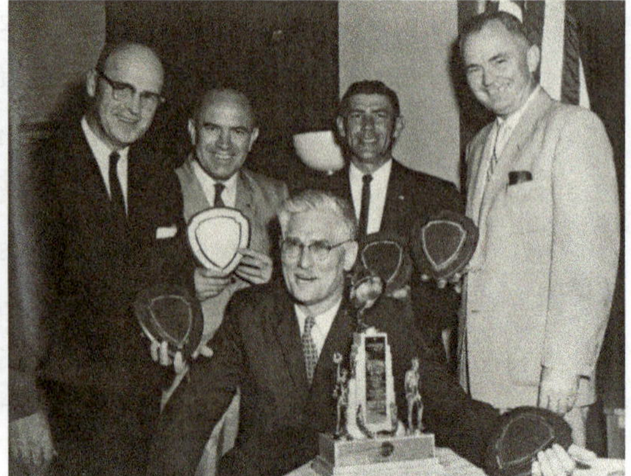

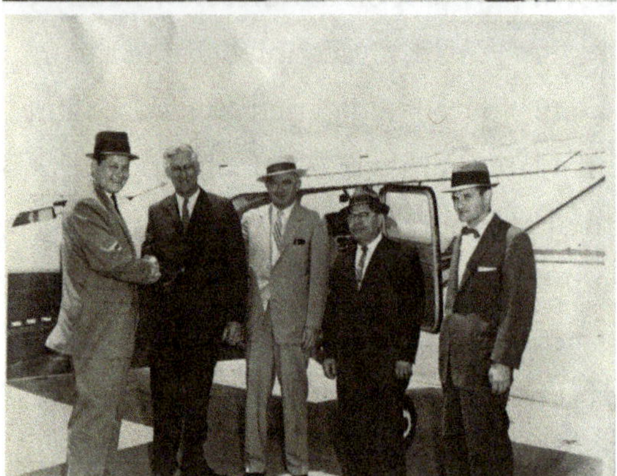

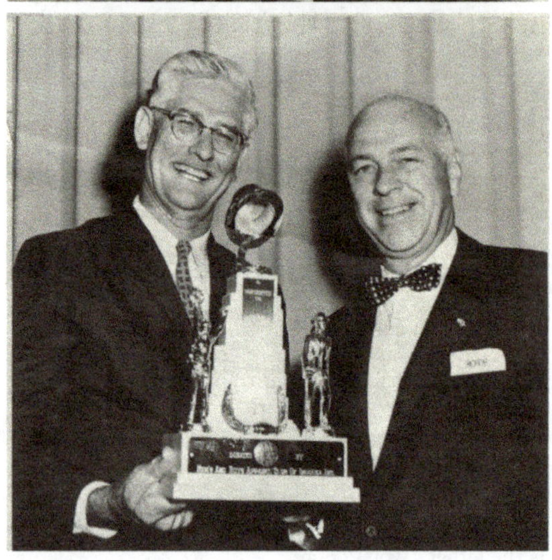

Top: Bloomington Daily Herald-Telephone photo of the jury which sat for the Emmett Hashfield trial.

Right: Clarence was selected as 1960 Indiana Father of the Year and was flown to Indianapolis to meet with Governor Handley (below) to receive the ward.

Photos: Photographers unknown, IU Archives.

For he'd love to snore
At the time when he should be arisin!
He must bring home the bacon
And do all the makin;
And fixin' and mendin' of toys,
He must treat all the girls
With respect to their curls
And must treat all the boys like they're boys.
My Dad is all this and much more
But, though I've said this times before
I'd like again to say
That, to us, Clancy you're really great!
As fathers go you really rate!
Happy Father's Day.

Out of many statewide entries, Clancy was chosen as "1960 Indiana State Father of the Year." He even beat out a County Sheriff and an I.U. Dean. He was photographed and featured in the local *Daily Herald -Telephone.* Kit won a three-month movie pass to the Indiana Theater downtown, and Clancy won $115 in merchandise from the sponsors. The impressive 15-inch high, brass-plated trophy crowned with a springy top hat, reads "Presented to Clarence M. Flaten, Indiana Father of the Year 1960 through the cooperation of Indiana Retail Men's Wear Merchants, donated by Men's and Boys' Apparel Club of Indiana, Inc."

On June 18, he was flown by private airplane to Indianapolis, picked up in an official "Indiana's Father of the Year" convertible and driven to a luncheon at the swanky Claypool Hotel in downtown Indianapolis where he accepted the trophy from Governor Harold W. Handley. Privately, our family was most amused by the irony that Dad did not own a proper suit (only one, very threadworn) and had to go buy a new one in order to receive the award from the Apparel Club of Indiana.

Two years later, he wore that same suit as he sat as the foreman on the jury of the most sensational trial Monroe County has ever seen, the trial of Emmett O. Hashfield. The crime, of which the defendant was eventually convicted, was murder in the first degree. He raped, killed, and dismembered an eleven-year-old girl in Warrick County and threw her remains into the Ohio River. The defendant pleaded insanity, which required the expert testimony of psychiatrists and physicians. All the while this murder trial lasted, from October through November, The Cuban Missile Crisis kept everyone on edge, and so Mary was challenged to maintain the house and calm our fears while the jury was sequestered.

Clancy was civic minded. He felt a great deal of gratitude to his community and knew that he could not have risen without the help of others. Having felt the lifeline of the YMCA while at Ann Arbor, he was inspired to give back as President of the YMCA Adult Board in Bloomington and he reorganized the Student Y, a part of the organization. During his term, the Freshman Record was begun, the Student Y reactivated its interest in I.U. Sing, and became more heavily involved in the annual Chimes of Christmas musical. He and Mary remained extremely involved in their Catholic Church, St. Charles Borromeo, in their PTA, and St. John the Apostle church, Little Sisters of the Poor, and Sisters of Providence, many times in fund raising capacities. Around the time that he completed his Ph.D. and won the Indiana Father of the Year Award, Clancy converted to Catholicism, a move that would have shocked his maternal grandfather, Han Bendick.

LONG JOURNEY WEST: THE MOVIE

Right after receiving the Father of the Year award, Clancy and his family packed up the (previously referred to) green Ford Country Squire station wagon and took a long journey East so that they could star in the educational movie called "Long Journey West: 1820." It was produced by the I.U. Audio-Visual Center, and the storyline was about a pioneer family who, in 1820, traveled by ox and wagon, then by flatboat down the Ohio River, from Sturbridge, Massachusetts to New Salem, Illinois. The pioneer family was

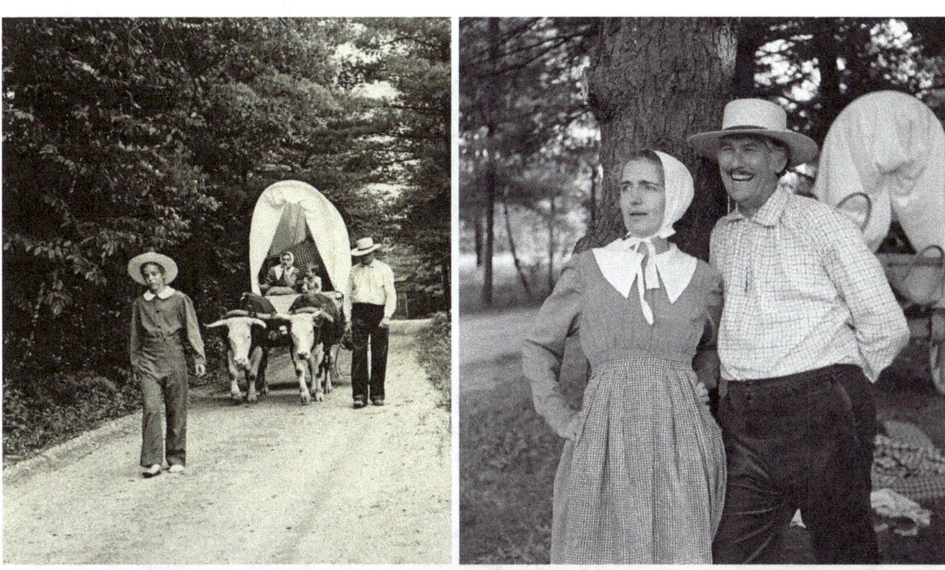

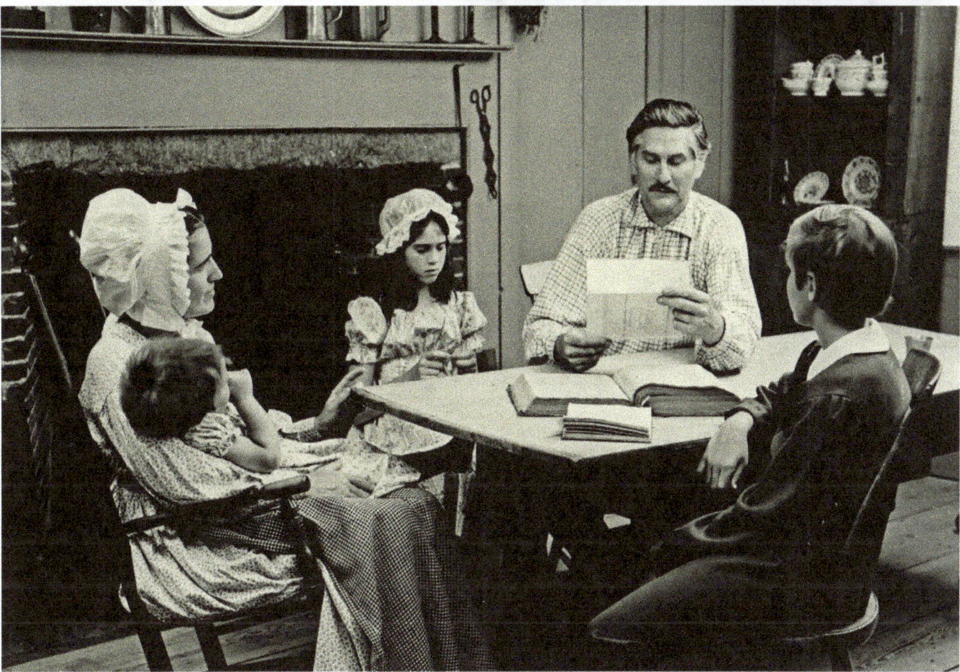

Still shots from the educational film produced by I.U., "Long Journey West: 1820". The Flatens portrayed a pioneer family who traveled from Old Sturbridge Village, Massachusetts to Illinois. Below, the family consults a Bible in order to make a wise decision regarding their move West. Above, they travel by wagon on the Pennsylvania Turnpike. Right: Mary and Clarence, pioneers. 1959. Photos: Indiana University, IU Archives.

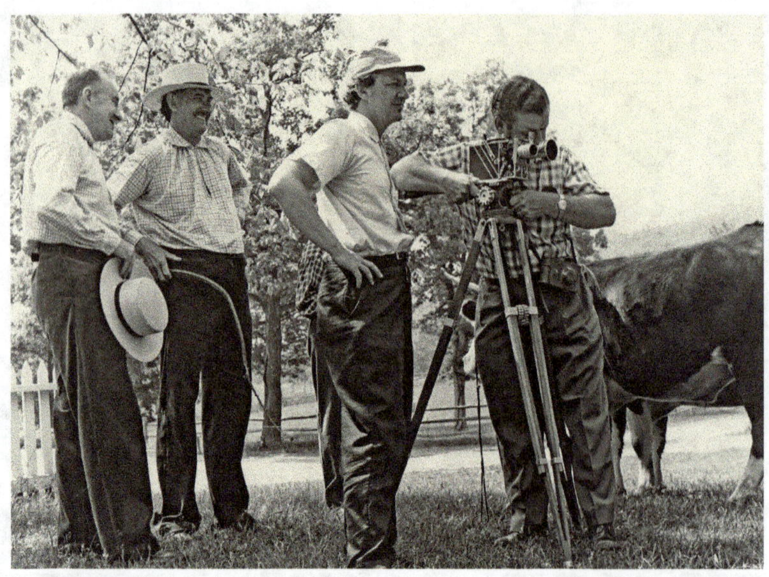

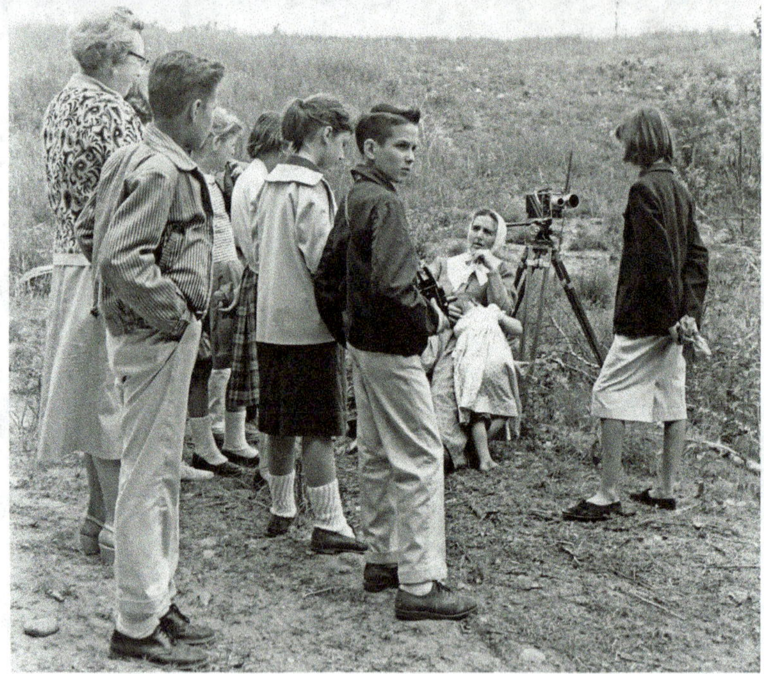

Above: Clancy works on the other side of the camera: L to R: unidentified man, Clancy, Bruce Buckley, Hal Skinner. Sturbridge, MA. Below, Mary answers questions from curious tourists. 1959. Photos: Indiana University, IU Archives.

moving west for better prospects.

Clancy, Mary, Larry, Peg and Tom were chosen for the cast, with Brian playing occasional supporting roles, and in order to make it all happen, Clancy and Mary packed up the new Ford Country Squire station wagon and drove out East, first to Far Rockaway, New York (where the three youngest girls were dropped off with Mary's Irish Aunt Annie Rowan), then on to Massachusetts.

The scenes were all shot in the same approximate locations as the fictional pioneer family might have traveled in 1820: Sturbridge, Massachusetts, to Cooperstown, New York, through the Catskills of New York and the Delaware Water Gap, through the mountains in Pennsylvania and on to Rockford, Ohio where they boarded a flatboat to the town of Rockport, Indiana.

On site, Clancy drove a team of oxen and navigated his covered wagon over corduroy roads, realistically re-enacting a hard life using skills not dissimilar from his own Grandpa Christopher and Narve Flaten's pioneering in Minnesota. During filming of a scene which took place on a flatboat on the Ohio River, Clancy caught a bad break. He fell down an embankment, and tore off his toenail on a boat fixture, and had to have it taken care of at a hospital. Meanwhile, 3-year-old Tom refused to wear his costume (which looked like a little girl's dress) unless he could wear pants underneath. To Mary's consternation, Clancy had died his hair black and grew it long for the role. On the plus side, however, she really did enjoy the fact that onlookers were asking for her autograph during camera breaks in the shooting. Her drama skills rose to the occasion.

Here is the link in case you want to see the movie.
https://media.dlib.indiana.edu/media_objects/xw42n811v

ON THE WAY TO WORK AND SCHOOL

When he built upward in the first renovation on the farmhouse on Airport Road, Clancy put in a stairway with sturdy handrails, and with a window halfway up the landing which overlooked Funkhouser Hill. The window was a daily lookout once school began, and we took turns standing guard to watch as the yellow school bus snaked its way down the hill toward our house. "The bus is at Dickies!" we would yell. This heralded us all to finish breakfast, grab our lunch sacks and books, and run to the bottom of the driveway for pickup.

Instead of the bus, sometimes Clancy would drive us to school. But beware those who dallied! When we heard his announcement "We're Off!" at the front door, that meant that if you were not in the car in one minute, you would be left behind by Capt. Flaten. He knew all about discipline and he never bluffed.

Sometimes he would drive to his office first, and we would wait around there until the school opened, often sneaking around the darkroom and spinning around on the old wooden office chairs. The darkroom was where the negatives were developed and printed. There were large stainless steel trays of developer and fixer chemicals and there was a red lightbulb on the door which, when switched on, meant it was forbidden to open the door and let light into the room. There were illustrations on the wall of his office of chicken embryos and other biology specimens. We loved running around there. To anyone who might ask, "What does your father do?" we were told to reply "He's a microbiological photographer," which was a wonderful mouthful, sure to elicit a puzzled expression. I knew this meant he produced motion pictures of cellular development at the microscopic level, known as photomicroscopy. But it really wasn't a great conversation starter.

Clancy's experiments with time-lapse photography at Indiana

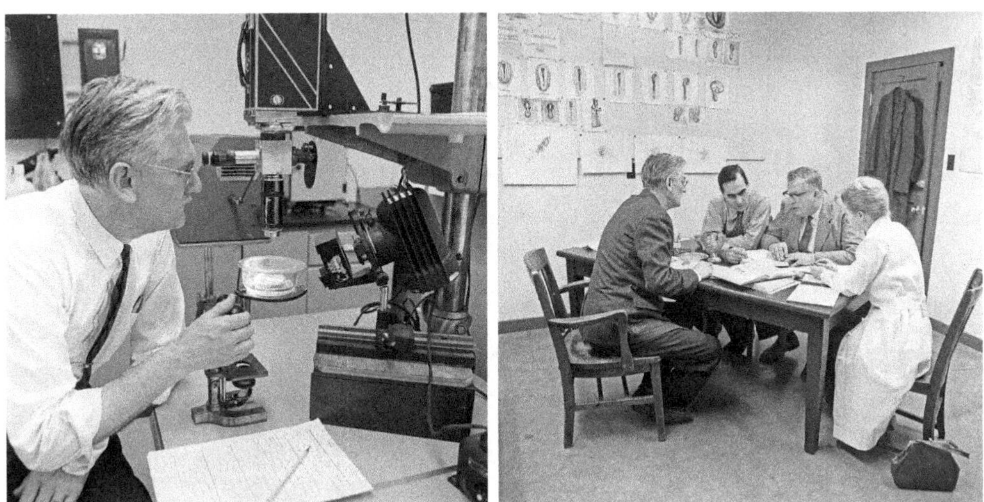

Top: Clarence in his lab studying the developmental anatomy of the chicken embryo. Right: Flaten confers with colleagues: Clancy, George Vuke, Harvey Frye, unidentified scientist. 1962. Photos: Woodfin Harris, IU Archives. Below: Flaten delivers a lecture. Photos: IU Archives.

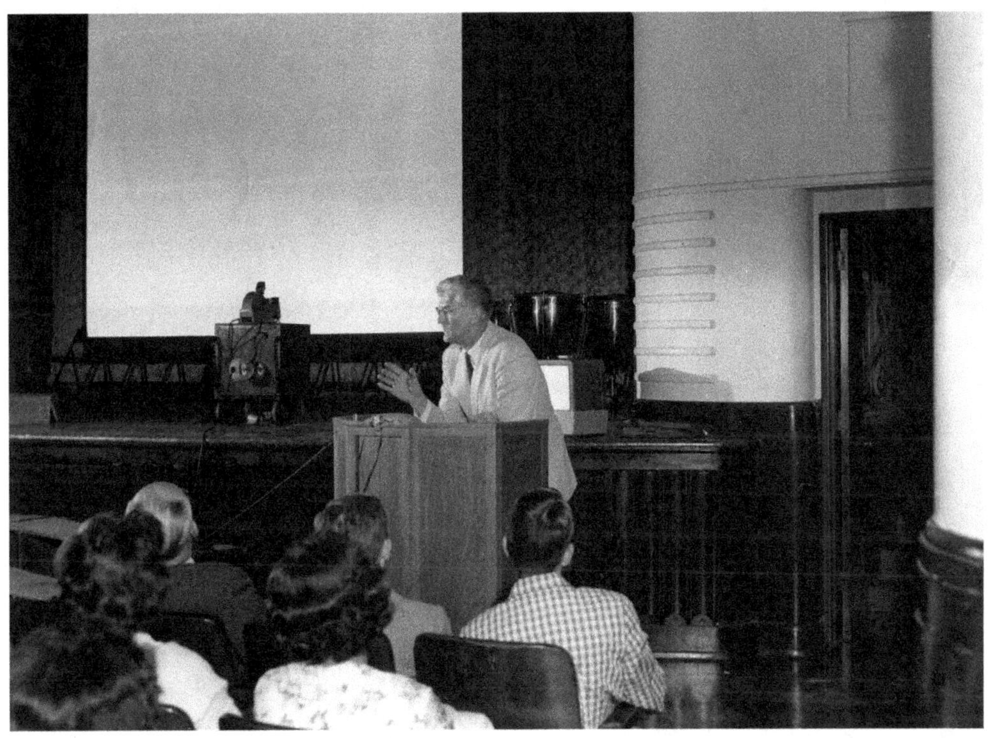

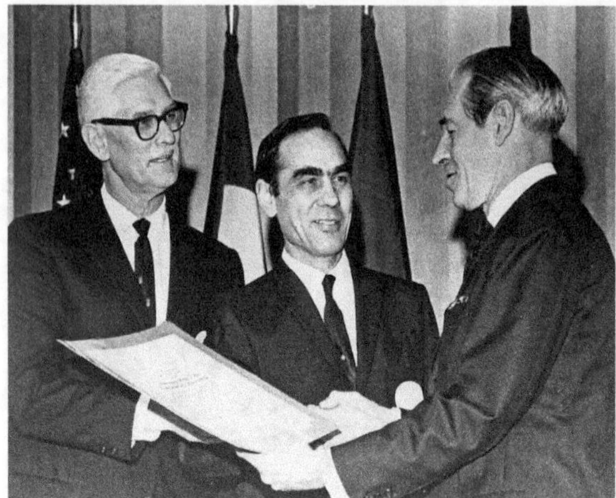

Left: Clancy and George Vuke receive the Golden Eagle Award at a ceremony in Washington, D.C. 1967.

Below: Harvey Frye and Clancy hold the the trophy after a volleyball victory for the Photo Lab. This contest was an annual tradition at the Cascades Park annual Audio-Visual Lab picnic.

Photos: unknown photographers, IU Archives.

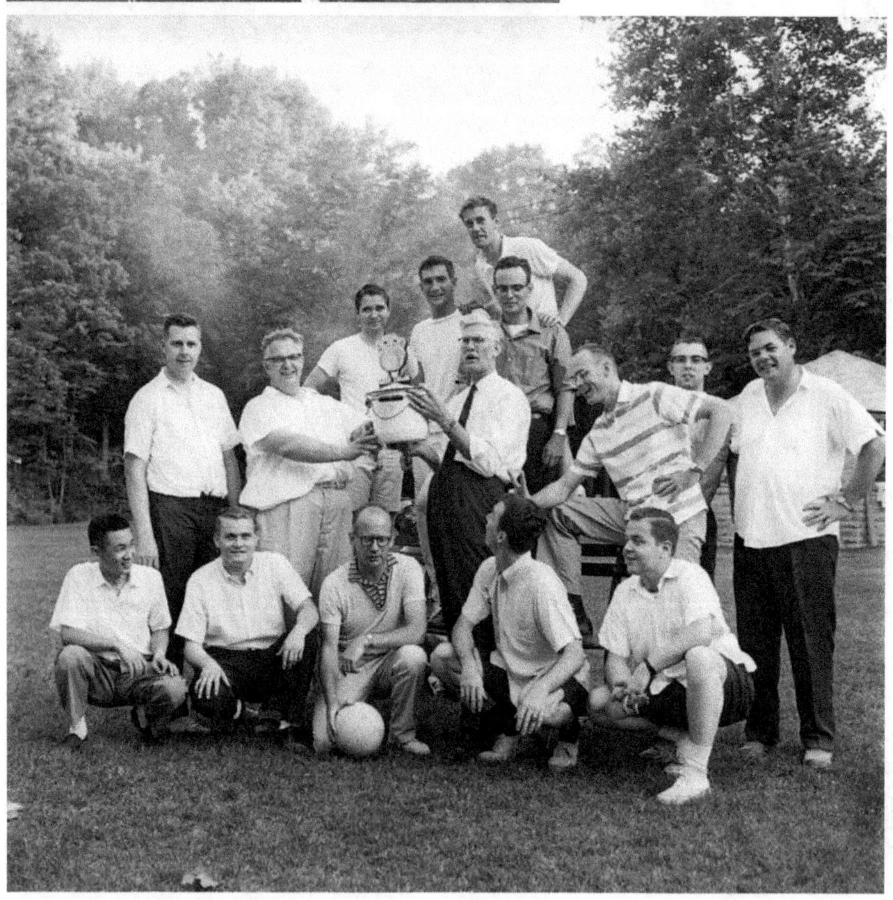

University meant that he worked with axolotls, crayfish, and chicken embryos. His original, award-winning work on the time-lapse photography of the development of the cardiovascular system of chicken embryos meant that he would often drive into town, sometimes in the middle of the night, to make sure the incubator was working.

Some days, he would drive up the driveway after work, get out of the car, and hand us an egg carton filled with eggs, both unfertilized and fertilized, left over from his work. He brought home a lot of these chicken eggs, as it took many to produce his films. We would gleefully dash out into the back pasture, and taking one egg at a time, lob it as high as we could into the air, so that we could watch the egg splatter to the ground. We would run over to the splotch and inspect: sometimes we could see a dead chicken fetus and we would curiously inspect the prize, insensitive to the aborted life. We poked at it with a stick, then ran inside. We had no qualms; we were not squeamish. We understood that these eggs were experiments, and that there was no further life for these chicks, since they had been removed from the warmth of their incubator.

THE 1960s: THE BIOLOGICAL SCIENCES CURRICULUM STUDY (BSCS)

In 1964, age 54, Clancy took a sabbatical as Chairman of the Audio-Visual Department to head motion picture production for the Biological Sciences Curriculum Study (BSCS) at the University of Colorado in Boulder. The BSCS, supported by the National Science Foundation, was formed to modernize biology curriculum of high schools. The text, manuals, guides, and all other instructional material were adopted nationwide. But it was all built on one guiding principle: that the Teaching Technique use both expository and inquiry projects in order to challenge students to their highest learning.

This philosophy also describes Clancy's approach to everything in life.

"The essence of inquiry is really a driving desire and never-ending curiosity. It is a kind of soul or spirit that carries an individual onward in a search for answers. It is a lifestyle in which the ever alert individual finds the challenge to learn irresistible," he once remarked in an article. And I think it brilliantly describes my father's character.

In addition to his work in Colorado, his film work at I.U. received an important national award. In 1967, Drs. Flaten and Vuke received *The Golden Eagle* Award, which was presented from CINE, the Council on International Nontheatrical Events, a non-profit organization based in Washington D.C. whose mission is to select an American film for international festivals. CINE singled Flaten and Vuke's work "*Development of the Chick: Extra Embryonic Membranes*" as wholly original, and they flew to Washington, D.C. to accept the prestigious award. This was an important recognition of their work in developmental anatomy of the chicken embryo. Also having received this award are, among others, Steven Spielberg and George Lucas. Clancy also worked with the BBC TV in London on the "Ascent of Man Series," contributing his knowledge of filming, cloning, and the development of axolotls.

Serious science aside, his cloning time-lapse sequence was also used in a 1975 Hollywood movie called *The Outer Space Connection*, narrated by Twilight Zone creator Rod Serling, whose grave voice opens the film with: "This may be the most startling and controversial film you will ever see." In it, science is sandwiched between flying saucers and Egyptian mummies who were, apparently, preparing to return to outer space. Did aliens visit Earth in our far distant past? Perhaps they still do! Clancy and Mary had a special date night at the Indiana Theater to see the early release. (Although the movie came out in 1975, they must have seen an early release.) They thoroughly

enjoyed the film and were amused at the outlandish assertions. You can see the film here:
https://www.youtube.com/watch?reload=9&v=PNmXUskujAQ

1972: COLORADO AND TRAGEDY

He was promoted to full professor in 1972, a promotion based on a detailed and extensive dossier of accomplishments. All seemed infinitely bright for he and Mary. They had marvelous plans for the next summer: they drove to Boulder and rented an apartment while Clancy did some work with the university. Tom came along, and their family vacation also included a joyful reunion with Kit, who had planned to drive from California to meet them. They stopped along the way in Missouri to visit their old World War II friends, the Funks. It was an incredible time. The skies were a clear blue, giving no hint of the horrible tragedy that suddenly appeared.

It was devastating. Clancy and Mary received the worst possible news in July of 1973, when they answered a phone call in the night from Liz telling them that she had just learned from a County Sheriff that Kit had died in an auto accident in California. Tom describes a walk he and Dad took the day after the tragic news was delivered.

> "So there we were in mid-July 1973 on a bright sunny Boulder, Colorado summer morning. The weather was perfect, the blue sky was brilliant. And we were in a state of shock. Eventually dad decided to go outside for a walk around the apartment complex. He asked me if I'd go with him. As we walked, I didn't say anything. Dad was weeping, repeating words which I cannot recall, mumbling, almost stumbling. Eventually when I became his age (65), I came to experience similar feelings. I realize now that on that July 1973 morning, I was walking

next to a beaten man. I remember his clothing - he wore what he always wore to the office. A crisp short sleeve, pattern dress shirt with tie, tie clip, dress pants, up over the waist of course, with black leather belt and dress shoes. It's what I'd always seen him wear - but I'd never seen him wear it under such duress. He looked out of place, surely thinking "this isn't happening to me." I remember he tried to engage me in conversation a couple of times, probably trying to find some solace from the presence of at least one of his children, but he'd just start weeping again. We walked along the chain link fence outside of the tennis courts. I'd played tennis there all summer, sometimes twice a day, and had gotten fairly decent at it. I really wished I was playing tennis that day, as I, too, was wondering 'why is this happening ?' We flew home through Denver. I remember dad running into someone he knew in the airline terminal, explaining what was going on, and the hurt expression on that person's face. There was nothing they could do but say how sorry they were and wonder 'what will happen?'"

Clancy, Mary and Tom flew back to Bloomington for the funeral, then to California to collect Kit's things and to visit with his son Brian, his new wife Judy, her parents Chuck and Fran Felkins, and his new granddaughter Kim. They also visited Kit's lab at Santa Barbara to meet Dr. Walker, head of the Physics Department, and to see the University. Then he returned to Boulder to finish his teaching.

In August, he wrote a letter to then-Governor Ronald Reagan, asking that the charges against the driver, Daniel Barlow Row, be increased beyond involuntary manslaughter, since Row had been driving on a suspended license, on the wrong side of the road, when he ran head on into Kit's 1964 Triumph.

He also responded at length to a letter from the Santa Barbara Probation Department regarding Daniel Row's sentence. In that letter, Clancy says the family experienced "...depths of sorrow and loss that cannot be described ..." and "...the family's hopes, dreams, and cares were shattered in an instant of time. That is emotion almost beyond endurance." He recommended a felony manslaughter charge, driver license revocation, mental health examination, and rehabilitation service work with victims, and suggested other ideas for new laws.

He returned to Bloomington for a final year at I.U. It was a very painful time. His mother, Ollie, had passed away only nine months before Kit's accident, October 21, 1971. The blows had been too much for his heart and he rapidly aged.

Only one and one-half years after Kit's death, Clancy passed away on October 23, 1974, of a sudden heart attack (fatal arrhythmia) right after he finished his lunchtime laps in the pool at the Indiana University gymnasium. Even though CPR was immediately delivered, it didn't make a difference. He passed away one year before retirement, at age 64. Mary and Tom, the last to be living on Airport Road, turned to the family once again to grieve. Too soon, the family convened for a second burial.

The university honored his service with a Memorial Stone next to a tree planted on campus in his honor, and the family received many condolences. The University also issued an official Commemoration.

I remember meeting many people at Dad's wake. Perhaps the most surprising was a visitor who identified himself as the man who used to deliver our coal. He had a distinctive face, one I remember way back from my childhood. There were so many people, from all walks of life, who were very fond of Clancy.

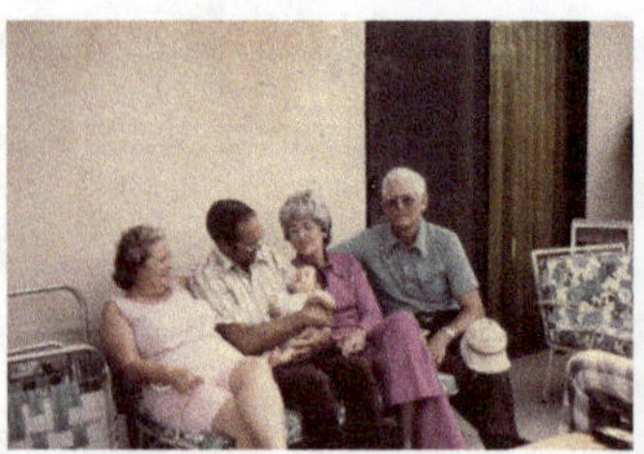

Top: Nov 1973. Clancy and Mary visit Chuck and Fran Felkins in Santa Barbara CA, and hold their new granddaughter, Kim Flaten. Photo: Judy Flaten, Collection of the author.

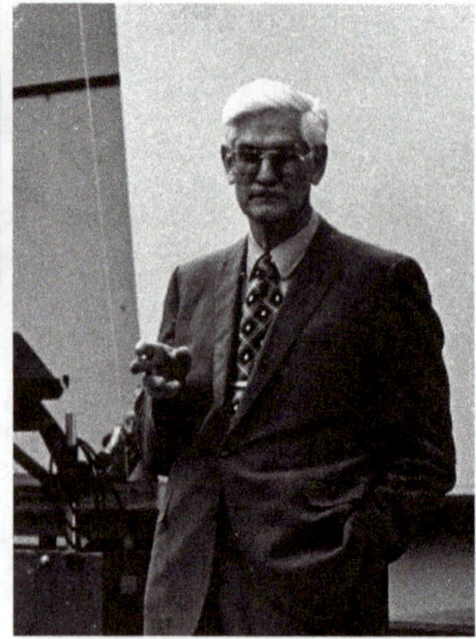

Right Clancy delivers a class lecture. IU Archives.

Below: the dedication of a dogwood tree and Memorial Marker in Clancy's honor, given by Mr. and Mrs. William E. Benckhart and Mr. and Mrs. W. H. McDonald, both seen in foreground. The family attended the ceremony on campus, June 15, 1975.
Bottom Photo: Anita Sperber. All photos: IU Archives.

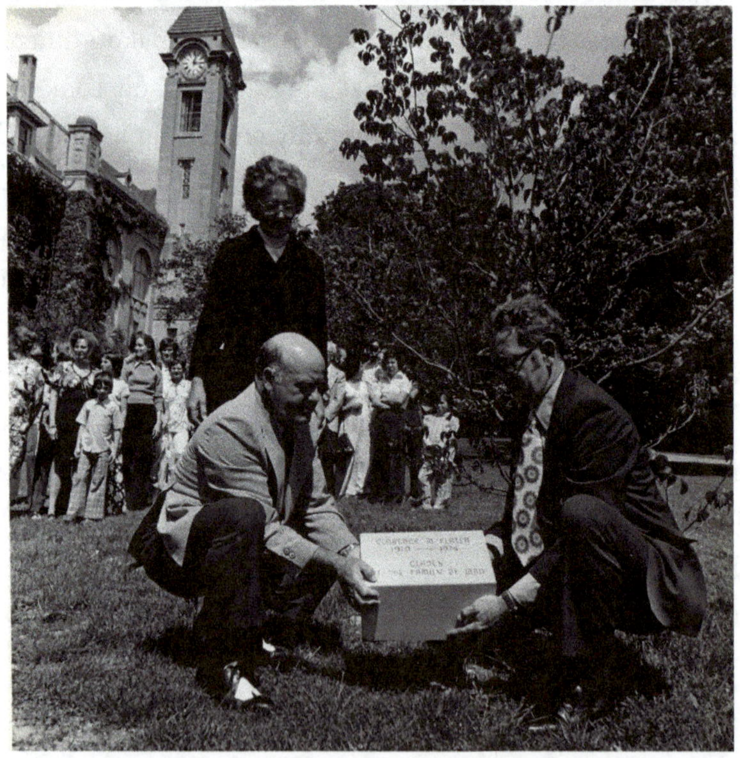

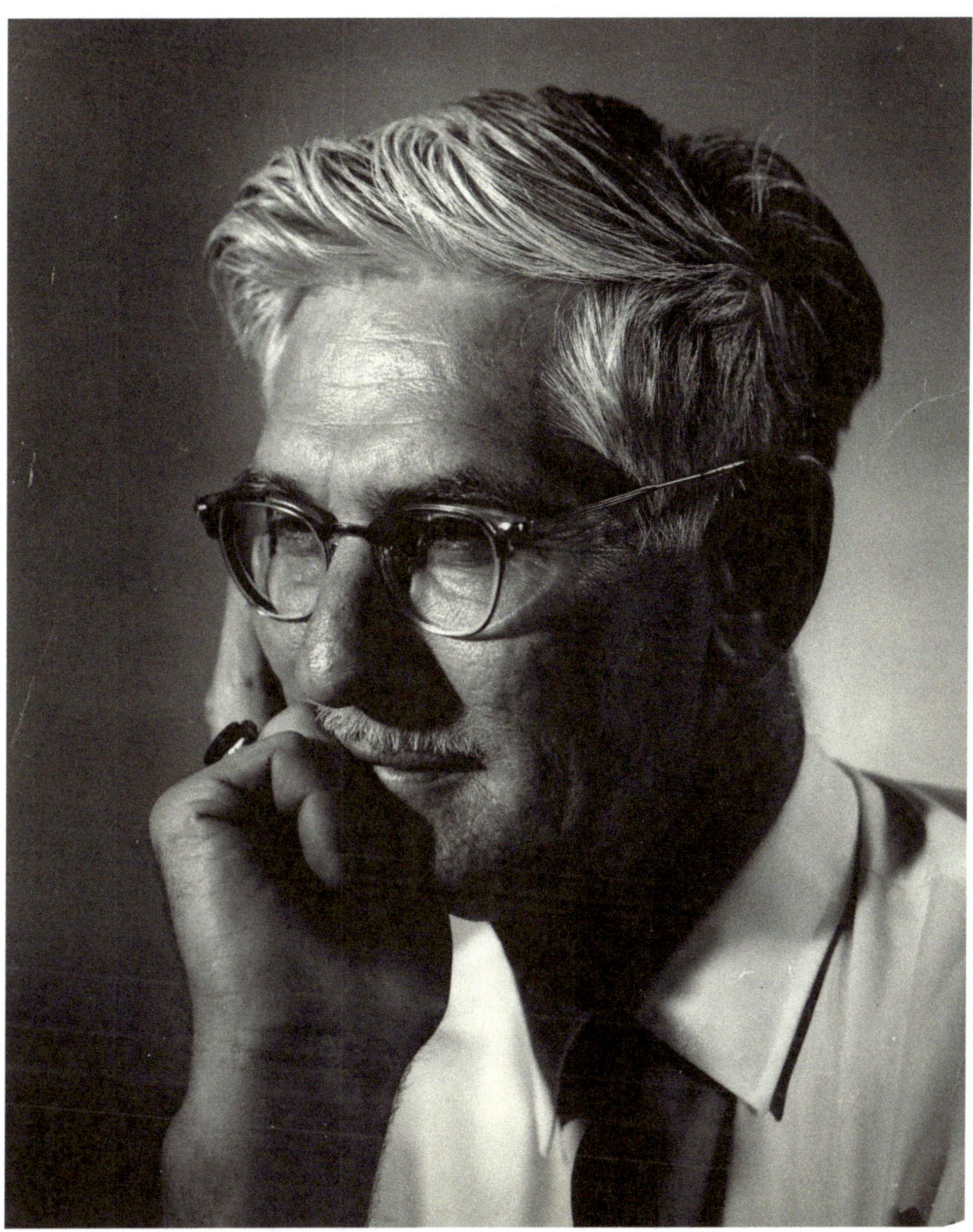

Clarence M. Flaten. Portrait, Photo: IU Archives.

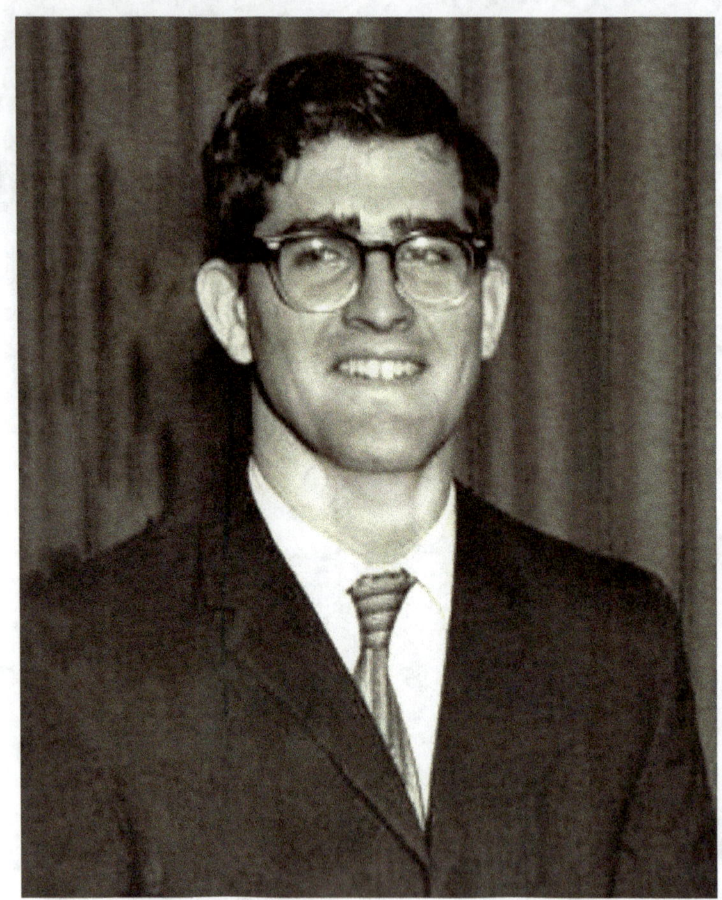

Christopher James Flaten. Photo: CM Flaten, IU Archives

CHAPTER FOUR

CHRISTOPHER JAMES FLATEN 1942-1973

CLANCY AND MARY'S FIRST-BORN SON, CHRISTOPHER "KIT" James Flaten, was named for his Norwegian great-grandfather, Christopher Aslesen Flaten, but did not favor the fair looks of the Norwegians. He had the darker features of his Irish maternal grandfather, Luke James Browne. Kit's life was tragically and violently cut short, at age 30, and there ended the legacy of the name handed down from Christopher Aslesen Flaten.

As I began to write this book, I came across a note from Dad written after Kit's death. It was a short list of goals Dad planned to pursue after he retired. Along with travel, this one stood out: a commemoration of Kit's life. It made me sad to know that Dad didn't live long enough to do something. So, although I began this book with only Christopher Aslesen's life in mind, it expanded to include his son and grandson and then, great-grandson. I decided to bring the family history all the way forward to include Kit's life. This final chapter is my tribute to Kit on behalf of my father.

It's a terrible thing to die young, before your time. Many people say expansive things about the dead—even of those whose accomplishments don't fill but half a page. Absence and aloneness and grief amplify the tragedy. But a burdensome sorrow sets in at the realization of the loss of what might have been, of exceptional character and great promise, all gone. Kit's loss was all of this.

Rather than let the tragedy of his death become his legacy, I turned to family stories, recollections and letters to illuminate the joys of having known him. I could not have written this without the help of my brothers and sisters and for their contributions, I am forever grateful.

Kit lived in six cities: Ann Arbor, Queens, Bloomington, St. Meinrad, Seattle, and Santa Barbara.

1942. ANN ARBOR AND QUEENS: INFANCY

Kit was a late Christmas gift, born December 26, 1942, at St. Joseph's hospital in Ann Arbor. He was a "war baby." Dad was away training in the U.S. Army Air Corps, stationed at Sheppard Field in Texas, which left Mom all alone in the hospital. John Joe Rowan and Winifred Browne drove there to act as godparents; Kit was christened in the hospital chapel since John Joe and Winifred could not make it there later.

Wars are fearful, terrible traumas. Mom suffered great anxiety and she didn't have the stamina to wait by herself in Ann Arbor for an uncertain end to the war. During Dad's first visit with Kit in Ann Arbor (when he was on furlough in May 1943 from Sheppard Field) they decided she would move back to Queens, New York, where her parents could help her. The next month, they moved back to Queens. Her mother, Margaret Browne, who had once been an Irish nanny to a wealthy family in New York, and who continued to foster children at home, was overjoyed to have Mary and Kit back home. And Grandpa Luke Browne continued to operate his grocery store while Mom made herself "useful as well as ornamental" by earning money selling ads for a radio station in Manhattan. Even with the love and support of her parents, her Irish aunts and uncles and "cousins by the dozens," the war years were so stressful that Mom set a pattern for herself of self-admitted worry and overprotection for Kit. She was not able to let go of her worry until three years

Top: Mary and Kit, 1943.

Below: Clancy met his son Kit for the first time in May 1943 when he came back to Ann Arbor on his first furlough.

Photos: CM Flaten. Top left from collection of the author. All others: IU Archives.

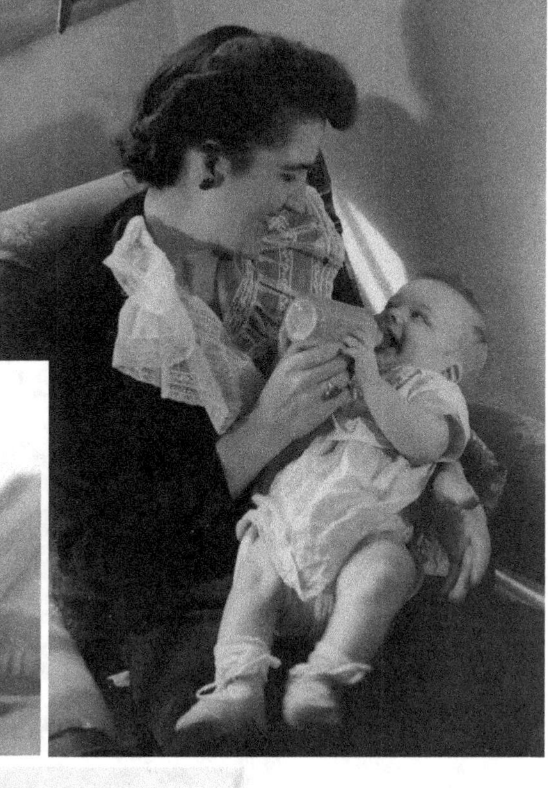

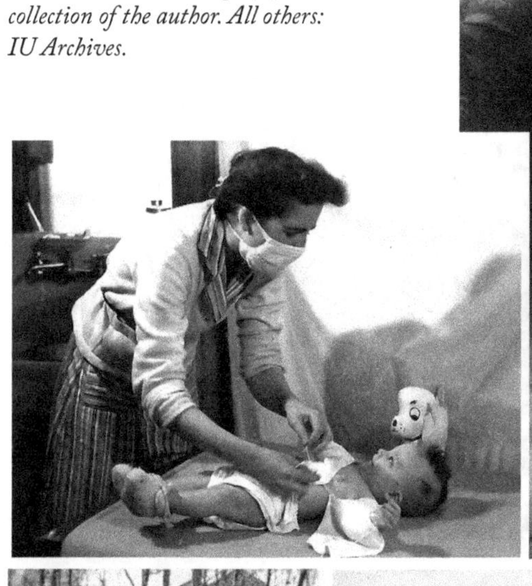

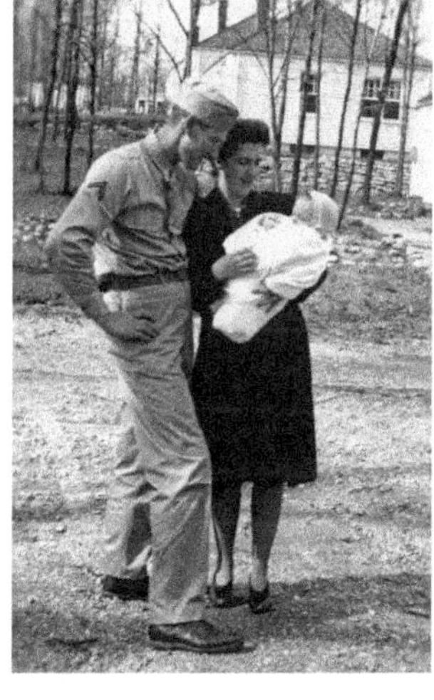

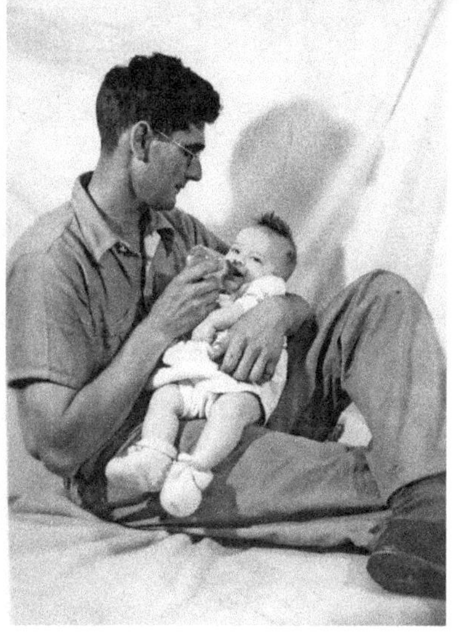

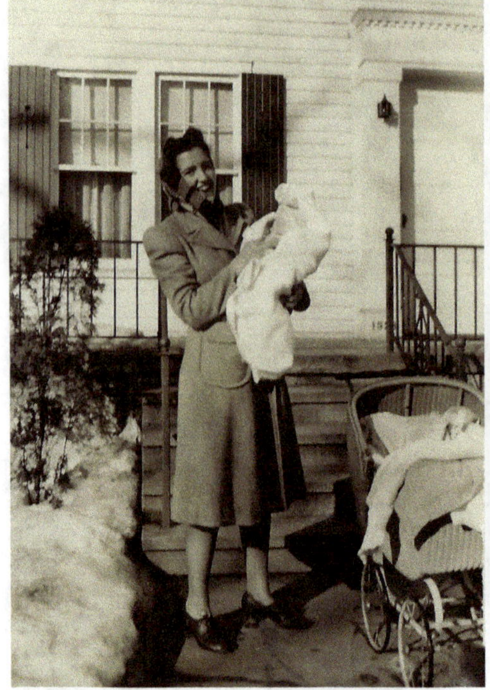

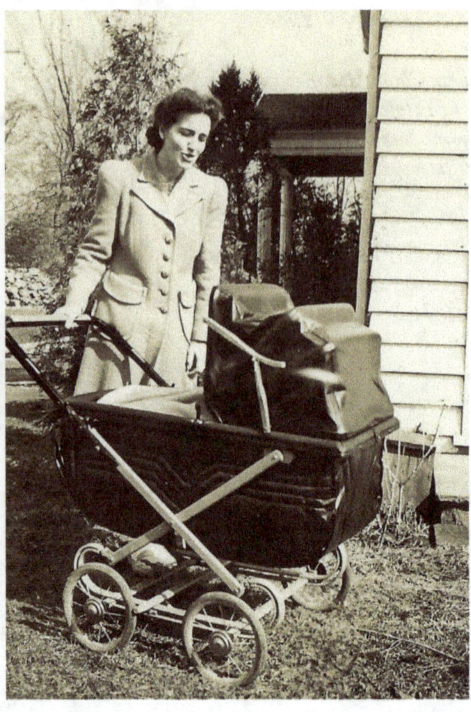

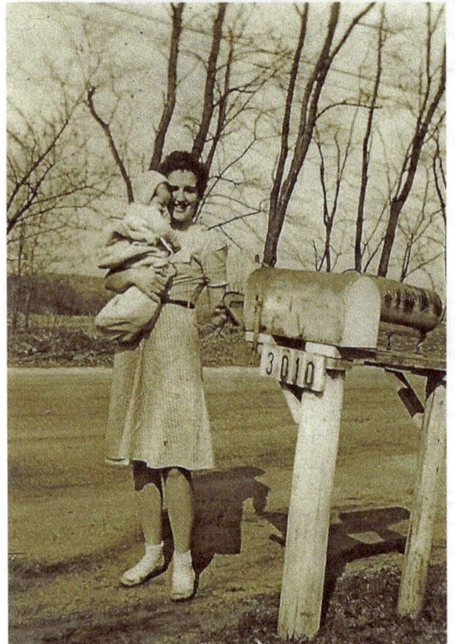

Left: Six weeks old, an outing to "Henrietta's house," Ann Arbor. Unknown photographer.

Right and below: home on Geddes Street in Ann Arbor, while Clarence was home on furlough, May1943.

Photos: CM Flaten. Photos in collection of the author.

Mary felt that raising Kit by herself was too challenging, so she and Clancy decided that she and Kit should move back with her parents in Queens NY during the war years.

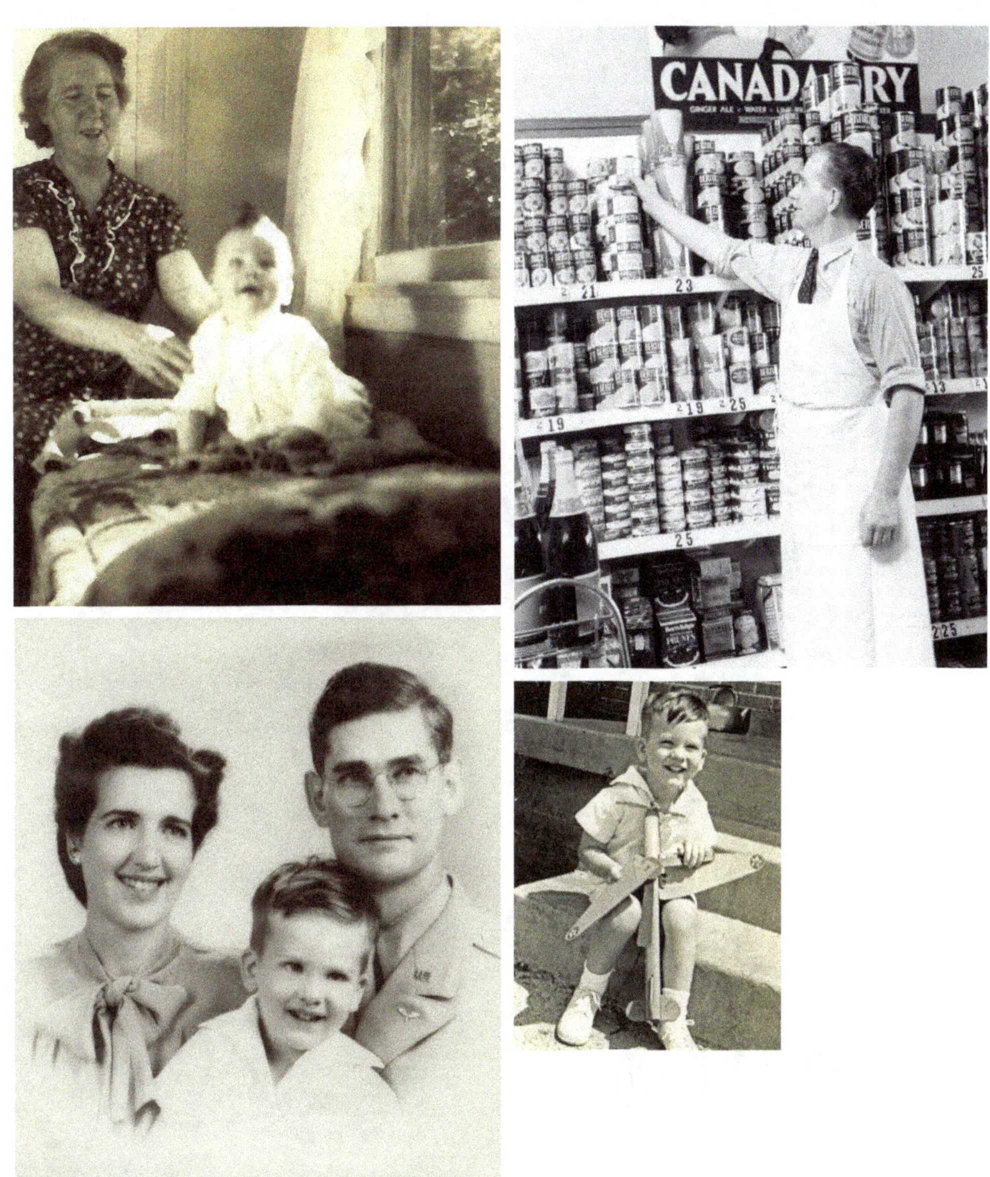

Clockwise from top left. June 1943. Margaret Browne with grandson Kit. Queens NY. Photo: CM Flaten, collection of the author. Luke J. Browne owned a grocery store in Springfield Gardens, Queens NY. Here he is checking inventory. Photo: CM Flaten, IU Archives. Kit plays with a small AAF toy plane. Possibly taken on a visit to a base. By the time the war ended and Clancy's commission ended, Kit was four years old. Photo: CM Flaten, collection of the author. Below left: Mary, Kit and Clarence. Ca. 1944. Photo: Photographer unknown, IU Archives.

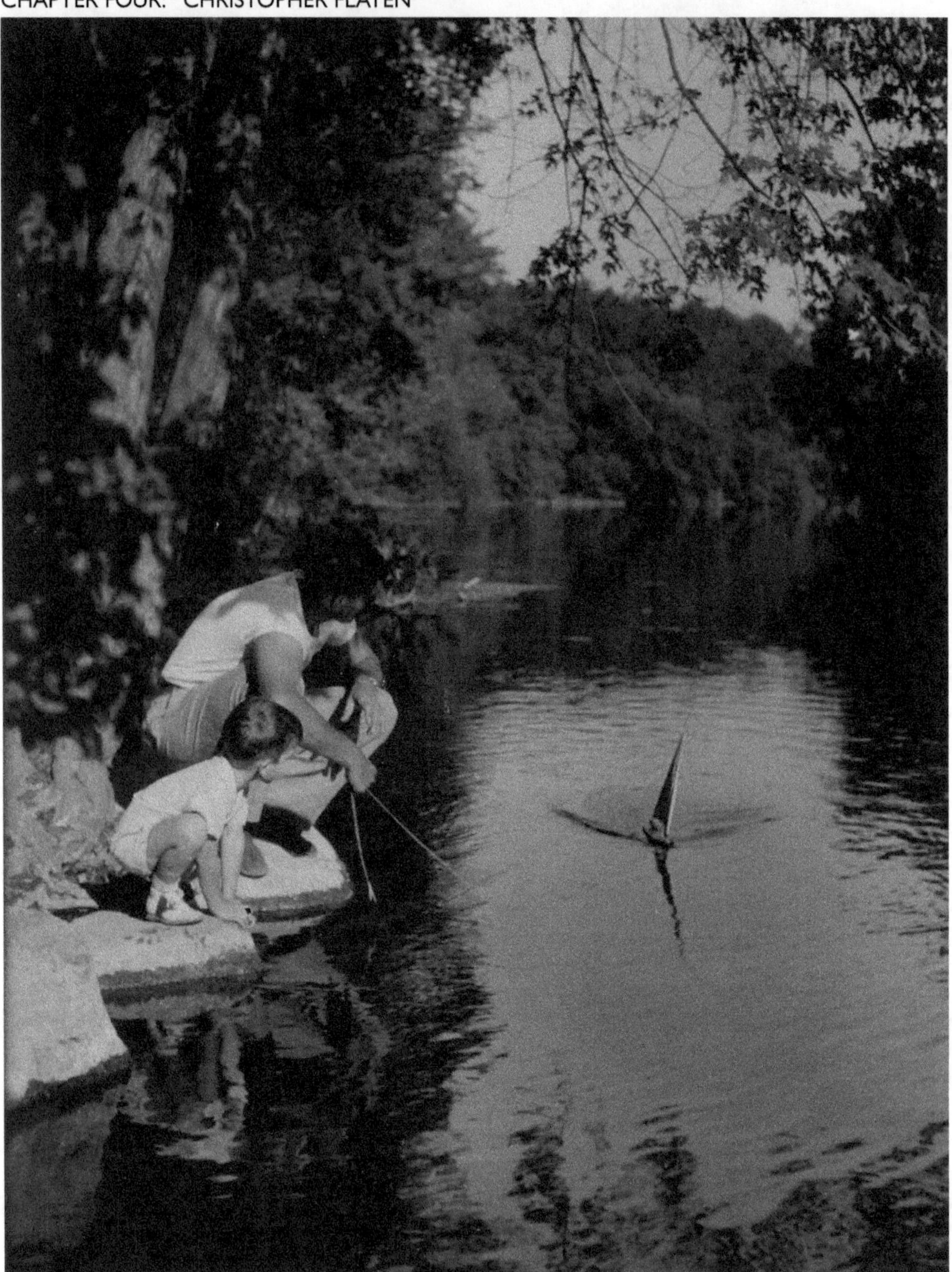

Father and son. Clarence and Kit enjoy nature and the blessings of peace after life returns to normalcy, post WWII, photo taken perhaps in Ann Arbor. Photo: CM Flaten, IU Archives.

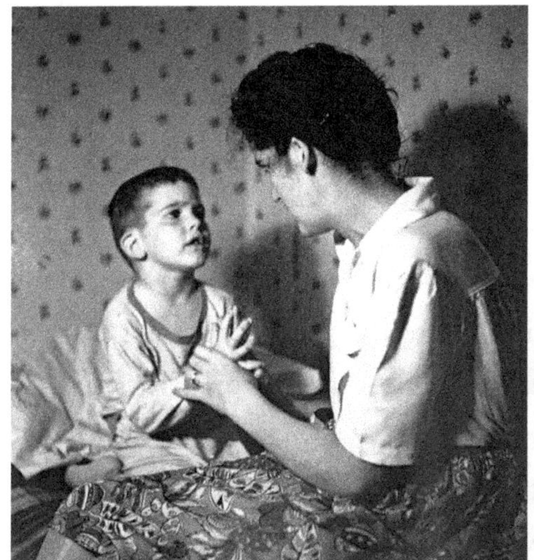

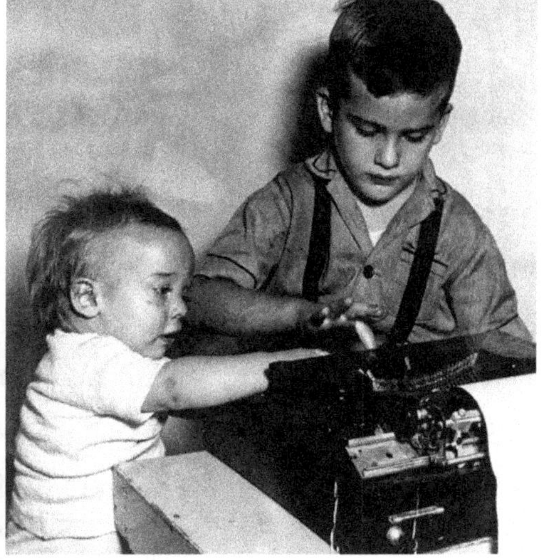

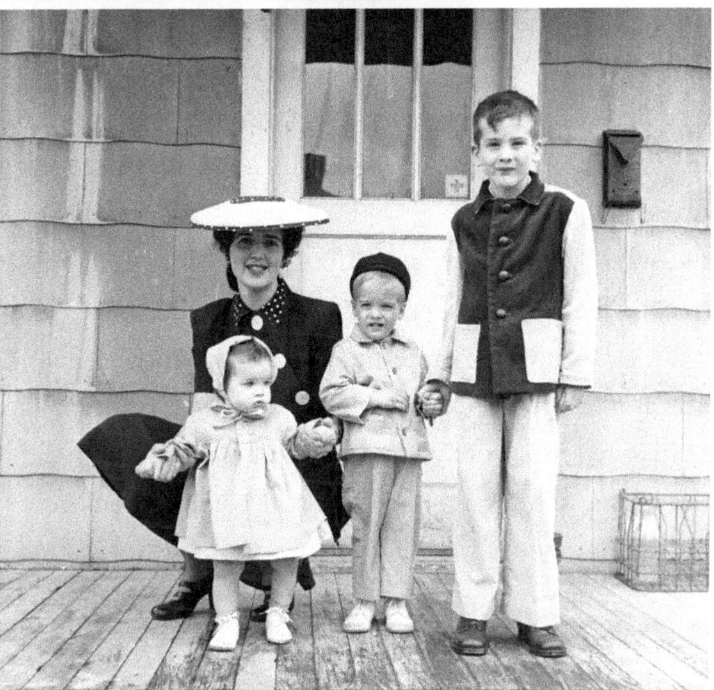

Top left:Kit and Mary pray together.

Top right, Kit shows his brother Larry the typewriter.

Bottom, Mary, Peg, Larry and Kit in front of their home on South Washington Street in Bloomington, Indiana. 1949. Easter Sunday.

Photos: CM Flaten, IU Archives.

later, when Clancy finally finished his service and they returned to Ann Arbor in June 1946, soon to relocate to Bloomington, Indiana, a college town, and a place they truly felt was home.

1947. BLOOMINGTON CHILDHOOD: BIG BROTHER

His childhood began in a simple bungalow on South Washington Street, where he lived from age five to nine. There, as the eldest child, he enjoyed the special attention of his mom and dad. Mom used her skills as a trained English teacher to impart her love of books, and she guided him to the Catholic faith. Dad taught him to study and appreciate nature. One time, Mom bought a parakeet at the downtown Woolworths to liven their home with the sound of birdsong, and while shopping, she bought Kit a small pet turtle. He must have had his love of animals early on, because he was so happy that he kissed the tiny turtle. But it clamped onto his lip, and he went running to Mom, crying, with the small turtle hanging off his lip. Mom often laughed when retelling that story.

The family grew larger (Larry, Peg, Brian, Liz), so they moved from South Washington Street to the farmhouse on Airport Road (and grew even larger: Georgia, Marianne and Tom) and there, in that wonderful place, surrounded by cornfields and temperate skies, our time unfolded together. Kit, who was always tall for his age, thin, wore glasses, and had a quick laugh, did remarkable things with eagerness: he was a young scholar who truly enjoyed learning. He memorized Latin names for birds and animals and insects. He collected exotic animals and had a county-wide reputation for being "the animal guy," the go-to person for critter questions. And he really liked sharing these things with us. Also, he was always a good writer. When he submitted the winning entry for the Monroe County Essay Contest in 1956 while in the 8th grade at St. Charles, he received a letter from the First National Bank

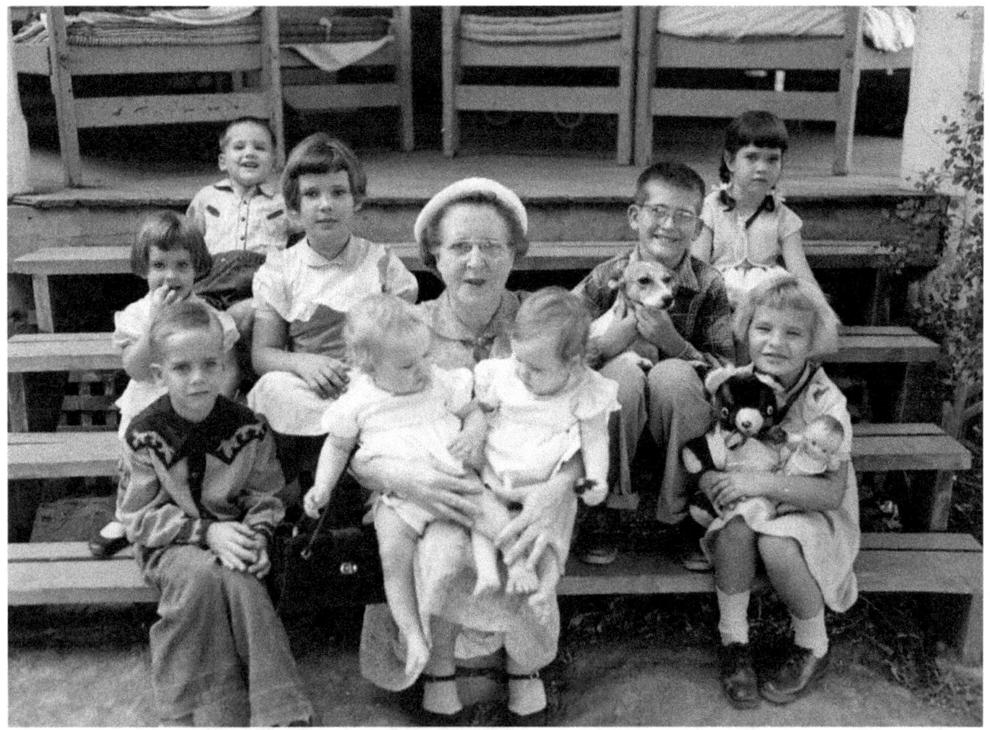

On Airport Road: Grandma Margaret Browne visits with the kids, Spring 1953. The house had not yet been renovated. The kids got to sleep on the front porch on wooden beds. L to R: bottom step, Larry, Grandma Browne holding Georgia and Marianne, and cousin Chrissie Piszczek. Second step, L to R: Liz, cousin Tanya Piszczek, Kit holding dog Sugar. Top step, Brian and Peg.

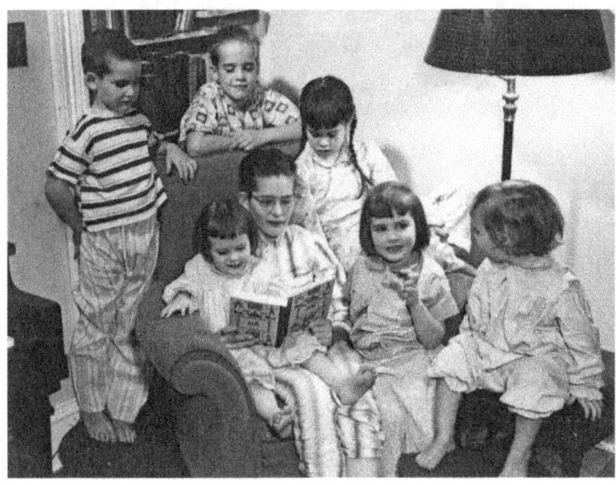

Throughout the years, Clarence sometimes used a book in portraits as an important added element of composition and message. His father, Gunerius, had used the same device in his portrait work.

L to R: Brian, Larry. Seated L to R: Marianne, Kit, Peg, Liz, Georgia. 1954.

Photos: CM Flaten, IU Archives.

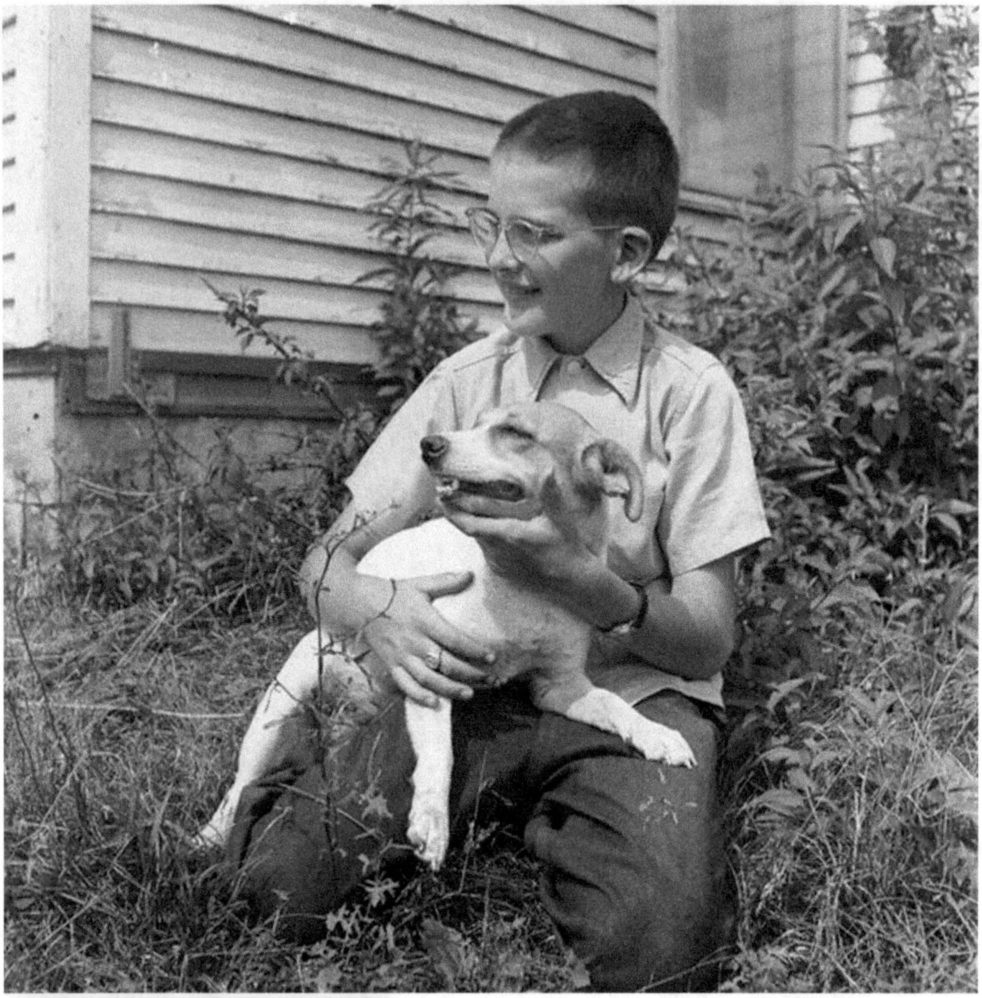

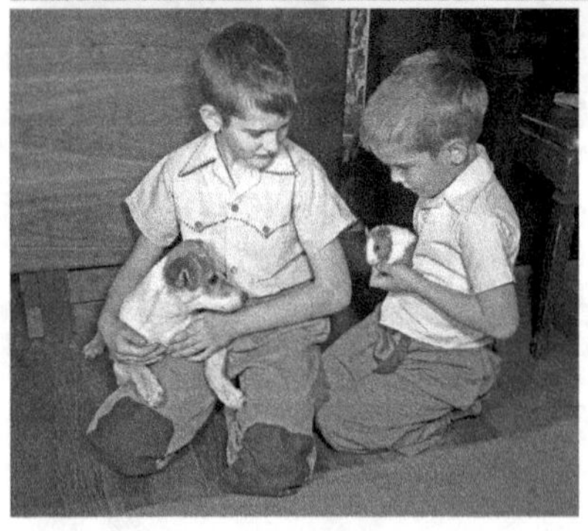

Above: Kit was well-known for his love of animals. Here he is with his dog, Sugar, a bob-tailed terrier. 1952

Left: Kit with Larry, Sugar and a hamster.

Photos: CM Flaten, IU Archives.

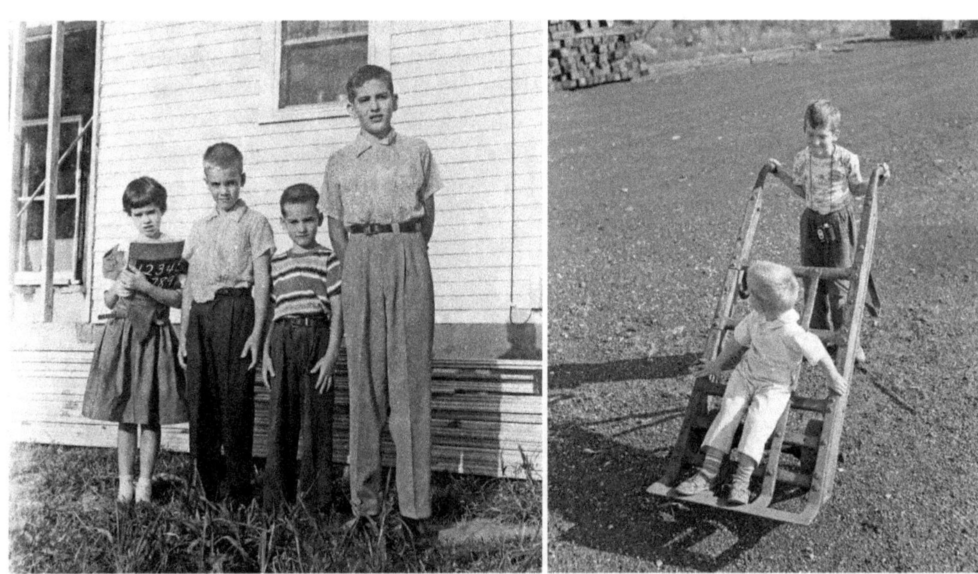

Top left: Ready for school, Peg, Larry, Brian and Kit will get a ride with their father to St. Charles Borromeo school. Ca. 1955. Right: Larry and Kit play with a transport dolly. Below left: Hoosier basketball with a homemade backboard in the backyard. Below right: Grandma Browne holding Liz, and Larry, Brian, Peg and Kit, who was always tall for his age. 1952. Photos: CM Flaten, IU Archives.

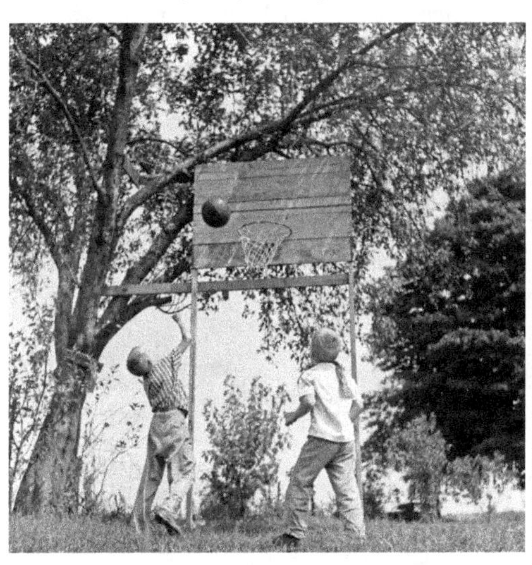

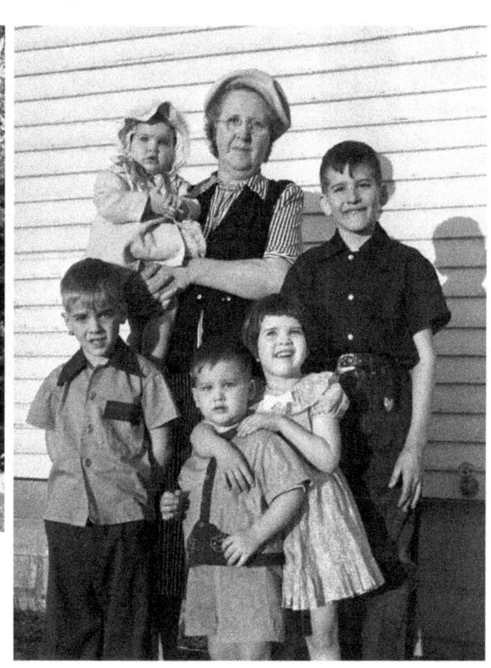

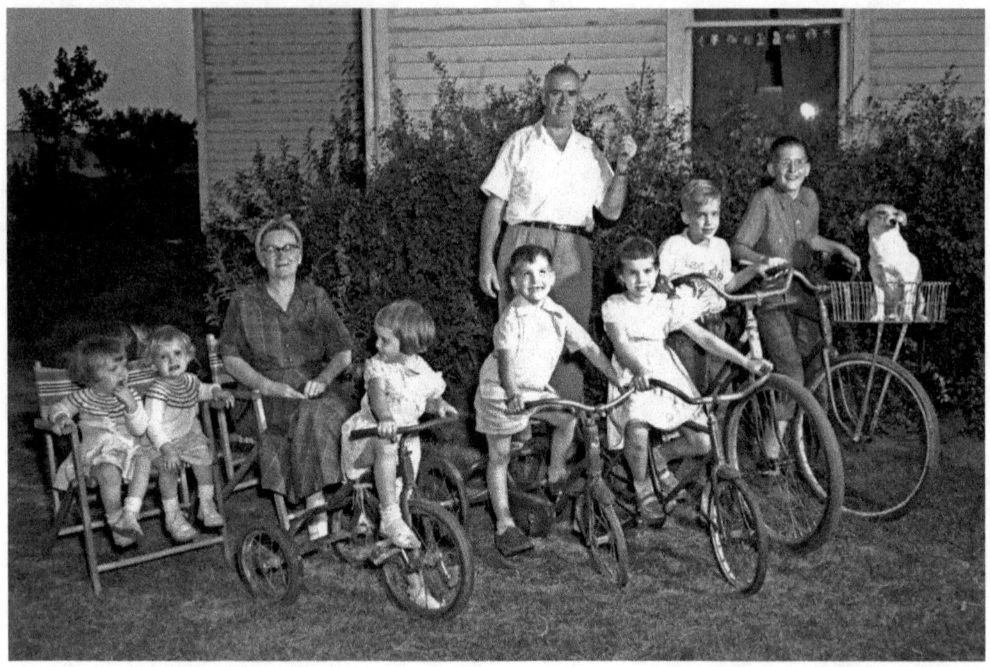

Relatives were frequent visitors. 1954. Johnny and Mamie Waldron from New York drove out to visit. Mamie was Mary's maternal first cousin. Seated in chairs, L to R: Marianne, Georgia and Mamie. Standing, John Waldron. On bikes, Liz, Brian, Peg, Larry and Kit with dog Sugar in basket.
Below: 1951. Kit sits at the dining room table in the dining / playroom. Right: Easter. 1955.
Photos: CM Flaten, IU Archives.

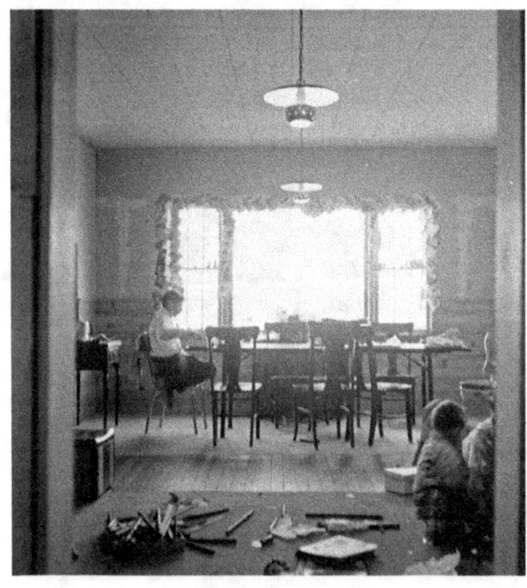

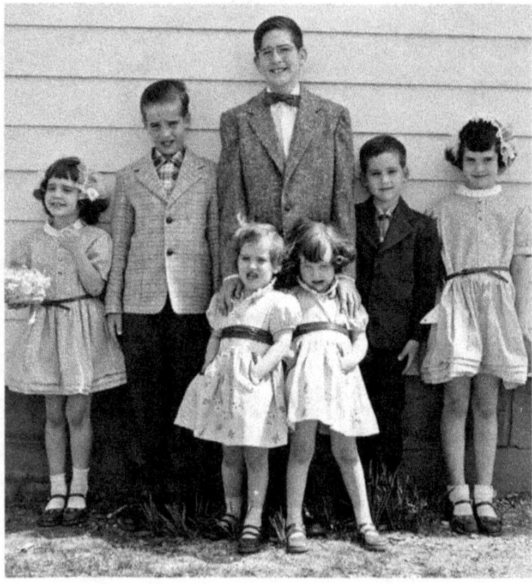

announcing his prize (a tour of the bank). Four years later he wrote a heartfelt, winning poem, "My Father," for a 1960 state-wide Father's Day contest. It was so convincing that it helped to sway a panel to select his dad as "Indiana Father of the Year." The whole family proudly posed for a photo which appeared in the local newspaper, *The Daily Herald-Telephone.*

His aptitude was encouraged by the Sisters of Providence at St. Charles Borromeo Catholic School (the old one at 3rd and Dunn Streets). All of us kids went to St. Charles School and were raised with conservative values which matched the old church of the times. The Catholic faith was not only important to our family, but to Mom it was paramount. Mom wanted Kit to go on to a Catholic high school but since there was none in Bloomington, he continued on to St. Meinrad Seminary in southern Indiana. A July 1956 acceptance letter from the Archdiocese of Indianapolis states: "This letter will confirm the acceptance of your son Christopher as a student for the priesthood of the Archdiocese." It's hard to believe now, but when Kit served as an altar boy at St. Charles church, he would ride his bike all the way into town and back home (six miles each way) to serve early Mass. That was quite a pedal for a young skinny boy!

Even though he received a very good classical education there, he felt no call to the priesthood. In fact, quite the opposite. He graduated in 1960 with a firm distaste of the St. Meinrad experience. I remember him telling me about several incidents where the students were treated very poorly. And Liz remembers hearing Mom cry when Kit broke the news to her that he did not want to go back. Mom took Kit's decision to reject his Catholic tradition personally, but Kit made a major decision when he turned his talents toward academics and a life of science, not faith. He decided to use his intellect to pursue a degree in physics at Indiana University. He joined Sigma Pi Sigma, the only honor society for physics, signed up at the YMCA, and while he

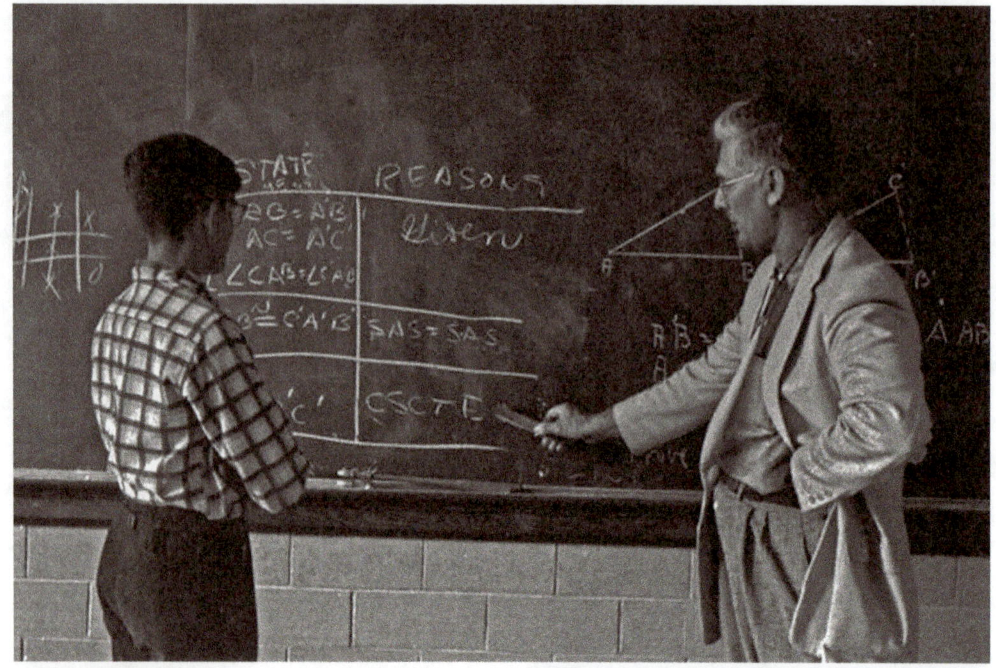

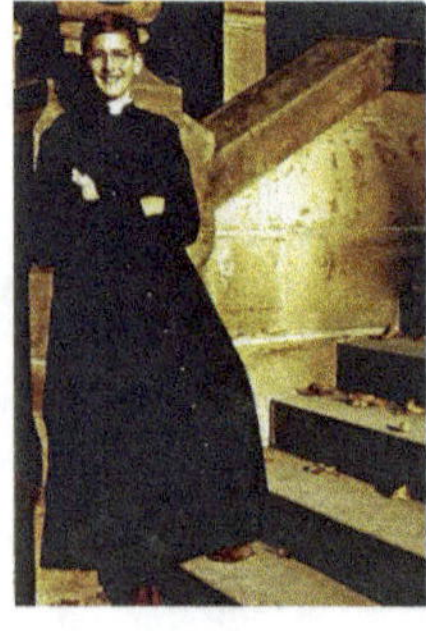

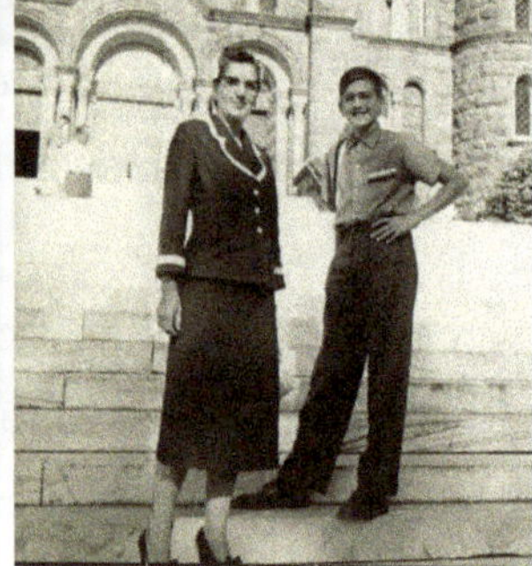

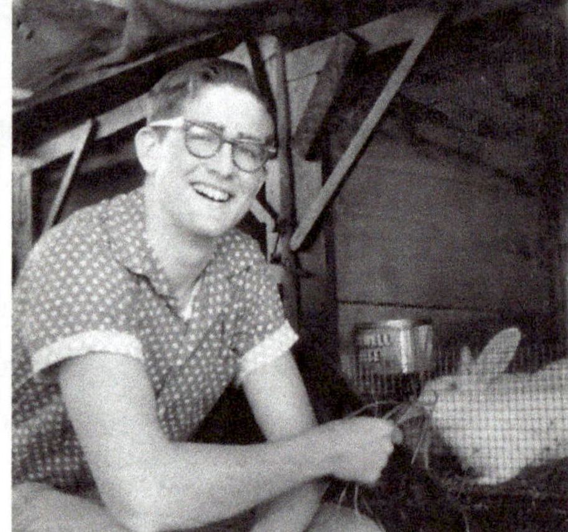

Kit went to high school at St. Meinrad Seminary. Top: Clancy and Kit work out a problem at the board during a visit to St. Meinrad. Ca. 1958. Left: Young seminarian Kit in his cassock. 1956. Mary and Kit in front of the St. Meinrad Archabbey Church. 1956. Photos: CM Flaten, IU Archives.

Right: Kit feeding a rabbit, photo taken his senior year for a 'Campus Chatter' article. 1960. Photo: photographer: J. McKinney, S. Downing, or R. Easton. Collection of the author.

attended I.U., came back to live with us on Airport Road.

We were thrilled to have him home again. This meant we could still play music together. We had our family orchestra and we also played folk music. Kit was very drawn to music. He had studied violin at St. Charles and sometimes I would ask him to play my violin tunes for me so that I could hear and imitate the tune while I was learning to read music. Later, he picked up the guitar, mandolin, and banjo, and he loved to sing. His childhood had been our childhood but when he got older, he was our mentor. He was such a very caring and loving person that we each remember him in our own ways with these special stories.

LARRY REMEMBERS

One weekend evening, Bucky and Eddy Crohn and myself and Greg Chitwood were together. Greg knew somebody at Lake Lemon that had a cabin and so we went out there just to spend the night. There was a railroad trestle not too far away, about 20 feet in the air, and there was a hawk that came and landed. It was eating something on the railroad track. Bucky said, "Let's see if we can catch it!" We took a blanket out, and that thing took off and then it came back and continued eating something on the tracks. Bucky went up to it and threw this blanket over it and picked it up! We walked back down to the cabin. There was a picnic table in the cabin, not much other furniture in it, and we let it out and it hopped up on this picnic table and Bucky found a dead snake outside for it, and it gobbled the snake up.

We decided, since nobody knew what to do with it, we would take it back to Kit. That's what everybody would say because Kit knew what to do with all these kind of things. Greg Chitwood was driving a Henry J, and Bucky put the blanket on this thing again. Greg Chitwood was driving, Eddie Crohn was next to him in the front, and Bucky was in the back holding the hawk, and I was in the back seat with Bucky. Bucky had this blanket around this hawk and he was smoking a cigarette and we were driving down the road when suddenly this hawk snipped that cigarette right off of his face! Bucky got scared and the hawk got loose and jumped up onto the back of the front seat. We were all too scared to grab it, so it rode all the way home on the back of the front seat. And as we went around corners, the hawk would lean to the right and left. When we got it home to Kit, he was able to coax the thing out. Mom even made a little hood for it, and it would fly and come back to Kit. The word got out around the neighborhood and some man came to claim it. It turned out that it was a trained hawk. Kit was pretty amazing.

Kit had this catalog. You could order any kind of reptile or exotic animal you could think of. If you wanted to order a hippopotamus, you could send your check in and about two or three weeks later, the truck backed up to your door and you had a hippopotamus!

He ordered something. I don't know what it was, but he was waiting for several weeks for this thing to come in. Meanwhile, in his bedroom, he built a large glass box for the thing. It was really elaborate. It had four glass sides and was about the size of a really large aquarium, and he put a twig and a little dish in it. Finally, this package arrived one day and he was really excited about it. I was up there in the bedroom with him. He took the top off the box and this thing—whatever it was—jumped out of that box from here to the table. I practically had a heart attack. This little thing stood up on its hind legs like a little tyrannosaurus rex, and Kit just went over and grabbed it by the neck. It was amazing. He had no fear. Later, he bought a gecko and an axolotl.

PEG REMEMBERS

On Airport Road, one year we actually got a pig, which we kept it in the chicken coop – fattened it up and had it butchered the next year. We also

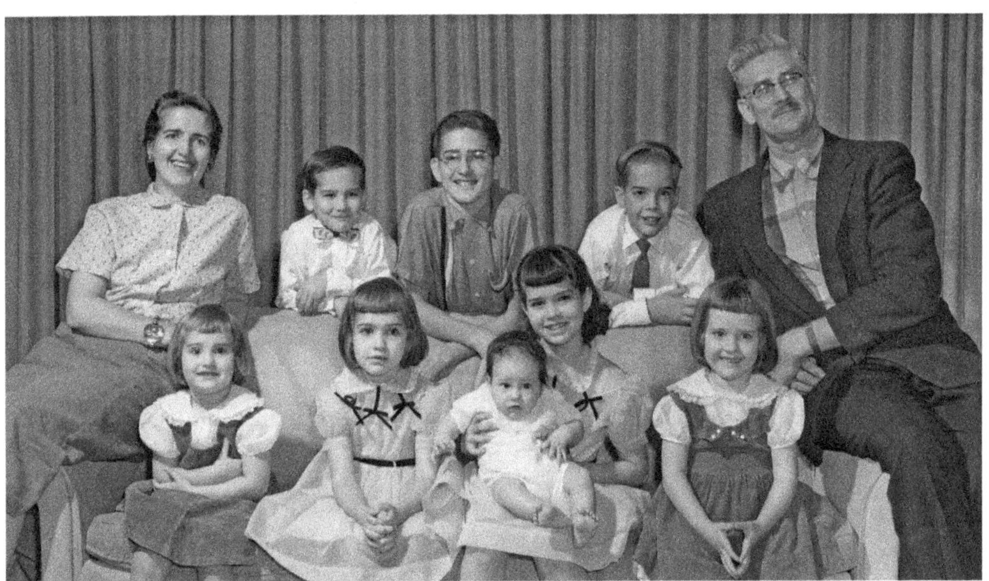

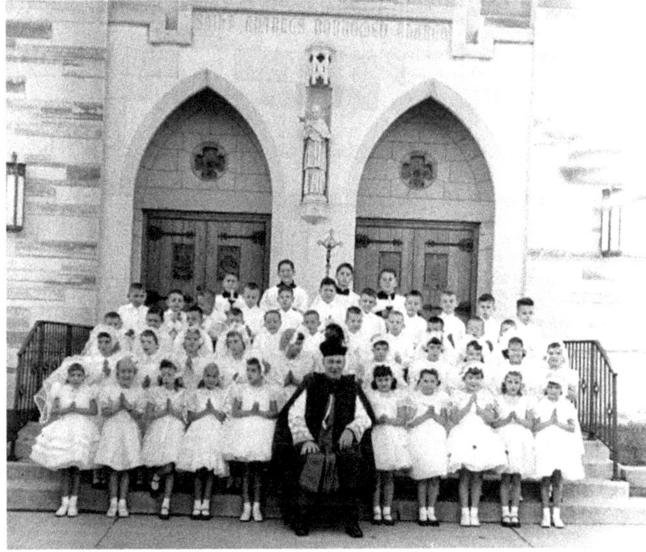

Flaten family portrait. 1956. Front row: L to R: Georgia, Liz, Tom, Peg, Marianne. Back row L to R: Mary, Brian, Kit, Larry, Clarence. Photo: CM Flaten, IU Archives.

First Communion at the "new" St. Charles Borromeo Catholic Church. 1955. The church was dedicated in 1952.

Kit, as altar boy, is in the back row, second from left. His sister Peg is in the second row, sixth from the left. Monsignor Kilfoil, front center. Kilfoil had been Monsignor at St. Charles since 1938. Kilfoil was from Vincennes, IN and a graduate of St. Meinrad.

Photo: unknown photographer. IU Archives.

used that chicken coop occasionally to play as if that was our "laboratory" and we probably got this from Kit who was into entomology in 4-H. Kit went many times to the State Fair with his entomology collections – with every bug perfectly pinned and labeled in the Latin and vernacular names. But our amateur attempts to be entomologists and scientists in a chicken coop laboratory involved catching lightning bugs or moths or butterflies or lady bugs, and experimenting with them in different environments. Would they prefer to eat grass? Or would they prefer to eat leaves? What happens if you give them no air? What happens if you give them two holes of air in the top?

Kit took me with him once when he was hunting for butterflies and dragonflies. He had a butterfly net and taught me how to use it, and helped me get over my squeamishness about touching insects. Besides being so interested in insects and exotic animals, he was a born teacher. There was a family that lived down the road from us, near the airport, in what was practically a shanty. The parents didn't force their four children to go to school. The oldest, Jimmy, who was just a bit younger than Kit, could barely read, and so Kit took it upon himself to teach him. Later we learned that Jimmy named his first child Chris, after Kit.

BRIAN REMEMBERS

In the Fall of 1970 while I was stationed in Vallejo, CA going through NIOTC, Navel Inshore Operations Training, in preparation for being sent to Vietnam, I was sent to Whidbey Island, WA near Seattle for survival training. This was very close to Seattle where Kit was living at that time and I wanted to get a chance to meet his wife Ellen and see my brother before I was sent to Vietnam. I flew to Seattle ahead of the start of the training and had a chance to spend two days with Kit and Ellen. We skied on Mt. Rainier, skipped rocks in Puget Sound, and went bar hopping with Ellen and several of Kit's Seattle friends. At the time I was only 20 and the legal drinking age in Washington was 21, so Kit got one of his friends to loan me his ID so I could get into the various bars. This was probably the first time I had ever spent any time one on one with my older brother and I got to see the really fun side of him versus the smart and studious side that I was so used to seeing growing up in Indiana.

In July or August of the summer of 1971, I flew back to Santa Barbara from Vietnam on R&R. This was the first time I was able to see my new wife Judy in over six months and I also got to see Kit who flew down to Santa Barbara from Seattle to see us. We had a chance to spend two days visiting and during that time we took Kit to the beach at El Capitan. We bought some cheap paper kites and lots of string and would let one kite out and then tie on another and so on. I think we had them flying so high that the airlines had to go around them. We laughed so hard that day in the sun and surf. Later that night, Judy and I took Kit to dinner at Cold Springs Tavern, an old stage coach stop over on San Marcos pass. It's a very rustic and beautiful site that we still go to when we are in California. I was so grateful to see some of my family again after being gone for those first six months in Vietnam, and again got to see the really fun and funny side of my big brother. This was the last time I got to talk with and see Kit before he was killed in the accident in Isle Vista, California.

It always seemed so strange to me how Kit ended up in Santa Barbara at UCSB teaching. This was the area that I met Judy and I had traveled the road he was killed on many times. I proposed to Judy on the Goleta Beach which overlooks the campus that Kit taught at. When we are in California, I remember those fun times I had the chance to have with my big brother. I miss him.

LIZ REMEMBERS

Kit was a tall, dark, handsome, tussle-haired teen, nerdy, smart and a lover of music and nature. I wish I had gotten to know him better. First, Kit was a nature lover. I remember walking into his room at the top of the stairs in my family's farmhouse in the country, and seeing cages filled with various reptiles, lizards and bugs. He even had a falcon in there. And of course, there is the infamous family story about the time Kit left for a camp counselor job on the East Coast. As he got into the car, he informed Mom that his snake had gotten loose and was somewhere upstairs. This caused quite a bit of fear in the household until the snake was discovered sleeping in the linen closet.

Secondly, Kit loved music. He learned to play guitar and I remember him playing the music of the Kingston Trio. One favorite was "Tom Dooley." I can still remember those tragic words and sweet melody.

Thirdly, Kit was going to be a priest. He attended St. Meinrad Seminary when he was in high school. The family visited him one beautiful Easter weekend (the pictures are quite lovely and everyone looks happy). However, I remember lying in my upstairs bedroom and listening to Mom sobbing as he told her that he was quitting the seminary. I always wondered what happened to change his mind. My family was not big on sharing emotional details of our lives.

We never interacted much, but I admired him as a little kid sister would. He became quite the family hero one summer. All the kids in the family were saving to buy a summer pass to Bryan Park Swimming Pool. We put our pennies, dimes, and quarters into a plastic duck and counted it religiously. However, we were still short when swim season was about to start. Kit came home from his job and put the final dollars in that we needed. Elation!! And we used that pass a lot. Our parents would drop us off at the pool in the morning and pick us up in the late afternoon. Who needed babysitters? Mom got herself a nice, well-deserved break.

Lastly, Kit was smart—very smart. He got his doctorate in physics smart. And I remember Mom reading us letters that he sent from Seattle, where he got his degree. He was pretty broke and miserable from all the rain. But then he got a job in Santa Barbara, California at the university there. This is where his story gets sad. He had finally gotten married when he was finishing his PhD. I never met his wife, Ellen, or her little daughter. But I remember that Mom and Dad made the trip to Seattle for the wedding. More happy photos. Then he got divorced. I never found out what happened. Again, my family didn't communicate such things. My last memory of Kit was when he came home after his divorce. I kick myself every time I think of this. We were sitting in the kitchen. Kit looked sad and honestly, I think he wanted to talk. But I didn't know how to talk to him. It was many years later that I allowed myself the luxury of my feelings. That's a different story. But I wish, I wish I had talked to him and told him that it was okay. We didn't care if he got married and divorced twenty times. He was still our brother and we loved and were proud of him. If he were sitting with me right now, I would tell him that.

GEORGIA REMEMBERS

My first memory of him was a lasting one. On a pleasant evening in June 1957, when I was five years old, as the sun was setting on another day of play in the yard, we were surprised to see the Hickmans, a big Catholic family from the parish, pull up in the driveway for a visit. Quickly, there were more children in the house and backyard. Out back, we had a sandbox and I decided to join the kids there. I often spent the day barefoot as I ran outside, then inside, then back out, running around the yard, climbing trees. As I was running through the damp grass to the sandbox I felt a sharp, slicing pain on the bottom of my right foot. I stopped and turned to walk to the house in order to use the bathroom. I went in through the back porch and passed through the old farmhouse kitchen on my way towards the downstairs bathroom. Once I sat down on the toilet, I looked at the bottom of my foot which was filthy from running around barefoot all day. When I looked at the ball of my foot all I could see was blackness, and then a thin, long opened line, a red line with white tissue surrounding it. I stared hard at it trying to understand. I did not feel pain, just puzzlement, and just as I sat staring at the cut, wondering what to do, Kit walked into the bathroom asking me what was wrong. He said he had seen a trail of blood on the floor and followed it into the bathroom. He looked at my foot and asked me what had happened, but I was only able to give a brief reply not knowing how the cut happened.

Kit left to find the cause of the cut. It turned out to be a sickle, a hand-held curved cutting tool which someone had left in the grass. After I got stitches the next day, Kit carried me everywhere, and I remember feeling very special. I was not allowed to run about and had to be carried most places. Kit took on the role of protector, and later in life, would reach out to me in with concern and kindness, a connection which began the night I stepped on the sickle. He was a good brother, one I felt I could confide in.

He loved animals. Sugar was "Kit's dog." She was a bobtailed short-haired terrier. One time, when she was nursing her latest litter, Kit added an orphaned baby bunny he had found in the field to her mix. Sugar nursed it, too, and as it grew bigger and bigger it finally began to hop away. Sugar would patiently leave her box, gather her errant "pup" in her mouth and bring it back to her litter. As the rabbit grew, back and forth and back and forth they went, but Sugar finally gave up.

Another animal project involved fish. Our Airport Road yard had many old flowering shrubs, the largest of which was an overgrown lilac bush. (Mom was fond of romantically quoting the first line of Whitman's poem,

"When lilacs last in the dooryard bloom'd ..." whenever we spoke of the lilac bush, though she always added that this poem was really about the Civil War.) Underneath the lilac bush Kit decided to build a fishpond from concrete, one of his endlessly enthusiastic projects, and once the concrete set he painted it aqua, and he stocked it with goldfish and lily pads. Such exotic things we had never seen out in the country. We were amazed by Kit's designs. One day, Kit cleaned the pond, but the fish were accidently sucked into the drainpipe which emptied onto Airport Road, and they spilled out the other end of the pipe all googly-eyed and dead. Even that amazed us!

Catholicism was an important part of our lives. I vowed to become a nun and used to spend hours with my friend Isabelle Murphy looking at a special book of detailed illustrations of the various orders showing the extremely distinctive habit each order wore. Based on costume alone, we tried to wisely choose how we wished to look for the rest of our lives, lives of obedience. I was fully prepared to embrace the idea of dedicating my life to an order (especially the one with the particularly fun wimple) until I mentioned it to Kit. "Why would you want to throw your life away like that?" he exclaimed. He told me that even though he had received good Catholic instruction at St. Meinrad, he disliked the blind obedience part. In the end, this was not a calling for either of us. I had complete trust in his judgment.

Since we grew up right next door to the County Fairgrounds, we hung around there all day long when the Fair came around every August. The only money I had to spend was lost money that I would find in the grass. Having no cash was a challenge. But the lure of the Bumper Car pavilion was mighty, so one time, as I watched in envy for quite a while on the side, I decided that once the ride was over and the drivers were leaving, I would slip in, unnoticed, through the EXIT area, and slide into a small car, telling the operator that I had decided to stay "for another ride." My plan worked, and the owner allowed me the free ride! How sneaky I thought I was! But to my surprise, when I got home, Kit laughingly teased me about stealing the ride, as he had been on the sideline all the while, watching my charade. It was a funny joke between us, and he never made me feel guilty about it. This is the best brother, I thought!

MARIANNE REMEMBERS

I must have been about four years old. I decided to touch the stove after Mom turned it off. I was curious to know "is it still hot when you turn it off?" The bright reddish-orange-red glow of the stove burner fascinated me when it was on. But to me, off meant off. I immediately heard a sizzle and my fingertip turned light brown. It hurt and I was scared. I ran upstairs to hide. As I lay in my bed crying, Kit came into the room. He must have noticed my quick exit. "Marianne, what's the matter?" he asked in a concerned voice. I was afraid that I had done something bad and would be punished. "Go away!" I demanded, which in hindsight I regret. Kit had a huge heart and was such a caring person—even with his siblings. Being the oldest of eight, he could have grown very weary of his little brothers and sisters at any time along the way. But ignoring me in this moment was not in his makeup.

Mom came upstairs—perhaps after hearing "from someone" that I was in distress. After much reluctance, she convinced me to come downstairs. Sitting in Mom's lap surrounded by my siblings watching with hushed concern, I showed her my finger. Kit immediately made a cold compress with ice and a washrag. After Mom wrapped the compress around my finger, she asked me what had happened. Convinced that I would get into trouble, I pointed to a big wooden box that Dad had made for our toys. I told her that a spider bit my finger when I was playing in the toy closet under the stairs. Kit and Mom were probably the only two in the room who could tell that I had fabricated this story. Yet everyone seemed to believe me. There was no laughter or teasing from my siblings, and no reprimanding from Mom. By bedtime when the drama was over and all was quiet, I felt safe enough to confess to Mom what had really happened. To this day, I am grateful that Mom and Kit responded to this incident with compassion and calm. There was no need for hysteria. I had learned my lesson and that was what mattered.

TOM REMEMBERS

For the majority of my time growing up, he wasn't there. He was either in the seminary, in college, or in Seattle earning his doctorate in physics. I mean, the dude was intelligent, talented, witty, and everyone who knew him loved him deeply. OK—high bar set for Little Tom from the start, for sure.

Like my dad Clancy Flaten, my brother Kit Flaten was a larger-than-life hero to me. I remember particularly the year Kit was home for Christmas during my junior year in high school. He gave me a very cool leather cap as a gift. And dad bought me my first "record player," but it didn't work and the tone arm just scooted across the record with no sound. Bummer? Not so with my hero brother. We set out during that holiday week to return the faulty player, and we found a quite suitable replacement. I still remember that new stereo with AM/FM radio and push-button functions (kind of like the old car radios with a dial that would light up when powered on.) The speakers and sound were far superior to anything I'd ever owned. Kit helped me buy hardware, and he soldered speaker wire extensions to mount the speakers in the corners of my bedroom at ceiling level. After he'd gone back to Seattle after the holidays, I'd spend countless hours in my bedroom listening to whatever LPs I could get my hands on (Long Playing record albums - 33 & 1/3 RPMs, as opposed to the Single Play 45 RPMs we'd been used to listening to as kids). Some of my favorites were Eat a Peach (Allman Brothers), the Carpenters, Carole King (Tapestry) and Santana (Santana!). As I evolved into rock music, I listened to Grand Funk, Black Sabbath, Deep Purple, and anything with loud guitars and drums!

Summer came, and I loaded up my guitar, record player and albums and headed to Colorado with mom and dad. Dad was working at University of Colorado in Boulder while we stayed at a condo/apartment. We stopped in Missouri on the way out to visit with the Funks, longtime friends of mom and dad. Their son, same age as Kit, was not living at home at the time, but his bedroom stereo was there and it was awesome! While the adults reminisced upstairs, I brought in some of my favorite albums, turned the stereo on and kicked back. It was a really nice stereo, the nicest I'd ever experienced.

By the time we got to Boulder and settled in, I had my stereo (the one Kit helped me get and assemble) all set up and I was jamming. There were other teenagers from families there for the summer. We looked forward to Kit's arrival that summer in July.

1960-64. COLLEGE YEARS AT INDIANA UNIVERSITY | SUMMERS AT CAMP GREYLOCK

Kit enrolled as a freshman at Indiana University in 1960 and continued to live at home. Since tuition was not a benefit offered to children of faculty, he needed to earn his tuition. So, when he was offered a job as a summer camp counselor (1962) at Camp Greylock ("A summer camp for boys in the heart of the Berkshires") in Becket, Massachusetts, he enthusiastically accepted. We were very impressed with his new job "out East" at a place where he would be playing touch football with the "Kennedy kids" and their privileged peers. This adventure would put him in touch with a wide world and he could bring stories home, first-hand accounts. Distance was no problem. To get there, Mom and Dad drove him into Bloomington and from there he hitchhiked all the way to Kalamazoo, Michigan to meet another counselor friend. From

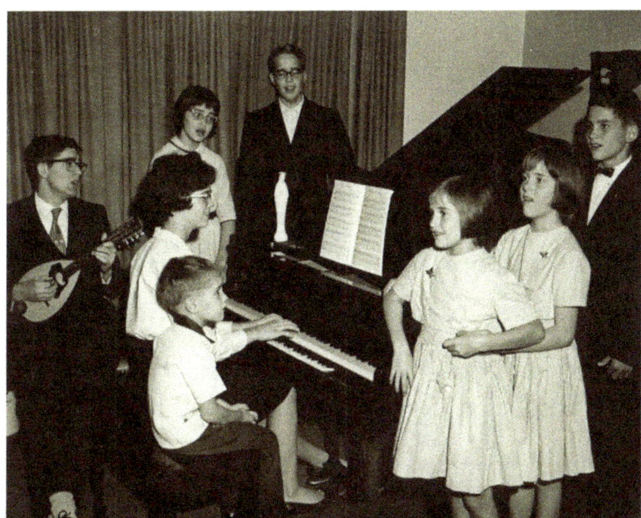

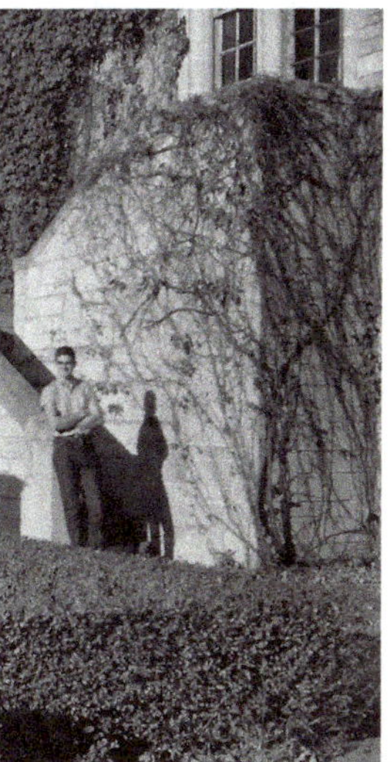

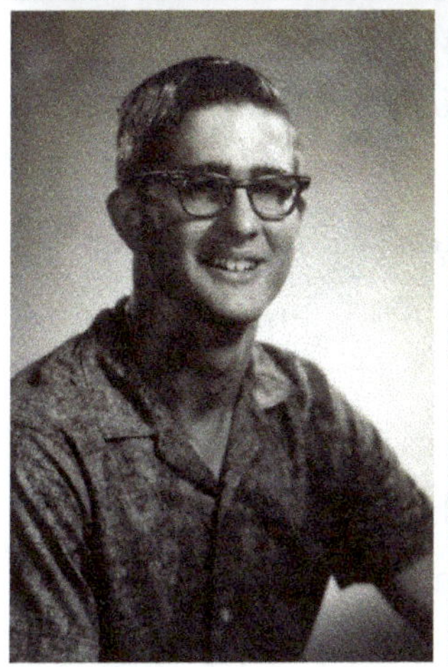

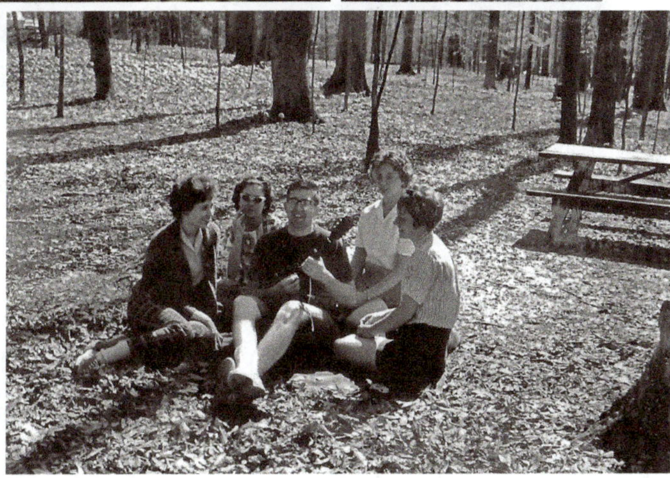

Top left: The Flatens enjoy making music together. Kit introduced us to the sound of the mandolin. Ca. 1961. At piano: Peg and Tom. Front row, L to R: Georgia, Marianne and Brian. Back row, L to R: Kit, Liz and Larry. Photo: CM Flaten, IU Archives.

Top right: photo taken by "Dave" of Kit perhaps outside of Swain Hall or the IU Memorial Union. Ca. 1961. Photo: Collection of the author.

Below left: Kit's portrait. 1963. Photo: Collection of the author.

Below right: Kit's caption: "Surrounded by beautiful girls, as usual. "Music hath charms... ." Karen, Ellen, Kit, Sally, Mia, Spring 1963. Picnic at Shades before dance at Wabash." Photo: unknown photographer, Collection of the author.

there, onward to Massachusetts.

Once he got there, he wrote marvelous letters back home with reports. The first few days of camp before the campers got here were fairly relaxed—the counselors spent time cleaning up the camp area and then swam and relaxed. But reality set in the day the campers got there. He said unpacking was unbelievably frantic. Over-solicitous parents helped unpack their kid's trunk while the kid obviously wanted his parents to get lost, a fact which the mothers just couldn't accept. It rained almost every day and the damp campers got restless. He made up special bunk challenges to push them. But he couldn't complain about the food, because, as he said, it was really delicious and plenty of it. And at night they had a campfire, sang songs. I even learned a new one for the occasion—*Puff, the Magic Dragon*, he wrote.

He said the worst part was cleaning up the bunk in the mornings. He said that since these kids were used to maids doing all the work, he had to devise a new system in which every kid (including himself) got a new name every day as dictated by a chart he cleverly drew up: (Superman, Perry White, Green Arrow etc.) and on the wall was another chart which told what jobs each individual Comic Book character must do such as sweeping, checking cubbies (Cubby Checker—get it?) and dusting bedrails. So far, the new system has worked well, he said, and I have my fingers crossed for the future.

His days on Airport Road had prepared him to lead a charge of youngsters. He was a frequent scout-ranger on chilly overnight hikes to Borden reservoir. Sometimes a "lazy day" was declared in camp. He wrote:

> "Lazy day means that everyone sleeps an hour and a half later and is served breakfast in bed. However, the kids didn't get much activity yesterday and as a result weren't too keen on the idea of staying in bed so I spent most of my supposedly lazy time yelling shut up or lie down at them. Then when the breakfast was brought to the bunk they got

so excited that they started to jump on their beds like trampolines. After a severe tongue-lashing by me, one of my boys demonstrated how effectively my speech had impressed him by asking me if I had seen him do the back flip and did I want him to perform it again. After the breakfast in bed we had a counselor basketball game in which I played every minute and got thoroughly pooped.

My kids were all mad at me because they had all bet candy bars on my team and had all lost. After that it was a lunch cookout for three of our bunks. The accepted rule at cookouts is that the counselor does all the cooking and eats what is left of the leftovers. At the cookout we had hamburgers and potato chips. So what did we have for supper this evening? You guessed it, Hamburgers and chips. In addition today was the day we had to (1) send out our dirty laundry, (2) put away our clean laundry, (3) put clean linen on our beds, (4) write home to parents, and as the final topper of the day the evening activity was bunk choice where the bunks all have activities with their respective counselors. By the time taps blew at 9:00 I barely had the guts to kiss them good night before taking a nice warm shower and settling down in the bunk bathroom, the only place within miles that is light enough and quiet enough to type in, which is where I sitting down at this moment writing this letter."

When he returned to I.U. in the fall he joined the Folk Song Club. The next summer of 1963 before he left for Camp, he purchased a banjo from Tom Pickett's Music Store in Bloomington. Ready to make more music! As he continued another successful year at Camp, he sent home more reports:

"I have taken out two overnite hikes already and the third would have been tonite except that it rained all day. It is becoming quite apparent that I have a rather poor bunk of kids. They all are worse than average (every Scout counselor has told me so) and most of them very much so. I have to pull out of 15 fights a day. Today Mark socked another kid in the stomach with a broom. There are two other kids: they just won't shut up at night. Then there is Frank who hasn't eaten a thing (honest) but bread, butter & water since the beginning of camp. Tom never comes down out of the clouds and wears glasses. Peter is very selfish, even for a child. Things are not all bad but I was certainly discouraged for the first few days. The first day we achieved the lowest mark in an inspection ever recorded at Greylock, a 2.8 out of a possible 5.0."

But he spent his weekends having a blast, going to see Tom Paxton, Tom Lehrer, and the Limeliters. When he returned to his studies at Indiana University, he had the cool factor, and he confided to us of his visits to a hangout in Bloomington called "The Wreck of the Hesperus" where coffee was served to beatniks. We listened to him with awe as we sat around our big dining room table.

In the summer of 1964, there was to be no hitchhiking to Camp Greylock because that June, he bought a snazzy, sea blue VW beetle convertible from Johnson Motors on South Walnut Street, packed it up, and headed out for a final summer at Camp Greylock.

But right before he left, as Larry later tells in this often-repeated family story:

"He had somehow got a six-and-a-half foot long black rat snake. And black rat snakes, their uniqueness is they can make a sound like a rattlesnake. They're not poisonous but they're scary enough. I was getting his room (the room at the top of the stairs) that summer after he left and apparently the night before he left for Camp Greylock, the snake got loose and he couldn't find it. That morning, I heard him tell mom about the lost snake as he got into the car to leave. He even carried the box with him so she was fooled into believing that his phrase "I lost the snake" meant that the snake had just escaped while he was outside. Anyway, after I had taken over the room and had been in there several days, I had totally forgotten about this snake. And then one day, I went into the closet and I pulled a blanket off the shelf and there was that thing right in my face! SSSSSSS SSSSSsssssssssssssssssssssssssss! So, I go screaming and Brian was home, and mom starts screaming at Brian and I, "KILL IT! KILL IT! KILL IT!" So, Brian and I went in there with a box and I mean that thing was moving and we were both hopping and I think Brian is the one who finally dragged it into the box and took it over to the corn crib and let it go."

Once on the road, he was jubilant in his new VW but reported that he had gotten a terrific sunburn on his legs by driving with the top down and wearing shorts on the way up here. ("The burn even had a line across it where the steering wheel crossed my legs. I looked pretty funny in a bathing suit for a few days.")

When Kit finally arrived at Camp on July 15, 1964, he wrote back to let us know about his road trip:

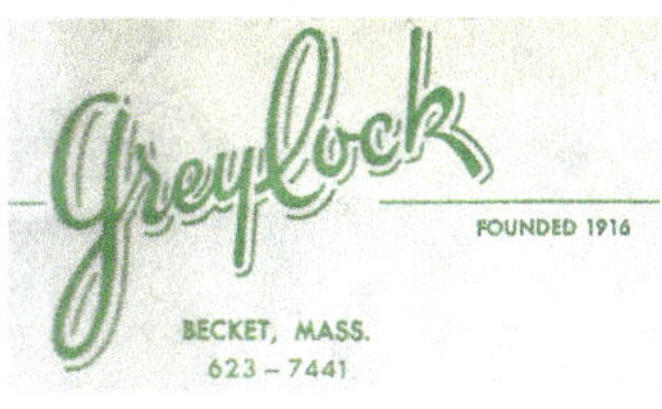
Greylock
FOUNDED 1916
BECKET, MASS.
623 – 7441

Dear Mom, Dad, Grandpa and Kids,

An exhausted and feeble hello emanating from the heart of the Berkshires. I took 3 days to get up here. Got to Pittsburgh the 1st night at

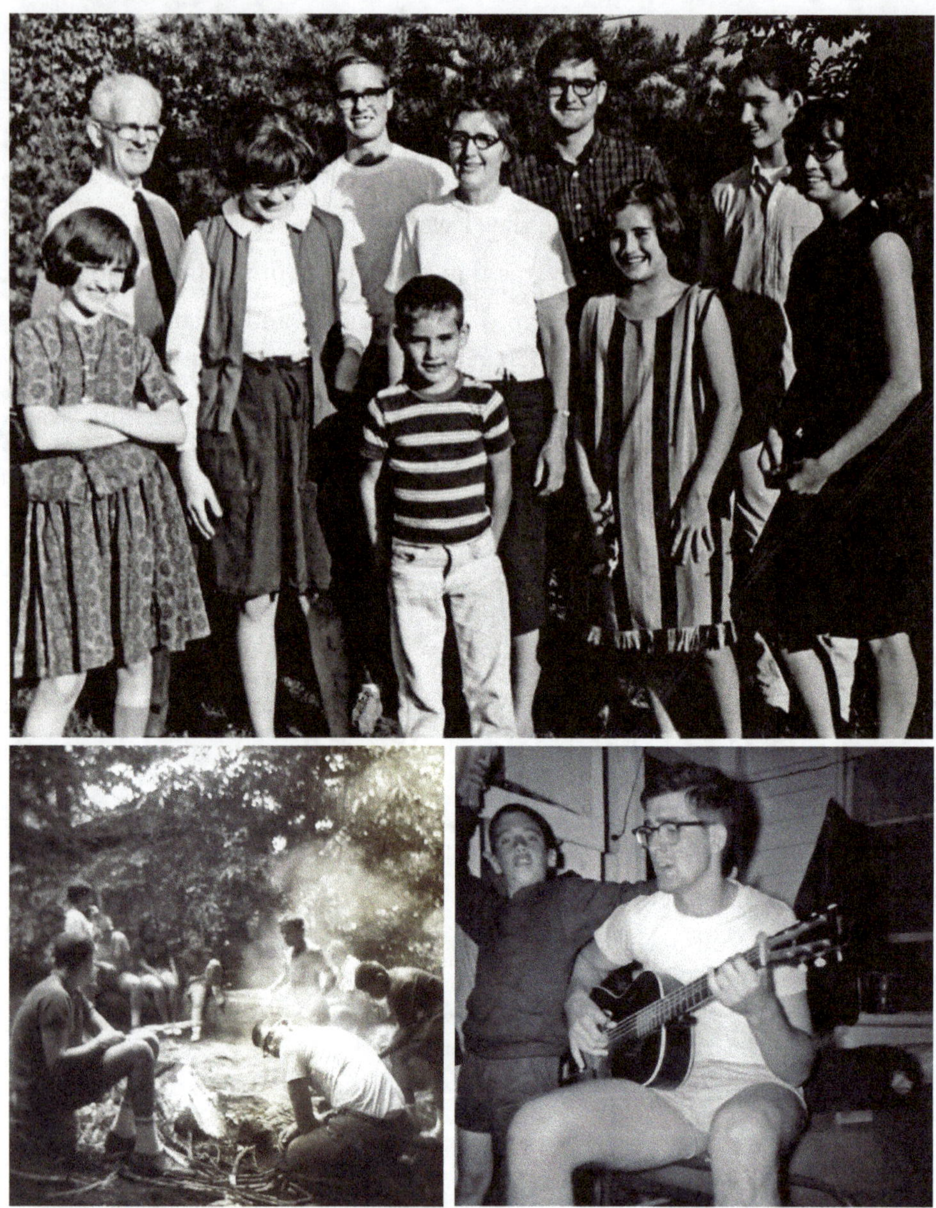

Kit prepared to leave for Greylock. Front L to R: Marianne, Liz, Tom, Mary, Georgia, and Peg. Back L to R: Grandpa Luke Browne, Larry, Kit, and Brian. Ca. 1962. Photo: CM Flaten, IU Archives. Snapshots from Kit's personal album. 1962. Left: Cookout in Tanglewood Tr. It had just rained, and we had a heck of a time getting the fire started. Right: Mike Leit, my guitar et moi in our bunk "NYU." Photos: photographer unknown, Collection of the author.

about 6 p.m. Philip had left for ROTC camp so didn't get a chance to see him. I went on & spent the night in a very cheap motel in Pennsylvania. Next day got to Willow Grove Pa. around 3:00 PM because his gal friend Lerna gave me the wrong address. We went bowling a few games, got to bed very late. I didn't get up till twelve next day.

It took me around three hours to get to Princeton where I stayed overnight with Howard Shoemaker, one of my old Physics buddies. Princeton is a very beautiful campus and most conducive to a study atmosphere. Howard is paying almost nothing for a beautiful room. The VW held up fine and gave out about 30 mpg. Only one sour note, someone put a dent in the right rear fender when I was parked overnight. It's not too big but it really broke me up.

I got to camp the next day around 4:00 PM. Not too many of the old counselors around but a lot of nice guys and quite a few guitar players. We got up a group and sang for a program last nite for the campers, yours truly on banjo. The program went over very well.

Love,

Kit

Music continued to be important. One of the counselors, Bob Foss, who was an expert bluegrass guitar player, teamed up with Kit as a duo, and they were allowed, according to Kit, to play in a local Pittsfield coffee house several times, and Bob showed Kit around Greenwich Village in New York (his "happy hunting ground") once camp broke up. There were others in camp who also enjoyed music making and it brought them together.

The legacy of his summers at Greylock was a boatload of new songs for the Flatens. While at Greylock, he had heard The Weavers perform at the Berkshire Music Barn, and sat around the campfire with other guitar players learning "Puff the Magic Dragon." He came home and taught us the basic chords and the beginner's chestnuts: "My Dog Has Fleas," "Little Brown Jug," "The Little Brown Church in the Vale," followed by blues chord progressions for "House of the Rising Sun" and "St. Louis Blues," and many folk songs from the Kingston Trio—"Tom Dooley," "The MTA," "A Worried Man," and "They Call the Wind Mariah." Kit added his mandolin and banjo to our sound. Even though we grew up in Bill Monroe's bluegrass country, we picked up only a few bluegrass/gospel songs from the radio, one of our favorites being "Do Lord, Oh Do Lord, Oh Do Remember Me!" which we harmonized to as we rode in the car together, singing with the radio or just by ourselves.

1964. SEATTLE

In 1964, Kit graduated from Indiana University with a B.S. and M.A. in Physics. His days in Swain Hall were finished and he no longer had to drill in the ROTC. (He joined the ROTC because it was compulsory for all male students at I.U. until 1964.) He was exempt from being drafted to Vietnam by the Indiana Selective Service System due to his graduate degree status. Kit was not eager to serve. He preferred graduate school and applied to the University of Washington in Seattle where he was offered a Teaching Assistantship in the Physics Department. He sent an urgent letter to the Registrar at the University in Seattle in June pleading with them: "Send to my draft board a notice of my acceptance. It is very urgent that they receive this notice early this month (by June 15) as I am uncomfortably close to being drafted." I don't want to leave you with the impression that he was a draft dodger. He was proud of Dad's service during WWII, and later of his brother Brian's service during the Vietnam war. But he was simply more interested in academics, a place where he was challenged and could contribute to society.

So, he left for Washington for his T.A. position the same summer that Dad left for Boulder to begin his year-long sabbatical at the University of Colorado. Once Kit arrived in Seattle in the Fall, he took preliminary exams for acceptance into the Physics program for a doctoral degree—a credential, he stated sarcastically in a letter, which would really "attract the babes." This was, after all, the heyday of physics; Oppenheimer and Einstein were household names. But he didn't pass his first prelims so he continued with classes and teaching and retook the exam.

It was all new and thrilling. Although he missed his family, he found Seattle to be "breathtakingly beautiful," though extremely hilly and with a constant drizzle. At a friend's house, his eye was arrested by the beauty. "When the sun was setting, it silhouetted the Olympia mountains on the left while Seattle twinkled in the dusk on the right with Puget Sound washing far below."

And he continued to be a faithful letter writer. He described a football game against the Air Force, and was particularly impressed with the Air Force's "beautiful white falcon mascot worth $6,000 on a leash. Every time, it seemed, that Air Force did anything spectacular the guy who was holding the leash would spin the falcon in a big white pinwheel. The bird, as you may have guessed, was somewhat excitable, but when your leash is only a foot long you can't fly far & fast." My, that falcon must have brought back good memories!

Mom read his letters aloud to us, and his letters were always entertaining accounts of his life. He was making his own way in Seattle, a place that seemed so distant to us, so far away that it could have been all the way across the ocean. He wrote about an earthquake (apparently common), and of his mixed feelings about Seattle as "very old-maidish with its customs and laws."

"The laws against drinking are very restrictive. (Can you imagine I.U. without Nicks?) You can't even buy meat in a market after 6 o'clock. In general one has a very cramped feeling when moving about because you never know what law you are breaking. And they are well-enforced—too well by my standards. It often seems that everyone has his own personal cop."

He continued to go to hear great music: Joan Baez, and Tom Lehrer at the Hungry i. And he enjoyed hiking. He took the prelim again but did not pass, but his grades were so good that his adviser encouraged him to try again next year. This time, however, he had anticipated failure and had applied and accepted a T.A.-ship at the University of California Santa Barbara for the next year. But he decided to continue at Seattle and canceled the contract with Santa Barbara.

1965-72. STILL SEATTLE

Here are some paragraphs from various letters home:

"Quite a few of the guys I hung around with last year have disappeared from the scene. Two have gone to Australia, one to Viet Nam and one to Europe. My old roommate is living out in an incredibly decrepit house with an incredibly decrepit roommate. He is the beatnik type and we couldn't agree on our standards of neatness. His, believe it or not, were below mine so we wallowed in a little filth. In addition he could subsist on extremely irregular eating habits. But we had a gas in our old apartment last year and sometimes I long for the good old days. The new crop of teaching assistants just don't have the character of last year's—or am I getting older?"

"…It would be a swell Christmas present if you would have my

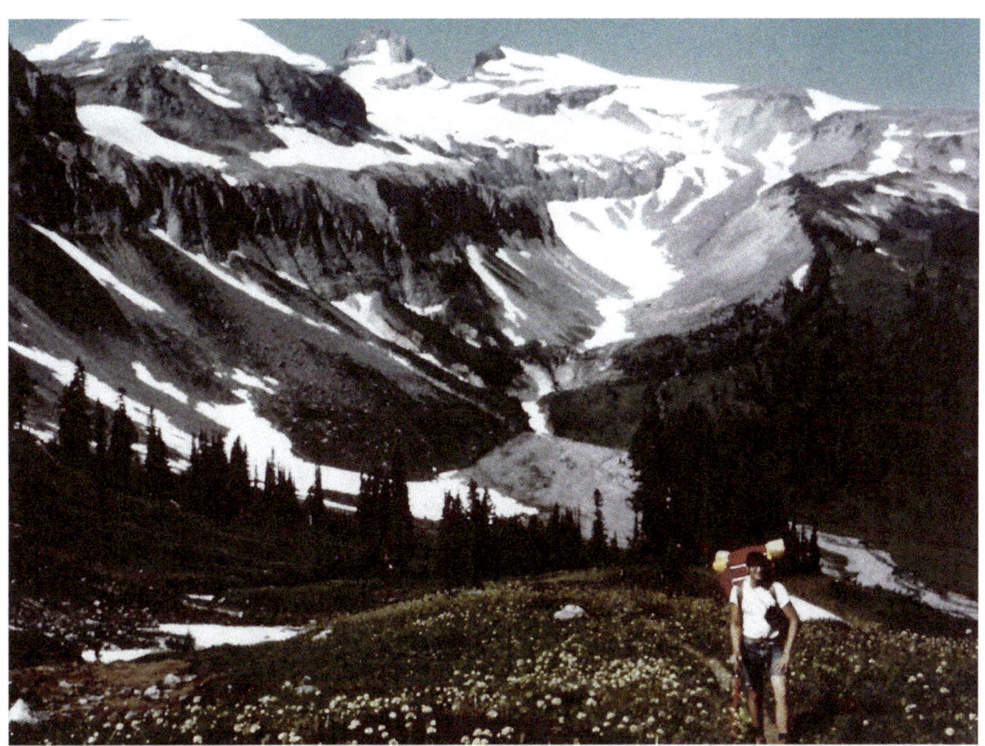

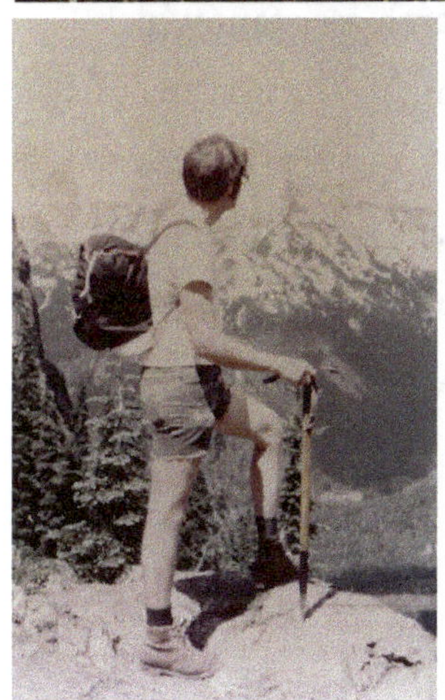

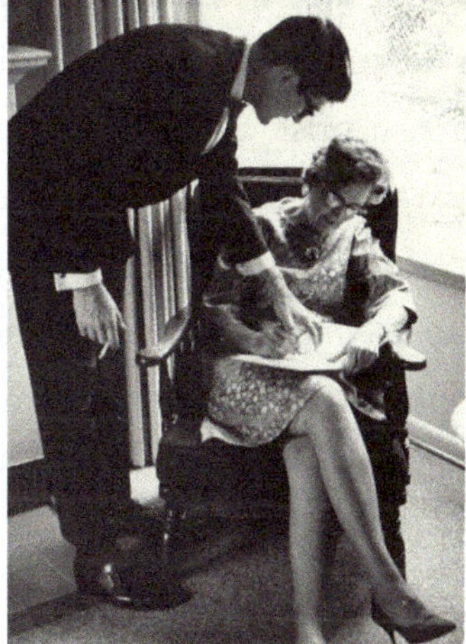

Top: Leaving Indian Bar, Mt. Rainier National Park. Oct 1971.

Far Left: On Eagle Peak, Mt. Rainier National Park. June 1971.

Left: Nov 1967. Kit talks with his mother during a reception after his wedding in Seattle. He divorced after three years in Oct 1971.

Photos: photographers unknown, Collection of the author.

guitar shipped out here if it is still in any condition to play. I don't know why I decided to leave it at home as I'd love to have it now. However I distinctly remember not loosening the strings before I left so I hope the neck has not warped."

"I guess you have heard about the great topless girl's disaster in Seattle. They actually got a couple started downtown. The city council of course immediately got into action and banned them. The big stink now is the question of why they haven't acted with half that alacrity in attacking the smog problem (yes Seattle now has smog which it didn't have last year), the freeway problem (to be complete in 1958) etc. A very typical situation in this progressive city. Well, only a few more years and I should be out of here. You wouldn't believe this state's motto —'KEEP WASHINGTON GREEN, USE YOUR ASHTRAY."

"Since I suspect this letter will reach you after Thanksgiving I hope yours was warm and filling and thoroughly relaxing."

"I am no longer a teaching assistant. I am a research assistant which is the next golden rung in the bejeweled ladder leading to the nirvana of PhDom. It came as quite a surprise as I was looking forward to a year with a dreary T.A. which was beginning to be a drag. I'm working for a fellow named Stern in solid state physics. The rest as of the present is indeterminate, the only hitch is that I have to take and pass the qualifying exam sometime. I'll probably give it a try in November. If I pass it there is going to be one of the wildest, drunkest, hallelujah parties ever thrown on the west coast. If I don't I'm not speaking to anyone for a year. Either way you see it has potent consequences. [1966]

"As the summer drew to a close I found myself anxious to return to Seattle, an emotion which two years ago I would never have put down for anyone, especially myself. But there's some sort of magic in the dreary routine of being a student and in Physics one occasionally feels that he is in on something which most of the world will never know. If only the standard of living was up to my impeccable tastes I'd probably stay in school forever. As it is if it takes me the average time to get my Ph.D. I have four more years of work, enough, I suspect, to sate the most craven glutton for punishment.

Well it's 9:00 AM and I have a class at 9:30 (Statistical Mechanics followed by Advanced Quantum Mechanics and Nuclear Physics—isn't that an impressive sounding array?) It takes 17 minutes to get from my place to the physics bldg leaving me 13 minutes for a cup of coffee & a cigarette provided I leave now. Please write when you can."

That summer, 1966, he gained Security Clearance to work at Livermore Laboratory near San Francisco. He wrote to Mom that "I'm still looking for myself and I suppose I probably always will be." But in the same letter, wrote: "When I saw Dad and heard his (slightly biased) button-popping discourse on the house happenings I feel at once very sad to be away from the center of the action and tremendously proud to be a member of that terrific ten-some, the FLATEN FAMILY."

"My only achievement so far has been to give a seminar on the work (ha ha) that I have been doing for Dr. Stern as well as a theoretical review of the optical properties of thin films and metals which is the type of study Dr. Stern has me working on. I am beginning to realize that the course work and general tests I have been going through so far are really a small part of a Ph.D. program and that research is the real bear. There you are usually trying to do something that hasn't been done before which makes you rely so much more on your own judgment and objectiveness. What one can draw up simply on paper usually appears very complicated in practice and little questions like what to hold one piece of the apparatus on to another part with or what sort of circuitry to use—which are outlined in other people's works as simply "clamp" or "amplifier"—are constantly coming up. You can waste weeks just trying to solve one problem like that and I am beginning to realize that this is where it really helps to have a handyman's knack which I have never had. But experience is slowly forcing me to learn such things. "[1967]

"I have been snapping pictures like mad with my new camera. Of course not a single roll has been developed yet but I sure get a bang out of taking them. Especially this last week and last weekend. We have been having the most breathlessly clear days lately (often only 8 hours of sunshine during December) and I have been taking full advantage of them. Seattle is such an exhilarating city when the weather is like that. Everywhere you go a mountain sprouts like some jewel on a near horizon and of course you are always within view of some body of water—be it Puget Sound, Lake Washington, Green Lake, Lake Sammamish or the murky Lake Union."

"Mount Rainier dominates the mood of Seattle until late afternoon when the sun begins to glint off the glaciers in the Olympic mountains forty miles away and across the sound. Then one can call up his girl friend and head down the new freeway to West Seattle and grab a couple of hot tacos from one of the three zillion "TACO TIME" restaurants scattered throughout the city. With the bag of tacos you race to Lincoln Park and grab a bench facing the sunset with the sound pounding at the base of a cliff like some miniature ocean 100 feet below. The joys of munching a hot taco and watching the sun glide down behind the skinny clouds—row upon row of them—making such glow a blinding orange in its turn; well you just have to experience it to know what a sheer sense of joy Seattle can produce in its gentler moments. Seattle

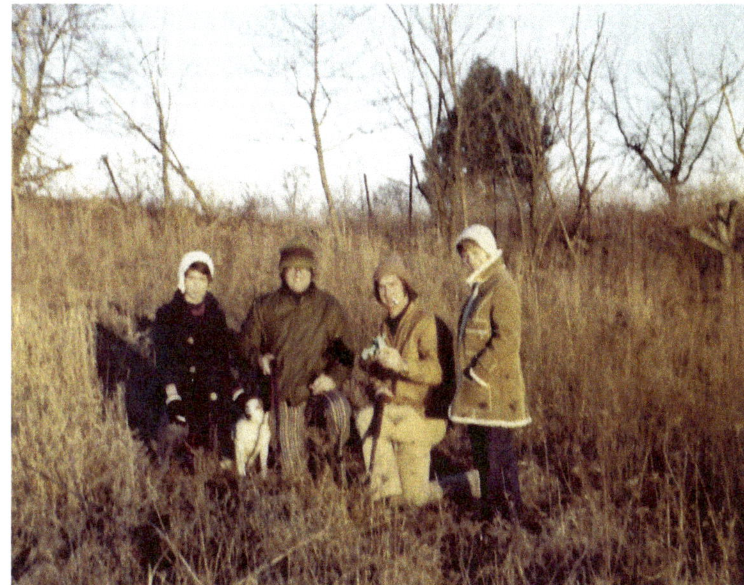

Kit returns home. Ca. 1972. Peg, Sugar, Kit, Brian and Judy go hunting. Photographer Ed Harrison?, Collection of the author.

The family strikes a comic pose during a portrait. Sitting: Brian; Judy; Clarence; Mary; Peg (holding Kelly); Ed; Ann; Larry Standing: Georgia; Marianne; Kit; Tom; Liz sits in front. 1972.

Photo: CM Flaten, Collection of the author.

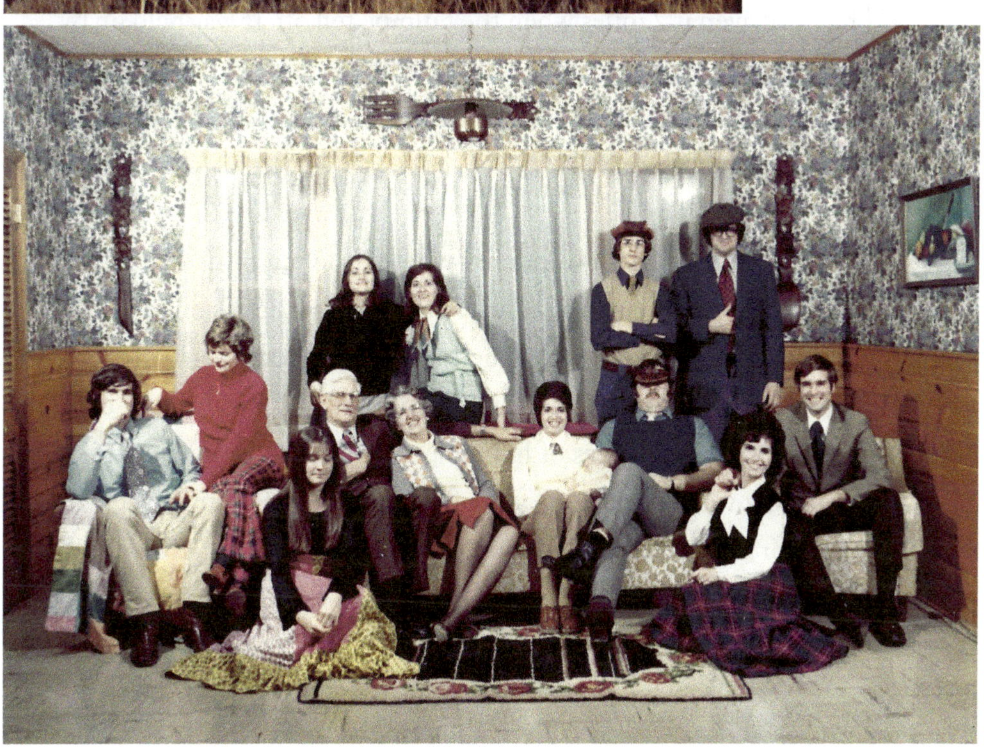

is an actress who favors gloomy parts and plays them too well but she shares the stage with no one when she plays anything but a tragedy."

A BRIEF MARRIAGE

In November 1967, Kit married a young 20-year-old who worked in the office of his physics lab, Ellen Ryall. She had a young daughter from a previous relationship and they tried to create a homelife. However, she was emotionally unstable. After an unhappy three and a half years, he paid for an expensive divorce. He was very relieved to be free of this ill-matched commitment. He turned to focus on his research, and he moved in with good friend Bruce Meyers, continued teaching Astronomy and Physics five days a week, and bought himself a used 1963 TR4.

"I hadn't driven it 2 miles when the tailpipe fell off. It was held on by a piece of string! .... but after fixes ... it's really fun to drive with a high-compression engine especially after putting around in Volkswagens and Ford Fairlanes all these years."

After soul searching, he wondered whether he might change fields and head into medicine. He got his Ph.D. in December 1972, but expressed doubt about his research, wondering whether he wanted to spend the rest of his life "studying the hair on the end of a gnat," which was his way of wondering about the narrowness of his subject matter. His solid state physics research involved a very specialized area of physics. His 1973 published article, "Exciton thermoreflectance of MgO and CaO" reflected this narrow focus. The answer to his questions came when he was offered a faculty position as teacher

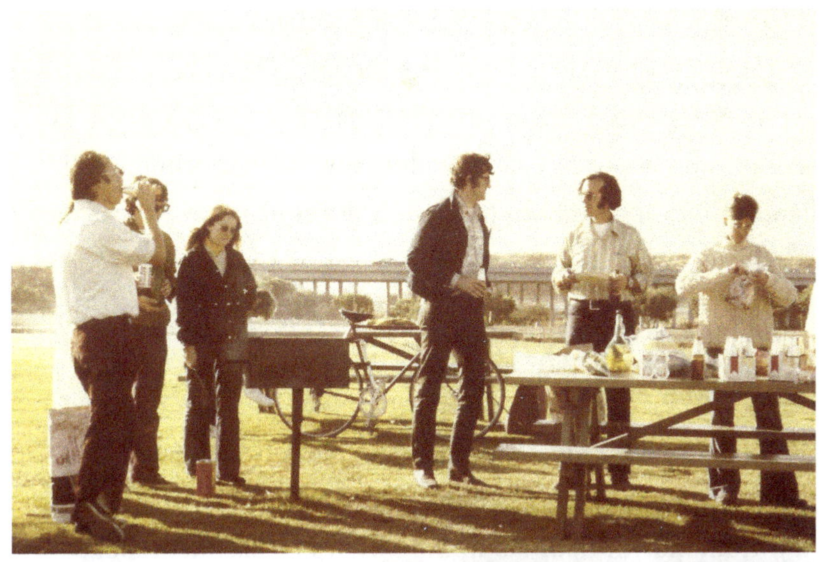

Kit at a picnic with friends, Dave Paquette, Doug Hogg, Eileen Hogg, Bob Bradford, Merrie Walker. June 1973.

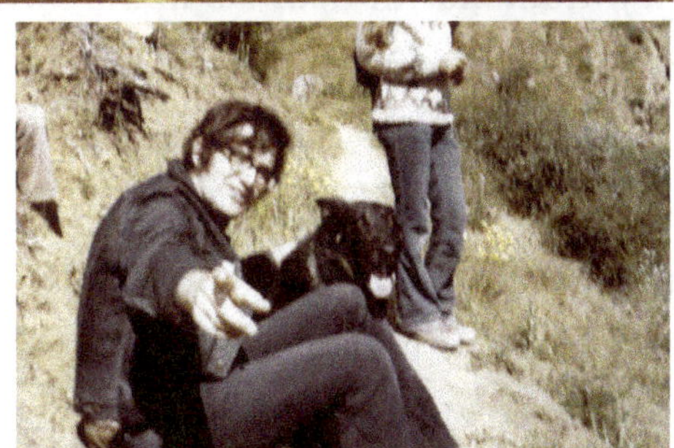

Kit hikes. Kit finds a canine friend along the trail. June 1973.

Photos: Photographer unknown, Collection of the author.

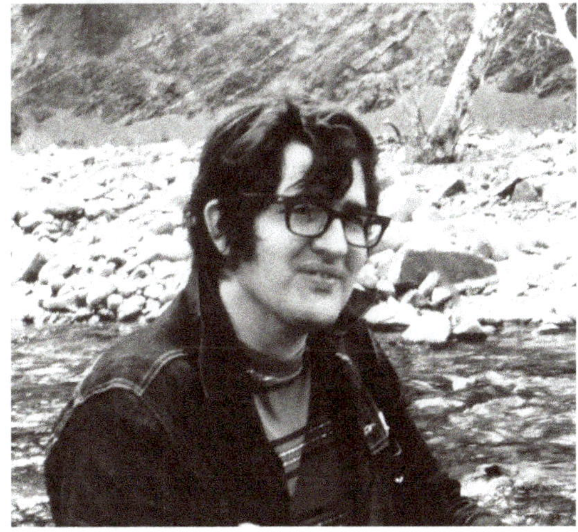

in the Physics Department with the University of Southern California at Santa Barbara. After years of study to become a theoretical and experimental physicist, after years of meager pay and struggles, his work was rewarded. He had found his calling, and wrote to Clancy, telling him of the excitement he found using Clancy's "inquiry method" to create a dynamic between teacher and student.

He came back for a visit on Airport Road, feeling that it refreshed his spirits. We sang together and then he left for California.

1973. UNIVERSITY OF CALIFORNIA AT SANTA BARBARA

Kit began a new teaching position in the Fall of 1973 at UC at Santa Barbara. The view from his 4th floor lab in the Physics Department looked toward the ocean. He was very happy and content to have made this move.

Dr. Walker, the Head of the Physics Dept. was his adviser. Under Walker, he worked on an experimental lab apparatus, a "Vacuum Evaporation System" (Alloys are evaporated onto glass substrates located near top of bell jar. An electron beam heats the materials. Film thickness monitors evaluate the amount of material evaporated.) Kit built the monitors and much of the equipment in the bell jar. After perfecting an automatic controlling system for evaporating alloys, Kit wrote "WHAT YOU GET IS WHAT YOU SET" in red lettering. He not only built much of the apparatus, but also helped perfect the x-ray techniques that were used in the physics lab to analyze samples.

He settled into his new position as teacher, using the Inquiry Method, and he received a standing ovation from his students for his classes. He missed Seattle but turned his thoughts to the students and new opportunities. He was a very popular teacher. So much promise. He was looking forward to Clancy and Mary's visit in July.

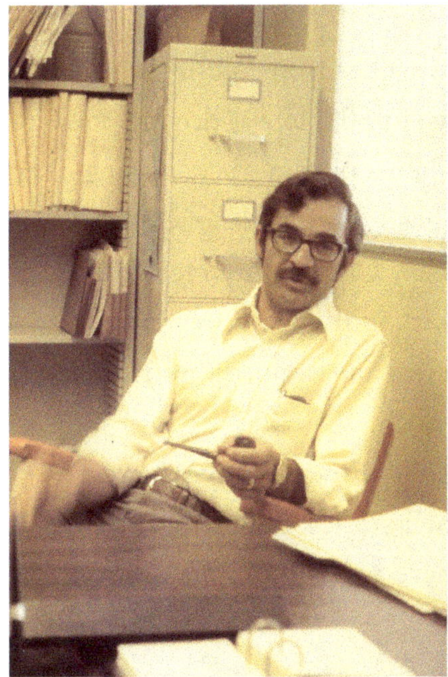

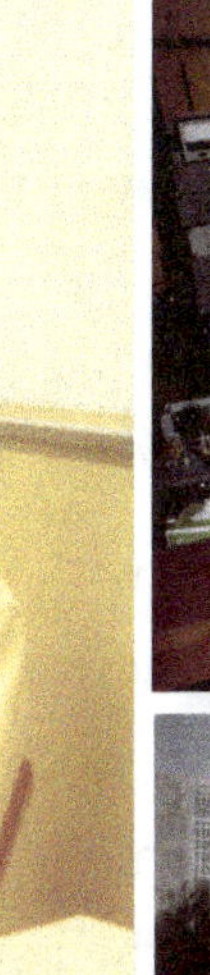

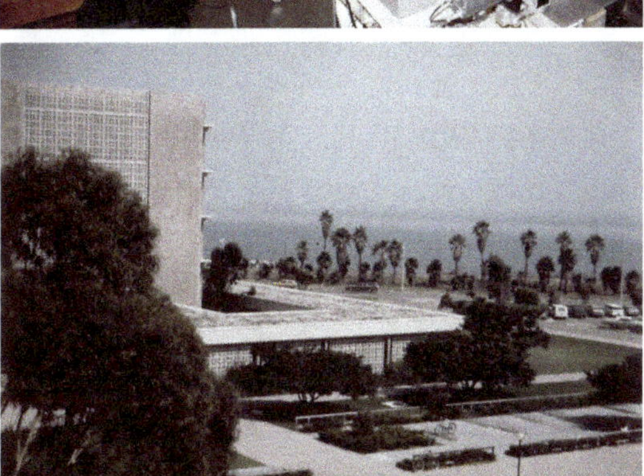

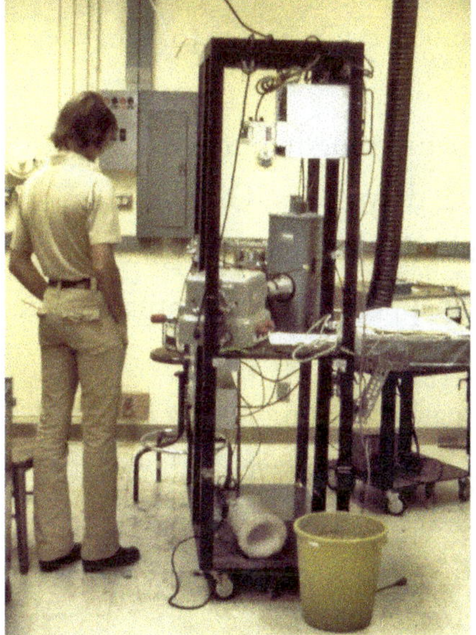

Top left: Dr. W.C. Walker, Head of Physics Dept. explains Kit's work to Mary and Thomas. Aug. 1973.

Top right: Kit's lab in the Physics Dept at UC Santa Barbara. Vacuum Evaporation System.

Above right: Kit's view from his window of his office at UC at Santa Barbara. View from the 4th floor of the Physics building, looking toward the ocean.

Below left: Thomas Flaten reviewing Kit's experimental lab apparatus in the lab.

All photos by Clarence Flaten, Aug 1973. Collection of the author.

DEATH

Suddenly and violently, Kit was killed in a head-on collision on Los Carneros Road, in Goleta, California at the age of 30. He was driving home in his '63 Triumph TR4 convertible sports car, when a pickup truck, passing a car and crossing the highway center line, plowed head on into his much smaller car. On July 1, 1973, at 12:37a.m.at Goleta Valley Community Hospital, he was pronounced dead from chest impact, with multiple rib fractures, a transection of the aorta and bilateral hemothorax, and multiple head and leg lacerations.

As painful as it is to remember a moment of tragedy, my sisters and brothers have once again generously shared their stories. I hope that you can see how much he is missed, but also that we have gone on in spite of it.

TOM REMEMBERS

That fateful morning was the day the music died. As Liz told me, her Camelot was over.

I was awakened in the wee hours of the morning in our Boulder apartment to the sound of mom and dad crying downstairs "Oh no, oh no, oh no" followed by weeping and sobbing. I was afraid to even go downstairs to find out what was going on. I'd never had this happen before. Eventually mom came upstairs to let me know Liz had called saying she had a visit from the police informing her that Kit had been killed earlier that night in a car wreck in Santa Barbara. I was numb. I couldn't process it. I don't even know what transpired between the time mom came and told me, to when I eventually got dressed and went downstairs. I'm pretty sure that they'd already begun making travel arrangements to go back to Bloomington where Kit's remains would be brought for the funeral and the burial.

We flew home to Bloomington and lived through the funeral, barely.

Then we flew out to Santa Barbara to collect Kit's household items and for the baptism of Kimmie, my goddaughter. (One of God's early lessons to me was this: no matter how dire the circumstances, there is always new life that will emerge from the darkness.) Brian and Judy took me to Disneyland for the day, and to San Francisco, Fisherman's Wharf, and we even panned for gold. We had a great time with Judy's parents, Chuck and Fran Felkins. Judy's family had gotten to know Kit, so this was really hard on all of them too. We flew back to Colorado, where dad finished out his assignment.

While we were still in Colorado, before going out to California, mom and dad spent the rest of the summer days watching the Watergate hearings. I still remember dad's bitter anguish crying out, "And I voted for that son of a bitch!!" I went back to playing my records in my room, tennis with my friends at the apartment, even fishing up in the mountains. How much fun it would have been to do all that with my big brother Kit, the dude that could do anything. I tried not to think about it but it was hard. Especially being around mom and dad ... especially dad. I watched him age 10 years in 12 months. After we got back to Bloomington and I started my senior year of high school, a package showed up with Kit's Gibson CF-100 guitar. Another arrived with a Sony sound-on-sound reel-to-reel recorder Kit had recently purchased. The next four years of my life through college included many late night sessions with that Gibson and the Sony.

Well, I kept that leather cap Kit bought me that Christmas. It's my keepsake from my hero big brother who I truly believe absolutely cherished having me as his very own brother, Little Tom. And I still cherish and appreciate good sound systems and tweaking the controls. And I still cherish my love for others and doing my best to maintain a good sense of humor, despite the circumstances. And although I never took up the banjo, mandolin, or fiddle, I'll always have Kit's CF-100 guitar, to cherish forever.

Fifteen months from the date of the accident, dad suffered a stroke while swimming at Royer Pool on the I.U. campus during his lunch break. I knew better though - it wasn't the stroke that got him. My big strong daddy died from a broken heart. I guess at least he didn't have to wait so long to join Kit in heaven.

GEORGIA REMEMBERS

I was in Lake Placid, New York on an art scholarship from the Maryland Art Institute at their summer campus when I heard the knock on my bedroom door early in the morning of Wednesday, July 1, 1973. My friend Alice came into the room and told me she had received a call. "I am sorry to tell you that your brother died in an auto accident last night." I immediately called home, and Liz answered and said that a County Deputy had knocked on the door of our Airport Road home and delivered the news. I was in a state of disbelief and did not know how to react. Later, I went for a walk around the lake, sobbing. I was so upset that when I got back to my room, I beat a hole through the plaster of my bedroom wall with a desk lamp. My teachers were forgiving. Instead of being sent home, the generous students and faculty took up a collection for me so that I was able to fly home for the funeral. I returned to Lake Placid to finish, but with a half-heartedness. That sense of disbelief has never entirely vanished.

LIZ REMEMBERS

It was shocking news that summer of 1973 when I was working at the hospital. I was getting ready for work when two policemen came to the door of our farmhouse and told my sister and me the news of Kit's tragic car accident at age 30. I had to call Mom. And then I went to work because I didn't know what else to do. And the viewing—seeing Kit in the casket and going through the funeral. Mom and Dad never really recovered from that shock. In some ways, neither has our family.

PEG REMEMBERS

About a week after the funeral, I had the most vivid dream about Kit. The family was driving home from the funeral, and I noticed a car beside us. Kit was driving. He was waving to us, trying to get our attention, trying to let us know that he was still alive. In my dream, I was so relieved, but when I woke up, I realized that it was just a feeling of denial on my part. It was so hard to believe he was gone. Especially since he had lived so many years of his life away from us, it was easier to believe he was just away somewhere and would, as always, return. Later, when I was experimenting with songwriting, I wrote a song about Kit and the forest green turtleneck sweater I had sent him the year before he died. In the song I recalled how I would lie awake in bed at night and listen to Kit in his room practicing one musical instrument or another—guitar, mandolin, banjo, violin—and when he was away, how we cherished the letters he wrote home, telling how his life was when he went out on his own. That big green turtleneck sweater was sent back to me, and I wore it myself until it finally wore out.

MARY REMEMBERS

It was just a few months after our son's tragic accident and death – and my husband and I were worn out trying to keep the family and job responsibilities going as usual. One evening he said, "let's go down to the lake"—we stopped for some sandwiches and fruit—then, on Lake Monroe, we got on our float boat [pontoon boat] which we shared with friends. The evening, a lovely autumn time—the withdrawal from shore—the water lapping quietly at the boat's edges—the feeling of remoteness—the quiet between the two of us—the gentle rocking of the boat—the echoes from the shore— the slow setting of the sun and the birds swooping back to their nests—their evening songs echoing across the water. All of this was a healing time for us, giving us the chance to pull our ravaged spirits together—to face with some courage and dignity what is demanded of us—to LIVE.

Dr. W. C. Walker, Head of Physics Department, wrote to Dad and Mom to tell them that they had established a Reading Room in Kit's memory, which was a nice tribute. And his article, "Optical properties of Gd, Dy, and Tb," JL Erskine, GA Blake, and CJ Flaten, was published in the Oct 1974 issue of *Journal of the Optical Society of America.* The journal *Physical Review* published his article, "Optical constants of some silver alloys," CJ Flaten and EA Stern. Jan 15, 1975.

We all seek inner strength to go on. His death marked the end of our lives on Airport Road. But the memory of his goodness, wit and love keep us forever grateful.

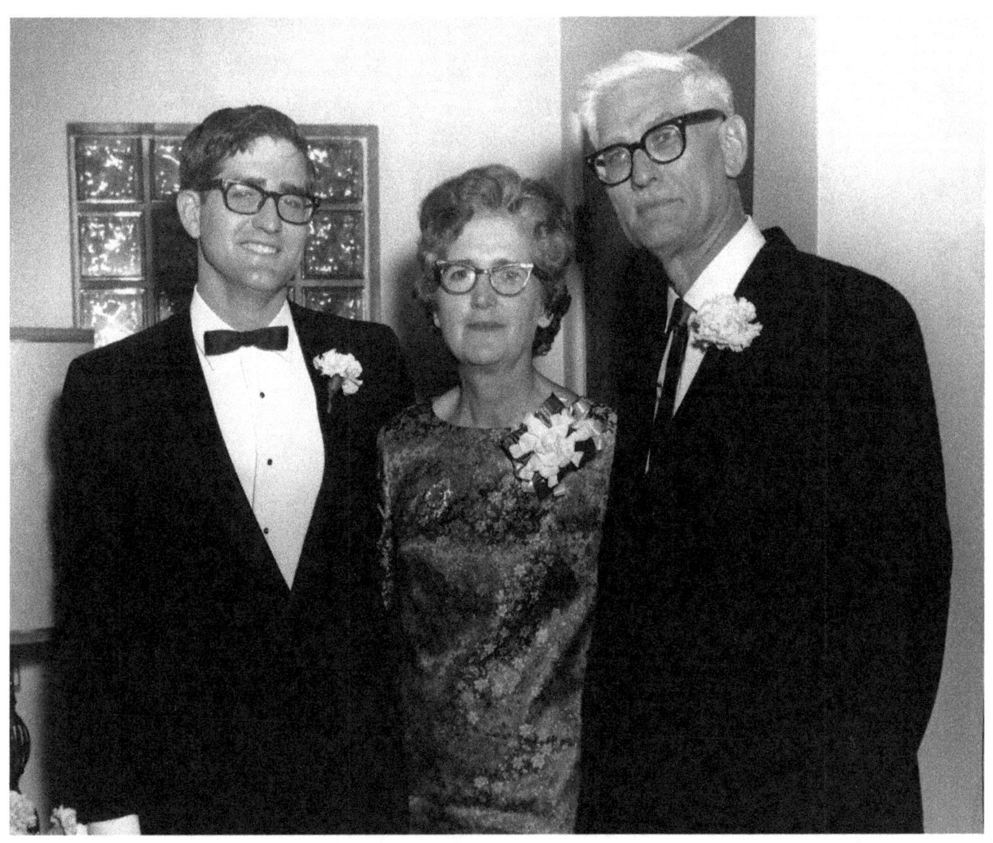

Kit, Mary and Clancy Flaten. 1967.Seattle, WA. Photo: unknown photographer, Collection of the author.

CHAPTER FIVE

CONCLUSION

THREE FLATENS ARE BURIED IN THE VALHALLA CEMETERY, in Bloomington, not far from the original home on Airport Road. The flannel grey granite headstones sparkle where they have been rough cut, but the faces are polished and chiseled. The headstones are warm to the touch and they sink into the earth at a slight tilt, flanked by metal urns which are polished from time to time by loving hands. (Recently, a beloved fourth member of the Flaten family, Cynthia Flaten, was laid to rest in the same section.)

CLARENCE M. FLATEN.

> August 27, 1910 – October 23, 1974. "He knew strength in God, Love in family, Joy in teaching."

MARY FRANCES BROWNE FLATEN

> August 23, 1917 – June 23, 2002. "Devoted to family and friends, Inspired by the arts and her faith, Beloved by all who knew her, She stands before God and smiles."

CHRISTOPHER KIT JAMES FLATEN

> December 26, 1942 – July 1, 1973. "Physicist – Teacher"

I have finished looking at the past. I see that love is learned and handed from one person to the next. Endings are sad and devastating. But beginnings, weddings, births, accomplishments are happy and joyous. I guess that is obvious. I conclude that each one of us is handed a unique life and it is best lived in the moment, with resilience, optimism, adventure, intention, faith, gratitude, bravery, and generosity.

REFERENCES

SOURCES

Franklyn Curtiss-Wedge, *History of Freeborn County Minnesota* (H.C. Cooper, Jr. & Co., Chicago, IL, 1911).

Rev. Edward D. Neill, *History of Freeborn County; including Explorers and Pioneers of Minnesota, and Outline History of the State of Minnesota* (Minnesota Historical Society, MN 1882).

Hettinger Centennial Book Committee, *Hettinger ND Centennial. 100 Years of Change and Challenge. 1907 – 2007.* (Hettinger Centennial Committee, SD 2007).

Anders B. Pedersen, *Sigdal* (Vol. 36, issue 1, Sigdalslag Saga).

Odd S. Lovoll, Todd Nichol, *History of Freeborn County. Norwegians on the Prairie: Ethnicity and the Development of the Country Town* (Minnesota Historical Society, St. Paul. 2006).

Oscar L. Flo, *A Town in Born ... Bricelyn.* (Graphic Publishing Company, Inc. 1949).

Andreas Holmsen, *The transition from tenancy to freehold peasant ownership in Norway* (Scandinavian Economic History Review, 9:2, 152-164. 1961).

Ingrid Semmingsen, *Norway to America, a History of Migration.* (University MN Press, 1978).

Allan Line Firm, *Emigrant's Prospects. Practical Hints and Directions To Intending Emigrants To Canada and the United States.* (1872)

The Adams County Record, compiled by, *30th Anniversary Booklet: 1907-1937. In Commemmoration of the Founding of Hettinger and Adams County.* (The Adams County Record. 1937.) Retrieved March 22, 2020 by Loren Luckow.

The General Land Office Circular showing the Manner of Processing to Obtain Title to Public Lands under the Homestead, Desert Land, and Other Laws. (Washington: Government Printing Offfice Issued July 11, 1899).

Mr. Loren Luckow, archivist. *School Records from Hettinger Public School Administration. (*Retrieved 2020).

Charles F. Romanus and Riley Sunderland, *United States Army in WWII. Cina-Burma-India Theater. Stilwell's Command Problems.* (Office of the Chief of Military History, Dept of the Army. Wash DC. 1956).

MNOPEDIA online, *Grasshopper Raids:* (https://www.mnopedia.org/event/grasshopper-plagues-1873-1877).

Daniel Buck, Esq, *Indian Outbreaks.* (Mankato, MN. 1904).

C.C. Andrews, *History of St. Paul, Minnesota*, (D. Mason & Co. 1890.)

St. Meinrad School, *Campus Chatter.* (SMAA, May 1960).
FAMILY STORY: Clancy and the Violin. Elizabeth Efroymson.
FAMILY STORY: Ollie Evans Flaten. Margaret Flaten Daisley.
Letter: Ebon Flaten to Mary Flaten. March 5, 1983
Email: Bill Flaten re: final sale of Flaten farmland in South Dakota. April 9, 2020.

ILLUSTRATION ATTRIBUTIONS
Norway Map: Norway Map by Vemaps.com

PHOTOGRAPHS and PRINTS

The Indiana University Archives Photograph Collection, Photograph Database Photographs by Clarence M. Flaten and Gunerius Flaten. Flaten Family Photographs Collection, Indiana University Archives, Clarence M. Flaten papers, Collection C660, Indiana University Archives, Bloomington.

https://webapp1.dlib.indiana.edu/archivesphotos/search/search.do?userQuery=Flaten

Sectional Map of the Territory of Minnesota. RG: 77, Civil Works Map File. NARA: 25464453. Q58 . War Department. Office of the Chief of Engineers. 1818-9/18/1947

Sketch Map of the Public Surveys in the State of Minnesota. RG: 49, Old Map File Manuscript and Annotated Maps of the United States and Its Territories. NARA: 6039426. Dept Interior. General Land Office. 1849-7/16/1946

The Peter Fox Sons Company (logo). https://www.buttonmuseum.org/buttons/peter-fox-sons-company

SHIP REFERENCES
https://www.wrecksite.eu/wreck.aspx?35520

http://www.norwayheritage.com/p_shiplist.asp?co=allan

http://www.clydeships.co.uk/view.php?official_number=&imo=&builder=&builder_eng=&year_built=&launch_after=&launch_before=&role=&propulsion=&category=&owner=&port=&flag=&disposal=&lost=&ref=21783&vessel=MORAVIAN#v
https://www.globalsecurity.org/military/systems/ship/passenger-19.htm
https://books.google.com/books?id=rRtis6DUY4wC&pg=PA24&lpg=PA24&dq=%22S.S.+Moravian%22+1865&source=bl&ots=muvs_cr0Ka&sig=ACfU3U3ZlicN2VYZcdvmZgYE0ooYZaFkEQ&hl=en&sa=X&ved=2ahUKEwi-ip3EhaDqAhXpoXIEHTzvC88Q6AEwAHoECAkQAQ#v=onepage&q=%22S.S.%20Moravian%22%201865&f=false

Enterprise and Prosperity of the Transatlantic Steamship Companies: The Great Ferries Across the Ocean." June 7, 1865.
https://www.nytimes.com/1865/06/07/archives/enterprise-and-prosperity-of-the-transatlantic-steamship-companies.html

WEBSITES

Dakota Buttes Museum in Hettinger
https://www.dakotabuttesmuseum.com/

Freeborn County Museum and Library
https://www.fchmmn.org/

Long Journey West:1820 movie
https://media.dlib.indiana.edu/media_objects/xw42n811v

The Outer Space Connection movie
https://www.youtube.com/watch?reload=9&v=PNmXUskujAQ

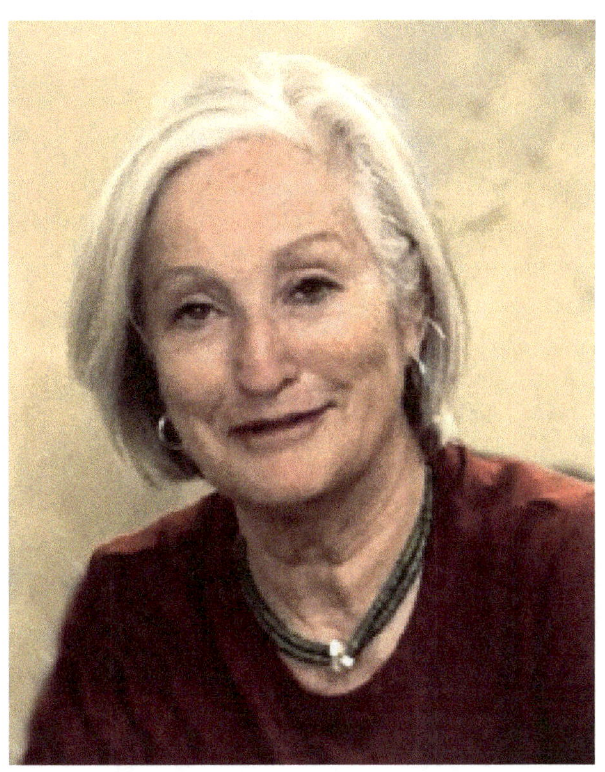

ABOUT THE AUTHOR

GEORGIA FLATEN SHAW, is a researcher at the National Archives, in Washington, DC, with a speciality in photography and images. She knows how important written documents and images are for affirming stories. Born with an innate curiosity about origins, her interest during her childhood was ignited with visits to an abandoned house and piqued by artifacts and photographs which her father, Clarence Flaten, brought back from his service in WWII. Trained in art and music, she has a B.A. from Indiana University and an M.S. from the University of Maryland, and after completing work at NIH in Bethesda MD, where she worked in medical illustration, she now writes about her family. She believes that having a knowledge of her origin is important, and the insights gained while reflecting on the past have explained her place and purpose in the world and put other cultures into perspective. She lives in Bethesda, MD, with her husband Patrick.
georgiashawemail@gmail.com

Photo by Barbara Shaw.

www.ingramcontent.com/pod-product-compliance
Lightning Source LLC
LaVergne TN
LVHW081258100826
845148LV00005B/912

9798986407517